BEHIND THE BARS; 31498

CHARLES C. MOORE

BEHIND THE BARS; 31498

CHARLES C. MOORE

Ex-preacher and convict, author of *The Rational View*
and editor of *The Blue Grass Blade*

Introduction by Madalyn O'Hair

American Atheist Press
Austin, TX
1990

Originally published in 1899 by Blue Grass Printing Co., Lexington,
Kentucky

American Atheist Press, P. O. Box 140195, Austin, TX 78714-0195

ISBN 0-910309-65-5

This book is most affectionately
dedicated to my

Wife and Children

Penitentiary, Columbus, Ohio,
March 10th, 1899

Introduction

Charles Chilton Moore was born in Kentucky on December 20, 1837, and died in that state on February 7, 1906. Robert Green Ingersoll was born in Dresden, New York, on August 11, 1833, and died on July 21, 1899. Although Moore retained his base in Kentucky, Ingersoll finally moved to Illinois where he established his reputation. His final years, however, were spent on the East Coast, primarily in New York. The two men were contemporaries for their entire lives.

Briefly, Moore was born into wealth. His minister father's estate at the time of his death was over $100,000 — a fabulous sum in the mid-1800s. He was educated with the social elite, graduated from college, and spent several years in Europe. He then accepted ordination in the church system which his grandfather had founded. However, having preached for several years he found that he could not accept what was presented in the Bible and abandoned his vocation, first labeling himself an "infidel" and later an Atheist.

Ingersoll was also the son of a minister, but his father was an itinerant and a poor churchman. Self-educated, Ingersoll undertook the study of law as an apprentice in a law office. Relying on the astuteness of his older brother, a politician, he soon associated himself with the Republican party in Illinois and began his career as an attorney for the powerful.

Both men married wealthy women. In the case of Ingersoll, his wife's family was a part of the marauding railroad empire and Ingersoll quickly became a "railroad attorney." But Ingersoll married a woman who was a "freethinker," and it was after his marriage that he became an "agnostic."

Ingersoll loved oratory and Moore loved writing. The former took to the lecture platforms and the latter began his own newspaper, each with the intention to have his views made known. Moore's father was a slave owner, but Moore himself embraced abolition. Ingersoll's father had thoroughly indoctrinated him into the abolitionists' stand. They both understood and appreciated the states' rights stance and the logical derivation of the right for a state to secede from the union. Ingersoll briefly served in the Civil War, with the rank of colonel, that having been obtained through political connections. Moore peripherally encountered some of the Civil War in several brief field hospital incidents. Both, sickened by the sight of death, retreated from the encounter. Ingersoll resigned his commission; Moore simply left the area. And, of course, Ingersoll was a tippler while Moore was a prohibitionist.

Ingersoll became nationally famous for his oratorical skills at a time when these were much fancied in the nation. "Elocution," or orational skill, was a standard college requirement course. And, ministers vied one with the other to develop a reputation of expertise in this ability. Ingersoll was more magnificent than any. He commingled political speeches in support of the Republican party position with those on agnosticism. Moore, founding his own newspaper — *The Blue Grass Blade* — billed it as "The only prohibition paper published by a Heathen; terms per year $2.00 for Rich People; $1.00 for Poor People." Ingersoll catered only to the rich.

The book in your hand is Charles C. Moore's personal story of his stay in prison during the year 1899 for a federal charge against him under the infamous Comstock laws. The official charge was that he had sent "obscene matter" through the mails, in that two different issues of *The Blue Grass Blade* had run articles on "Free Love." All concerned in the case knew that the trial had to do with his open Atheism and that it was an extension of harassment directed against him by the religious forces in Lexington. He had, before this indictment, been in court on a blasphemy charge which was in the appellate process at the time. Several other court appearances and short jail sentences had been occasioned by his advocacy of Atheism also.

At the time that he first issued his paper he was physically assaulted in the streets of Lexington by Christian gentlemen acting from aroused emotions. On one such occasion, fearing that he was going to sustain bodily injury, Moore fought back. For this he was charged also, being briefly incarcerated.

Again, once when asked where hellfire was, he replied that if he wanted to find it, he would dig close to a particular church. For this he spent two months in jail.

At another time a plot by very highly placed persons (including three judges!) for his assassination was revealed to him and it was necessary to take extraordinary precautions to save his own life while attempting to defuse the plot of the conspirators.

On one of these charges he had thought of obtaining Robert G. Ingersoll for counsel and had the funds to do so. Consequently, he wrote to him outlining the matter and received back what was to him a shocking reply. This single encounter, after a lifetime of Moore's devotion to Ingersoll, soured C. C. on "the great orator." The exchange of letters between them, after the first request, was printed by Moore in the May 20, 1894, issue of his paper.

Col. Ingersoll's Letter to
Me and My Answer To It
by Charles C. Moore
(Reprinted from the *Blue Grass Blade*, May 20, 1894)

New York City
400 Fifth Ave., May 8, 1894

My dear Mr. Moore:

I am sorry that you are in trouble — sorry that you touched the feelings of your neighbors — but I do not think you have violated any law — though you may have lacked courtesy.

It is impossible for me to take your case. My time is already mortgaged. Besides, if I should appear it might injure you by fanning into flame all of the bigotry in your section.

I guess you will not need much help.

Yours always,
R. G. Ingersoll

Lexington, Ky., May 14, 1894

Col. Robt. G. Ingersoll.

Dear Sir: In candor I must say that your letter dispels from my mind much of the illusion that has for years hung around your name, and I believe it will have the same effect upon many of your friends in Kentucky.

Before I ever heard of you, and when I did not know, or know of, an infidel in Kentucky, if in the United States, I walked down out of a pulpit,

iii

when I was at the height of my popularity, and loved by a highly intelligent and appreciative congregation of which I had charge, and took hold of the plow handle, when I had not been reared to work, because I had discovered all unaided, and just from reading the Bible, the "Mistakes of Moses."

It not only broke my mother's heart, but broke my own heart; and I saw, in prospect, as plainly as I now see the thirty years in retrospect, the Iliad of woes that my departure from the faith of my fathers has brought upon me.

I had not the genius to successfully defy the world as you have so heroically and successfully done. I had nothing to support me but the knowledge that I was right, and the courage of my convictions.

When you, like Minerva from the thigh of Jupiter, sprang, at one bound, full panoplied into the arena and astounded and startled, like some wondrous brilliant meteor, the whole civilized world, and dashed from your assailed flanks the legions of howling hypocrites, as some Nemean lion would a pack of curs of low degree, you were a revelation to me, and I bowed at the shrine of your mighty genius, with an adoration and idolatry far more genuine than that which the average Christian feels for his god.

I read your books, traveled to a distance to hear your lectures, cheerfully paid high prices to hear them, sought and obtained interviews with you, and to you and to others, in season and out of season, utterly regardless of all that it was costing me in money, in social recognition, and in every interest of every kind save that of mental liberty, out of the abundance of my heart my mouth spake my unbounded, wild enthusiasm for you. It cost me my position in a bank, and my position on a newspaper, and came nearer costing me the love of the dearest wife that ever plighted troth than all else together.

But by years of pure life I have lived down all of this, and my neighbors saw that a man could be an infidel and be a good man.

The conviction that I was right grew with my years, and ripened into defiant courage as my hair began to silver with the frosts of years, and I wrote a book in which I said kind and enthusiastic things about you. I became a prohibitionist, and when as the editor of a prohibitionist paper, the way to eminence and financial success seemed clear if I would only pander to Christian ignorance, bigotry and hypocrisy, I would not desert you because you were right, though letters came by the hundred, repudiating me and refusing me support, and time and again, until I cannot now count them, Christian men threatened to murder me with the same breath that proclaimed their faith in their religion. Christian men caught me in the public highway, and in the name of the church subjected me to such outrage as no other Kentuckian ever suffered, and finally a church that worships god and believes that Jesus was born with a god for his father, fined me and put me in jail, locked in a stone and steel cell for two months with Negro thieves and murderers, for saying in the defence of good morals what every intelligent man in the Blue Grass region knows was true.

Many good Christians and good infidels came to see me and wrote me kind letters, and they came from all over the United States, but none of them were ever signed Robert G. Ingersoll.

I went to my farm and worked hard for two years to recuperate from my losses, and to let my wife recover the health that her sympathy with me had almost destroyed; she once lying at the point of death when I was locked up in jail and refused by Christian men the privilege of going to see her under a guard for just one day.

Four times I have started my paper, and though no man has ever lost a dollar by me, I have lost money every time and this last time in about three months I have lost, out of my own pocket, beside my time and labor, about $200.

Lately I said in my paper that Jesus Christ had a father and mother just as I had. A Methodist preacher and a Commonwealth's attorney indicted me for blasphemy for having said this, and stated in the indictment that I was editing my paper "for lucre."

I was taken through a rain, a gray-headed man, and put in a cold and comfortless cell in jail, right here in Lexington, where I and my family and two generations of my ancestry have lived lives of purity and excellence second to none that ever breathed the breath of life — in this city of Lexington represented by W. C. P. Breckinridge.

Not long since I read that your profits for last winter's lectures had been $50,000. And now you, Robert G. Ingersoll, write to me that you are sorry that I have touched the feelings of my neighbors. When I have read your replies to Gladstone, I have said that you were the prince of irony and that Juvenal was not your peer in satire; but little did I think that I your humble friend and admirer would be the victim of the most scathing of all that has ever flowed from your gifted pen.

I have now some adequate appreciation of what "The grand old man" and the lovely Dr. Field must have felt, and what must have been the sense of pain with which you actually killed old judge Jerry Black. But they were your enemies and I was your friend. They got only what they had a right to expect. They were rich and had millions of friends. I stand alone, and moneyless and troubled, and seeing the almost certainty of my conviction when my trial comes in July.

I was silly enough to boast how you would come to my aid, though I was ashamed to have to say that I would have to pay you for your services.

You could not have been ignorant of my case. It was in the Associated Press dispatches everywhere; and when I asked you for bread, even for money, you gave me a stone.

The last issue of my paper tells how a Catholic priest of Minnesota, who had never seen and talked to me half as much as you have done, sent me $5.00 to help me, out of a $600 salary, and wrote a splendid article which was published in my paper, and twelve pages of beautifully and closely written private letter to me, full of such tender love and brotherly affection that my aspiration is now to have him come and see me in my humble but sweet and romantic country home, and sit on our famous Blue Grass under the very tree where for years I have had the dream that someday you and Mark Twain would sit with me and my wife and children.

This priest, Martin Mahoney, did this when he was in the habit of reading in my paper that I was an Atheist, and that I did not believe in the immortality of the soul, as you thought possible at the grave of your brother.

I have no more faith in any kind of Christianity, Catholic or Protestant, than I have in Buddhism, and not as much faith in either of them as I have in Mohammedanism. I do not believe that Jesus Christ was any better man than Martin Mahoney, or that the mother of Jesus was any better than my mother, or my wife; and yet see what kind of a fix you have left me in to boost infidelity and blast Catholicism.

Where did you get the idea that I had "lacked courtesy?" You are the first man that has ever suggested it. Certainly no Kentucky infidel has said it, and if Christians may have said it, are you absolutely certain that the whole Christian world has concurred in the sentiment that you were absolutely courteous?

Though I am a gentleman to the manor — and manner — born, I have lately worked with the Negroes, and I have been imprisoned and treated as if I were an outlaw; and if, under these circumstances, I may not have lived up to my Chesterfield so punctiliously as you who have lived on grand stages and "Fifth Avenue" may have done, is a little lack of courtesy a thing for which I ought to be imprisoned?

I hope that your time is all of you that is "mortgaged," and that your soul is not in the same fix, with the devil as the mortgagee.

It was so considerate in you to suggest that your presence might injure me by fanning into flame all the bigotry in my section.

Of course, nothing of that sort exists here now where they have had me in jail twice and will try to get me in jail or the penitentiary the third time, and where last week a Christian editor threatened to kill me, and where vilification and lies about me constitute a large feature of the newspapers.

Your guess that I would not need much help was an exceedingly bad guess for a man of your distinguished perceptive powers, but I guess I will try not to need yours.

A sadder but a wiser man I am yours respectfully,

Charles C. Moore

Moore went to the Federal Penitentiary in Columbus, Ohio, on February 26, 1899. He had acted as his own attorney at his trial where he expected a fine but received, instead, a two-year jail sentence. The reports of that trial reproduced, in part, in this book are shocking and incredible.

The Ohio Liberal Society, a group of "freethinkers," immediately voted to enter an appeal and employed the law firm of Phares and Keller, Cincinnati, Ohio, for that work. A retainer of $100 was paid, cash in advance. Various other freethought groups then began to publish accounts of what had happened, all being solicitous of Moore.

Because of his work for abolition, a Black editor of the *Lexington Standard* newspaper began a petition for clemency to the president of the United States, William McKinley, since Moore was in the penitentiary on a federal charge. Putting his name first, the editor asked that every Black person in Kentucky also sign the petition. This work was later taken up by others and in early July 1899, the president commuted Moore's sentence to six months, with one month's time off for good behavior. He was released early in the morning of July 7. But he could not forget that Ingersoll refused to be his counsel and subsequently made some harsh remarks at his "Welcome Home" celebration. On page 279-80, he notes:

My allusions to Col. Ingersoll . . . (were) not unpremeditated. I can, and will, forgive Ingersoll, but I can never forget that in the hour of my need of his friendship, he deserted me as no brave and grand and generous and bold man would have done.

Moore, of course, continued with his writings, producing three books in addition to articles and the *Blue Grass Blade*, much of which was his

vii

own composition. Prior to this book he had written *The Rational View* in 1890, a serious attack on supernaturalism within the Christian religion. In a way emulating Mark Twain, his final book written in 1903 gives an account of his journey in countries bordering the Mediterranean. Ingersoll continued with his lectures which later were published in book form by his brother-in-law. Ingersoll died of heart failure approximately two weeks after Moore was released from prison. Subsequently Moore noted:

> *Before Ingersoll died it was hard for me to forgive him that he had never come to my assistance, but after his great death, which ended the greatest life of any man known to history, I have mingled all my reproaches of him with his ashes and scattered them to the winds.*

In this book Moore does not get to the matter of his legal difficulties and prison stay until chapter 10, beginning on page 212. Prior to this, the book is full of anecdotal accounts of his boyhood and youth, some fragments of his life and vignettes concerned with incidents of his life or evaluations of persons in closed situations. Yet, his is a free-flowing pen with a grand and interesting style. He could easily have been classified as one of the best writers of the day. But, alas, accolades are not for those who challenge majoritarian views.

Madalyn O'Hair
1984

Behind the Bars; 31498
Chapter I

My maternal grand-father was Barton Warren Stone. He was one of twenty children of the son of the Earl of Surrey. He was the founder of the religious sect variously known as "Christians," "Disciples" and "Campbellites." This last name was given them from the fact that about three years after my grand-father had organized this sect Alexander Campbell came from Scotland to America and, accepting the distinguishing religious tenets of my grand-father, added to them the doctrine known as "baptism for the remission of sins," and urged that doctrine with such special force that it, being quite unpopular, attracted much attention, and resulted in the religious body being called "Campbellites" and in Mr. Campbell taking precedence over my grand-father as the leader in the religious denomination. Stone and Campbell were respectively like Melancthon and Luther in "The Reformation," as the new sect was called; my grand-father being mild, gentle, retiring and unobtrusive, and Mr. Campbell being very ambitious.

I can only remember my grand-father on two occasions. Once he was smoking a cob pipe in the front porch of the large home of my parents, and once my father was counting out to him about a hundred silver dollars. I thought they must be very rich people. My paternal grand-father died many years before I was born. My father was Charles Chilton Moore, the Chilton, and I imagine the Charles also, being for my paternal grand-father's Captain in the Revolutionary war.

My name is Charles Chilton Moore, as it was recorded in the large old family Bible, that had in it the apocryphal books of the Old

Testament, that I read with the canonic books when I was a young boy, and that was burned in a fire that destroyed "my old Kentucky home," soon after our civil war.

On an adjustable kind of a door plate that hangs on the outside of the heavy steel doors, that now lock me in, my name is "Moore, 31498," the figures indicating the number of convicts in all, that had been in this prison when I came into it. I am a Government prisoner. This is the first position I have ever held under the Government, except that I have twice been Census Enumerator.

My eldest son is named Charles Chilton Moore, and his only child has the same name, and we call the little one Charles IV.

(Just then a man called to me through the grating of my cell door, and said, "Good evening, sir; I believe this is the Colonel from Kentucky," and I said, "No sir; I am the only man who ever came from Kentucky who was not a Colonel," and he laughed and said, "Oh, beg pardon.")

Heredity and environment and pre-natal conditions are the architects of our fortunes, despite the proverb to the contrary, that I offer this in apology for some further information about my ancestry. It seems fairly certain that I am kin to the Duke of Argyll, and the family name is in my immediate family. In the current rage for finding distinguishing ancestry, some late book on that subject, I am told, has made me kin to Charlemagne and William the Conqueror. I don't know, and don't care, but suppose it is no better sustained than such pretentions generally are.

Beside Adam I know of no other prominent ancient to whom I am related. He was a gardener and seems to have raised apples and to have had domestic infelicity with his wife, but belonged to the first families of his country.

My father was brought by his parents from Virginia when he was six months old, to his parent's home, eight miles north of Lexington, Kentucky, which is almost in sight of the fine "Blue Grass" farm of 850 acres that my father subsequently owned, and 347 acres of which my family now own. Our home is a nice and neat frame house, called "Quakeracre" from its simplicity.

My mother was a woman of strong common sense and had inherited her father's strong religious convictions. Her father was not rich, and even if she had had the finest opportunities of her day, in other respects, she could not have had great literary advantages, as she was married before she was sixteen years old. She was much esteemed for her own sterling qualities and for the great love that many had for her father. In one sense my father's education was limited; in another sense it was not at all so. The school facilities of his day, in Kentucky, were poor, but through a life that ended at 71 years he was a close and retaining reader of the best literature. He loved "Sir Walter Scott," as he always called him, and as far back as I can remember I have seen him shake with silent merriment as he read Dickens. He was a fine business man; began life on a patrimony of one thousand dollars as a merchant in Winchester, Ky., and ended as a farmer. Politically he was a great admirer of Henry Clay. He played no game but backgammon, but I have heard it intimated that rather than have Mr. Clay embarrassed my father helped to pay debts that Mr. Clay made at cards.

My father's only dissipation was chewing tobacco, though he was very neat about it. He nearly always chewed tobacco while he was reading newspapers. When he died one of the old Negro men came to me and said: "Now, Mars Charley, ole Marster's dead, an' I jes' want ter tell you one thing; you'se got to learn to read de newspapers and chaw terbacker." He thought that "ole Marster" got his business knowledge out of newspapers, and that "terbacker" greatly assisted in under-standing any good reading. In his young days my father was quite a beau. He was one of the "attendants" at thirty-two weddings, and in a Thespian society is said to have played "Tony Lumpkin," in "She Stoops to Conquer," in fine style. In his old days, he would sometimes, half in merriment, and half in the stilted dignity of his young days, bow exceedingly low to a lady and say, "Sarvant, Madam." He nearly always wore a dress suit, including white cravat, with an expansive and expensive bandanna handkerchief. In talking, which he did well, his habit was to plait and to unplait his handkerchief. When he would go to relate some of his early experiences, as he would do, by special solicitation on occasions when we had a pretty large visiting company, and especially in winter nights, the Negro women and children from the kitchen would frequently steal in and take retired seats on the floor of the sitting room. I cannot tell a story as well as he did, and so I will just give you the substance of one of his stories.

It was at the Battle of the River Raisin, or Dudley's Defeat, I don't know which — they may be two names for the same battle. Colonel Dudley was commanding the regiment in which my father was.

(At this point I bought from a newsboy at my cell door, a copy of the Columbus, Ohio, Press-Post of this date, Sunday, February 12th, 1899. In it are two columns of an account of me, and five pictures of me, and under the five, that are in a group, there are, in large letters, the words, "Versatile Charles C. Moore." In this group of pictures of me the largest one is simply of my head and bust, with my prison number, "31498," in

3

large figures across my breast, as I sat to have my picture taken according to the requirements of the "Bertillon system" used in the prison. One of the pictures represents me in the conventional penitentiary stripes. This is inaccurate. While some of the prisoners have these stripes, the large majority of them including myself, have uniforms not unlike those of the Confederate officers in the civil war. The other two pictures of me are anachronisms, as they represent me as a preacher and as a European tourist with long gray hair and beard as I now have, which in those days were as black as a crow. The article in the Press-Post, headlines and all, is as follows:

REMARKABLE

IS THE LIFE STORY OF CHARLES C. MOORE, EDITOR OF THE BLUE GRASS BLADE. — HIS PRESENT TERM IN THE OHIO PENITENTIARY MERELY AN INCIDENT IN THE NUMEROUS CHAPTERS OF ROMANCE AND ADVENTURE. — PHILANTHROPIST, TRAVELER, EDITOR, INFIDEL, AND NOW A CONVICT. — THRILLING EXPERIENCES OF THIS UNIQUE CHARACTER IN HIS STRUGGLES TO SATISFY HIS AMBITIONS. — TELLS HIS STORY TO THE PRESS-POST.

Charles C. Moore, the gray-bearded, silvery-haired prisoner who entered the penitentiary Wednesday evening to serve a sentence of two years from Lexington, Ky., has a life's story that fairly teems with romance and adventure. In brief, he has traveled the course from the son of a wealthy Kentucky gentleman, with means to gratify every wish, to an inmate of a felon's cell. That he is now in the penitentiary is due to an error in judgment, rather than in purpose.

Shortly after his arrival at the institution he related the following story to a Press-Post reporter. It is a very small part of his history. Complete, it would fill a book. Said he:

"I was born 61 years ago on the farm where I have resided all my life, about eight miles from Lexington, Kentucky. My father was a wealthy man and I was an only child. I was left with all the money I could wish for and my check was honored all over the State when made payable by my father. But I did not spend much money. Rather than go into society and spend money, I lived as a recluse, spending most of my time in study and reading. I had two intimate companions. One was the brightest boy I have ever seen and the other was about the dullest. One is Judge John G.

4

Simrall, of Louisville, and the other is General John B. Castleman, also of Louisville. I received my early education from a private tutoress whom my father secured in New York. She was a woman of remarkable abilities, and we regarded her almost as one of the family. When I grew old enough to go to college I started in at what was then known as Transylvania College, at Lexington, but I did not like the place and later went to Bethany College. It was in the year 1856 that I entered there, and two years later I graduated with the degree of bachelor of arts. During my stay at college I was ranked as the most popular man there. I was popular with the professors and best students, as well as with the most harum-scarum boys enrolled. I was into every bit of mischief.

"After returning home in 1858 I started in to preach, and throughout the war I was regarded as one of the foremost preachers of the State. At one time I preached at the same church with James A. Garfield. I did not know at the time who he was, but remarked that he was a very unusual man and a good one, but a politician rather than a preacher. During the war I was an abolitionist and a secessionist and I did a great deal of good work for both sides.

"Shortly after the close of the war I made up my mind to walk to Palestine, starting on my walk from Liverpool, England. I did not complete my journey, however, for reasons which I will describe later. I went across the water, however, and started out from Liverpool on foot. I went from London to Paris, walking all the way, and I made a host of friends doing it. One rather interesting thing happened after I left London. I had been walking all day and when night fell I reached a small town in which there happened to be a great number of Her Majesty's soldiers, and I could not get a place to sleep for the night. I consequently left the town and a short distance out of it I came across the mansion of an English lord, whose name I can't recall. I was determined to stay there that night, and so on approaching the place I walked right past the porter's post and into the house where I met his highness, the lord. I told him of my mission and said I could vouch for my honesty. He doubted me, and, after some little parley, said I could not remain there. Then I said I would sleep in the roadway in front of his house. Meanwhile his wife came out, and after a short talk with her, he called to me to come back and stay there. I accepted, and our evening was a most pleasant one. Next day, when I left, they gave me a hearty invitation to return, and the lord gave me one of his cards, which I still have. One day while near Paris, at the suburban town of Bois de Boulogne, I saw a man drowning in the Seine, and it afterwards proved to be an attempted suicide. I saved his life by swimming in after him. After getting him out I helped him to his home and there discovered that the affair had come out of some domestic trouble. But the man when I pulled him out thanked me in his French tongue a thousand times.

"Shortly after this I received word that my sister had died, and I became so homesick that I gave up my journey and started for home. After reaching my Kentucky place I preached for a year or so at the Christian Church, Versailles, Ky. During my ministry there the most remarkable thing of my life happened. It was my change from a preacher of the Gospel to an infidel. One of my most intimate friends was William J. Hatch, who was a son of the ex-president of the university, and one of the most learned persons I have ever met. He was an infidel, while I was a Christian. He came to see me while I was at home and the pre-eminent question of our lives immediately sprung up. We mutually agreed not to argue on the question, but to get the very best books on infidelity and Christianity, and read them carefully. He was at my home six weeks, during which time we studied the question constantly. I converted him, and at my next Sunday service I baptized him. This is what that operation cost me: A few Sundays after that I was preaching at my usual place, when, at the close of the sermon, I closed the Bible and walked down from the pulpit and out of the church. I called a meeting of the elders next day and informed them that they would have to get another preacher, as I was skeptical and could not preach what I did not believe. I was an infidel, and that after a most careful study of the subject. It was not my intention to say much about my change of belief at that time, but the question was so often put before me that I did finally make a public avowal of it.

"After that I drifted into journalism, acting in the capacity of reporter and also editor of the Lexington Transcript and Daily Press. Both papers, however, have since merged into other papers, so that they are not known by that name now. I followed that vocation off and on until 1886, when I started my own paper. I did that because I was unable while on the other papers to express my thoughts. I was a moralist, and, although an infidel, I have done more for the demi-monde of Lexington than any other person that ever lived there. One night when I was walking home from town, it was a cold, snowy night, I lived eight miles from town, I turned the whole matter over in my mind and decided to start my paper. Almost at the same instant of my decision I decided to call it the "Blue Grass Blade," and it still bears that name.

"In my paper I fought the liquor question, but did not have the support of the professing Christians of the town. I also opposed the campaign of Colonel W. C. P. Breckinridge, who was a distant relative of mine. My paper had a wonderfully wide circulation. It had as many readers in Massachusetts as it did in my State, and in Nebraska, a State I was never in, it also had a very wide circulation. But the people were not in sympathy with my publication, and I was too much of a moralist for them, and finally I was unable to get my paper printed in the town. Then I took it to Cincinnati, where it was printed for some time, and I finally got things to running in Lexington again, so that it could be gotten out there.

"In 1893 I was locked in jail in Paris, Ky., for two months for publishing the following statement in my paper: 'If I had a contract to bore for hell fire, I would build my derrick where the earth's crust is thinnest, in front of the Christian Church of _____, Ky.' While I was in jail I wrote a book entitled 'Behind the Bars.' I worked on it day and night, and finally in a fit of despondency, after I had completed it, I tore up all the manuscript and threw it into the fire. Some time after that I was assaulted by a man and jailed for fighting. At the time of my trial, my attorneys were Christians, while the judge was an infidel, and I was cleared. Once again after that I was jailed for blasphemy, but released after a short imprisonment. The article which caused the arrest resulting in my being here was published in October, 1897. My life has been one of adventures and I can not but look upon my present condition as just one of the notable occurrences in my history. The keepers here at the prison have been just as kind to me as they could possibly be, and I am very grateful to them for all of it. The warden has told me that I will work in the prison printing office, where I can do proof-reading, and occasionally write a little squib of some sort, and that will be very enjoyable."

An allusion was made to the recent exploration of the John Morgan tunnel and the investigations such as have been published, and he made a start, exclaiming with surprise that he had forgotten all about its having occurred at this place. He expressed his desire to see the cells occupied by Morgan and his

7

men, and hopes to be able to write an article for his paper on the subject. Considering his position, he seems to be delighted with his prospects. He said the place did not seem to him like a prison at all; everybody was so courteous to him. Moore presents a very picturesque appearance in his prison garb. He looks like a statesman, and is a most fluent talker. His travels over the world and his previous excellent schooling, supplemented by diligent reading, have given him a magnificent education, and he is very conversant on almost any subject. He is very musical in his tastes, and, although when younger he was quite an expert as a pianist, he has done nothing with that for years. All of his folks are likewise musical.

One of his sons is a chemist in the Department of Agriculture at Washington. Another has recently returned from Porto Rico, having served in the late war, while still another is at home with his mother. His acquaintance throughout the South is something remarkable, and if he is not known by name, he is known as the editor of the "Blue Grass Blade."

* * * * *

I now resume my story at the point where I was interrupted by the newspaper incident. It was in 1812 and the weather was cold enough then, or soon after, to freeze the spray on the ropes of a ship on Lake Erie, and the scene of the battle was in the wilderness and I think not far from Lake Erie. My father, who was subsequently called Captain from his connection with the militia service, and his brother Thomas were privates in the war. There was a river between the American forces on one side and the Indians and the British on the other. The Indians were commanded by British officers. The river was so narrow and shallow that, had there been no opposition, the Americans could have waded across. The Americans, adopting the tactics of the Indians, broke ranks and, as far as possible, hid behind trees, each side firing whenever a man on either side could get a shot at the other. My father was behind a tree that was barely large enough to protect him, and a ball from an Indian knocked particles of the bark off the tree into my father's eyes.

By degrees the boldest of the Americans began running from behind the trees that concealed them so as to get closer to the river and to the Indians and their British officers on the other side. The Indians stayed still behind their trees, and killed and wounded the Americans as they

8

ran toward the Indians. The Americans showed a disposition to cross the river to the Indians, while the Indians were disposed to retreat from the river. It was a piece of strategy on the part of the Indians, and it deceived the Americans. When the Americans had thus been enticed to come close up to the banks of the river so that the Indians in front of them could shoot them if they attempted to cross the river, it was discovered that the Indians were coming up in the rear of the Americans, so that the Indians in front and behind were protected by trees, while the Americans could not be.

(At this point a prisoner postman of the prison post-office brought me the following letter from my wife:

LEXINGTON, KY., FEBRUARY 9, 1899.

MY DEAR HUSBAND:

I have been so shocked and dazed by what has happened that I can scarcely collect myself enough to realize that it is true. Last night was almost a sleepless night and was spent in tears. The inhumanity of man to man and the infamy that is perpetrated in the name of religion are enough to make one's blood boil.

Daddy, be brave and keep a cheerful heart. It is hard to bear, but I am proud to be a convict's wife under existing circumstances, and I scorn such characters as the hypocrite Rucker. I do not wish him any bodily harm, but I hope that derision and scorn and contempt will be heaped upon his head by true men. Leland seemed to boil with rage last night when he got home. I would be almost afraid for him to meet Rucker now. We are going to do all we can to get you back home.

Campbell told Leland that this would make you many friends, and that he would do all he could for you. How I hope the warden is a kind-hearted man and will respect your gray hairs. I feel that it is the greatest blot on civilization that ever happened. If your friends do not rally now, and do what they can they will not deserve freedom, if they ever had any.

How are you? I have thought of nothing but you since you left, but I am going to try, mighty hard, not to let it make me sick. You see my hand trembles so that I can hardly write. The nights are so long and lonely. It seems an age since you left us. There are a good many letters here for you. Must I send them to you? Tell us about yourself and let us hear from you as often as you can. I hope you are well and comfortable. There will be a day of retribution, I hope. The house seems as if we have had a funeral. The servants

9

all seem to feel for you deeply. Brent seemed dazed — just sat for a long time with tears in his eyes.

Willis is waiting for this, so I will stop. Brent joins me in love to you, dear Daddy. Let us know if you want anything.

Your hopeful wife,   LUCY P. MOORE

Leland and Brent are our sons, aged 23 and 21 years, and Willis is a faithful Negro man in our employ as a farm hand. Our other children are Charles C., aged 27, and Lucile Campbell Moore, aged 18, both in Washington, D.C.; the first in the employ of the Government as a scientist, in the Agricultural Department, and the latter at school. Beside these our only other child was our first born, Eliza Campbell. She died when she was eleven years old, and her death put the first gray hairs in my head.)

To continue the story of the battle, in a few minutes more the Indians came rushing, with wild war whoops, up behind the Americans, while the Indians on the other side of the river ran up to the river from which they had retreated, and the Americans began to fall fast from the rifle shots of the Indians. Col. Dudley seeing that defence was impossible, jerked a ramrod from a musket, tied a white handkerchief on it, waved it in token of surrender, and ordered his men to lay down their arms. The Indians, from both sides, rushed on to the surviving Americans and captured them all. My father had on a fine military overcoat, the lining of which was so quilted in squares that each square had a gold coin in it, that he had thus concealed for an emergency. An Indian snatched this overcoat and put it on without knowing that there was any money in it. My father never saw it any more, and used to wonder what became of the money that was in it.

The Indians then stripped all of the Americans stark naked. My father had a very handsome and bright colored pair of suspenders, with fine buckles on them. An Indian unbuttoned these suspenders from my father's pants and tried to fix them on to his own buckskin breeches; which, of course, he could not do, as the Indian's breeches had no buttons, being intended to be held up only by a belt around his waist. The Indian tried to buckle the suspenders around his waist, but could not. He threw the suspenders, with contempt, back to my father, who stood and held this only remnant of his toilet. The Indian started off, but soon turned back and snatched the suspenders from my father and tried to use them to hold his powder horn. Not succeeding in this he threw them a second time to my father and started off again. He soon turned back, however, and, a third time, snatched them from my father, and went off, and my father never saw him again. My father said, in telling this story, "He was an Indian giver." It was soon evident that the Indians were going to make all the prisoners "run the gauntlet." There was a long trench in the ground, which, from my father's description, I imagine was about four feet deep, eight or ten feet wide, and from a hundred yards to two hundred yards long. My father thought the ditch was either an old and abandoned mill race, or an old deep worn road. At one end of the ditch was a fort that my father called a "block house." The Indians marched the naked prisoners down to the end of the ditch, away from the block house, and told them that if they could run down that ditch to the block house and get into the block house, they would after that be saved. Many Indians then stationed themselves on the banks each side of the ditch to kill the Americans as they ran by. My father's most intimate friend was named Grant, and my father and Grant determined to hold each other by the hand and run together. When their time came to run they bid each other an affectionate good-bye and started together, running their best. They passed a number of Indians without getting hurt, and then my father saw ahead of them, on his side of the ditch, an Indian, with a bright, new rifle, who was fixing to shoot as the two should run by. As they drew near him the Indian drew his gun and fired, apparently at my father, when the two were nearly opposite the Indian. My father felt Grant's hand jerk loose from his, and glancing back saw that the ball had struck Grant in the naked breast, and the blood was spouting from his mouth as he threw up his hands and fell back. My father never saw Grant again.

My father continued to run, as fast as he could. He approached an Indian who, he could see, was getting ready to split his skull with a broad-sword, holding the handle in both hands. As my father passed him the Indian struck, and my father dodged so that the sword struck him across the shoulders. It was a glancing stroke, but knocked my father down. He lost but little time by the fall, coming down on his hands and knees, and going ahead all the time, until he regained his feet. He ran on and got into the block house, and used to say that the only wound he ever got in war was in the back, and while he was running. The prisoners who had gotten into the block house, knowing that the Indians had a special aversion to red-headed men, hid all of that kind under the wounded and dead men, but the Indians came in and found all red-headed men, and killed them and scalped them. While the Indians were scalping these red-headed men, my father could see that something at a distance was creating an excitement among the Indians and their British officers, and my father managed to get a view in that

11

direction, and saw an Indian on a horse, that had on him the harness of an American cannon carriage, coming toward them as fast as the horse could run. The Indian ran the horse at full speed right into the midst of the Indians and their officers, and began a most excited speech to the Indians. From the dogged and mean appearance of the Indians, it was evident to the Americans and British that the speaker, who proved to be Tecumsey, was abusing them for killing the prisoners, and even the British officers did not dare to resent what he said.

My father said "Tecumsey was a low, ugly, Potawatomie Indian." My father used to say that he never had seen but one man who would brag and fight, too, and that was General Leslie Combs of Lexington. Gen. Combs was in that battle. Years after my father was dead, I met the old General one day and asked him to tell me about the battle. His description of it was so nearly identical with that of my father that it is hard for me, in memory, to separate them.

(—I am in "Banker's Row;" ground floor. There are four stories of cells above me. At that black mark a prisoner near me called to one several stories above me and said: "Oh, Morgan; have you anything up there for me to read?" The prisoner above said: "Yes; I've got a Bible," and the man below said: "Oh, you go to hell.")

*   *   *   *   *

Summer before last Mr. and Mrs. Vincent H. Perkins, of Chicago, were at our home, and as we sat out under the porch, under the honey-suckles, I told them the story of Parker Craig Nicholson. Mr. Perkins said that, someday, I ought to write it for a magazine. I will probably never see my home again and will tell the story here.

My father had a brother named John, who did not go to the war. As far back as I can remember, and to his death, Uncle John was a rich farmer, living about six miles from my father. Later, I may tell you, if I do not forget it, how James Lane Allen wrote his first magazine article from a story that I told him, at "Quakeracre," about Uncle John. One day, long before I can remember, there came to the home of my Uncle John an entire stranger. He told my Uncle that he had known his brothers, Thomas and Chilton — my father was always called by his middle name — in the army. The stranger said that his name was Nicholson and everybody called him Major, as far back as I can recollect. Uncle John was familiar with the war experiences of his brothers, and soon saw that the stranger knew about them, though, as it proved, neither my father nor my Uncle Thomas could ever remember to have known anything of Major Nicholson in the war. Uncle John had a plain and not very large house, but he was famous for his hospitality. Uncle John invited the stranger into his home. The Major was dignified and agreeable and gentlemanly, and accepted my Uncle's invitation to stay for dinner. The Major and my Uncle became so engaged in conversation that they talked until near supper time, and the Major accepted an invitation to supper, and to spend the night.

The next morning they met at the breakfast table, and the Major and my Uncle talked on to dinner, and when dinner was announced, walked together, into dinner, without breaking their conversation. The Major spent the second day and the second night, third day and third night, and so on, until on the sixth day my Uncle proposed to take him to a public sale in the neighborhood. Nothing had ever been said about any terms upon which the Major was staying at my Uncle's, and no allusion had ever been made to it by the Major, or by any of the family in his presence. At the sale my Uncle introduced the Major to various friends. One of them asked, "Major, where do you live?" and the Major said, "At Captain John Moore's, sir." The reply astonished my Uncle, but he said nothing about it. Some days after that the Major came to see my father. He was kindly received. My father had a large house. The Major spent the day there, and at night was taken to the best guest chamber in the house. He spent several days at my father's, and each evening of the summer days, immediately after supper, he would, without any light, walk off to that room, before any arrangement had been made for others going to bed, simply saying, "Good night." He was always ready for breakfast, dressed with scrupulous neatness.

At the end of a year from that time the Major was living just that same way at my Uncle's, coming to spend a few days with us every two or three weeks, and he lived there and at my father's just that same way, for forty years, until he died, at seventy years of age, at my Uncle John's, honored and respected by all who knew him. He never paid anything for his living. He was buried at "Old Union" Church, of which the families of my Uncle and my father were members, and of which the Major had been, for years, a member. A nice monument was put over him, and it and funeral expenses were paid for out of about $800.00 the major left in a Lexington bank. Though my Uncle Thomas had a fine home and was wealthy and hospitable, and lived not more than twenty miles away, I never heard of the Major going to see him. None of us ever had any clue to the Major's history further than I have told you. For some years before he died he would say that, next year, he was going back to "Jersey," as he called New Jersey. He said that so long, that it

13

got to be a joke, though none of us dared to ask him about it.

One summer day, sure enough, the Major started back to New Jersey, and we supposed we would never see him again. He was gone only a month or two until he came back. He never said anything about his visit to New Jersey. The best room in my father's house was called "Major Nicholson's room" until after the Major died, and it was assigned to me. There were two other very poor men who occasionally came to our house to spend a day or two. The Major would not recognize them, and if he found either of them there when he got there, he would leave in disgust.

The Major had, nearly all the time, one or two fine mares at my father's farm, but he never paid a cent for their keeping, and from the sales of their colts the Major always had plenty of good clothes and saddles and bridles and pocket money for his moderate habits. His only jewelry was a breast-pin in his nice shirt-bosom. The pin was two hearts with a dart through them. As a boy I used to want to ask him about that pin, but, like my father, he was so dignified and reserved in his style that I never dared mention it to him. In later years I have wondered if there was not something about that breast-pin that connected his peculiar life with some love affair.

Chapter II

Before I go further with my own special biography, I am going to tell you one of the strange stories of the great variety of crimes that have been committed by my companions here, as they have told them to me. The man who tells me this particular one is here for a burglary that has no connection with his story that I am going to tell you. I told him that I wanted to put the story in my book, and he gave me his consent. He is fairly good looking and speaks English and German equally well. He was working in a tobacco field in Mexico, in April, 1898. He is now 26 years old. He had a Spanish sweetheart named Meda, an uncommon name, he says, in Mexico. The tobacco field was in a plain and Meda's house was on a very high bluff a considerable distance away, but in full view of the man in the tobacco field, who is now my fellow-prisoner. One day while the prisoner was working in that field he saw a man go into Meda's house, and knew that she was there alone, for he had seen all the other members of the family go away from home only a short while before. The prisoner then saw Meda run from the house, and jump off a high cliff, and kill herself on the rocks below. He saw the man go out of the house and ride away on a horse, and soon after that saw that the house was burning.

The man who is now a prisoner followed the other man, and saw him go into a dense forest and hitch his horse in a secluded place, and then go behind a large rock. The prisoner had a machete with him. He went up to the rock on the side opposite where the man was sitting, and, creeping around it, found the man and jumped on him, and cut him several times so severely with the machete that the man could not rise, though he did not seem to be mortally wounded. There are there very large ants called Hormiga Colorado. They travel in myriads, in a little path, and will attack, with great fierceness, any man or animal that obstructs their course in that path. They are an inch long, and their bite is very severe. The prisoner saw a stream of these ants as he approached the rock behind which the man was. He dragged the wounded man to this stream of ants and fastened him to a small tree with the man's stirrup leathers, so that the man's body would be across the stream of ants. The ants rushed over the screaming man until his body was covered with millions of them. The prisoner watched them until they had cleaned all the flesh from the man's bones.

* * * * *

The home of my parents was a two-story brick, having thirteen rooms, seven halls, and a two-story porch in front and a one-story porch behind. It was not a fine house, but was very commodious and splendidly adapted to the hospitality for which it was famous. It was destroyed by fire soon after the war, and a smaller one, belonging to my sister, the only remaining member of the large family beside myself, now occupies a part of the site of the old one. My sister's husband, Major Thomas Y. Brent, of the Confederate service, was killed at the head of a regiment of which he was an officer, on the morning of July 4, 1863, as they charged a Federal fort at Green River bridge, in Kentucky. He was the grandest looking soldier I ever saw. He was in the command of Gen. John H. Morgan, whose escape from this penitentiary, with a number of his men, is one of the traditional stories of this, the largest prison in the world, containing twenty-seven acres of ground and over 2,300 prisoners.

Through the middle of my father's farm ran a beautiful creek about seventy feet wide. On this creek I spent much of my young boyhood, walking, sitting, swimming, fishing and skating, much the greater part of the time alone, and my mind generally occupied in "air castling," in the common sense of the expression and much in a more literal sense, for I have spent much time thinking about the navigation of the air. In after years when I was a preacher and traveler afoot, through the mountains of Kentucky, I looked down upon the backs of buzzards sailing near abrupt precipices below me and have believed from then to this day, that there is, in all soaring birds, a dynamic force, the secret of which is, as yet, unknown to man, but which, some day, will be discovered, and it will be surprising that so simple a thing as a man's

16

traveling through the air was not sooner known.

A place on the farm that attracted much of my attention and thought, and where I spent a good many hours, was known then, as it is now, as "the fortification." It is evidently a prehistoric fort, the oldest trees of the forest in my earliest recollection growing in the bottom of its ditch and on the top of the bank which has been thrown up around it. The ditch is now eight or ten feet deep and three hundred feet in circumference. Strange-looking prehistoric relics and many flint arrowheads and numerous stone axes have been found near there in my memory. To this day I watch for any clue to its history, but have never found any. The old family home is named Forest Retreat.

The nearest and most intimate of our neighbors was Mrs. Polly Breckinridge, the mother of Rev. Dr. Robert J. Breckinridge, and grandmother of the "silver tongued" orator, Hon. W. C. P. Breckinridge. At the time her house was built it was among the finest in this country. It was very quaint and was very old when I first knew it. She was strongminded, but her education was only what was common for the day and country in which she was born. Notes that she wrote my mother were given away as literal curiosities. Their spelling and chirography were original. My mother generally managed to find out what was in them by asking the Negro servant, generally small and loquacious, what the old lady said. A broad avenue from her house ran, at a right angle, into a broad avenue from our house, and there was scarcely a day that a servant did not bring some nice thing, generally something to eat, for my mother, and my mother sent many things to her. She gave to my sister and me, each, a little tin plate, to eat off of, and around the margins of these plates were the letters of the alphabet with an & at the end, as all alphabets had in those days, and, as I now recollect, it was from those plates that I first learned my letters. If I had never learned them I would probably not be here. The man who made those plates, like Cadmus, carried letters into grease. When I can first remember old Mrs. Breckinridge, she had been blind for many years. She sent so many things to my mother, sometimes two or three times a day — among other things the first oysters I ever saw, then very expensive — that my mother became afraid that the old lady forgot how much she sent, or that possibly the Negro servants were just bringing her things on their own responsibility. So, one day my mother determined to tell the old lady about it. Mrs. Breckinridge affected a severity of style, just as her son Robert J. did.

My mother, with some misgivings, and fear of the old lady's tongue, went to see Mrs. Breckinridge, and, in an embarrassed style, told the old lady about how many things her servants brought to our house. Mrs. Breckinridge said, "I am blind, Madam, but, thank God, I am not a fool, and if you will just attend to your own business, I will try to attend to mine;" and nice things came on, every day, the balance of the old lady's life. I have known many Breckinridges, and what I have said of the old lady was characteristic of all of them. I remember the first time I ever saw John C. Breckinridge, subsequently Vice President of the United States, and more immediately than any other one man the cause of our civil war. The first room I ever had for my own, in my large old home, was a small room at the head of a back stairway, in which John C. Breckinridge and his widowed mother had lived when he was a small boy.

About three miles from my old home a man, without permission, had gone onto the farm of another man and had cut down a "bee tree" and had taken the honey. Probably under the earlier unwritten law of the country all wild honey belonged to the man who found it, but now a man was claiming it because it was found on his farm, and the owner of the tree demanded $5.00 indemnity. The suit was brought in a magistrate's court in the country, the complainant employing John C. Breckinridge, and the defendant employing Bob Woolley, now of Louisville, and, at that time, promising to be as distinguished as Breckinridge; the two just beginning to attract attention. There was a general impression that there was going to be something rare in oratory, and a large crowd of people came and sat upon seats of planks on logs, in the woods. The only witness in the case was for the prosecution. He stated that he "surrounded the bee tree," in the night and saw the accused chopping it down. Woolley attacked the idea of any one man "surrounding a tree," and attempted to invalidate his testimony on that ground, and Breckinridge defended the testimony. The people laughed and applauded, first on one side and then the other, until "order in the court" was impossible. The famous speech of "Sargeant Buzzfuzz" in the case of "Bardell vs. Pickwick," was equaled by either of the orators in this bee tree case, and I think from that speech, largely, began the fame of Breckinridge.

I had noticed that the two orators came from Lexington, in the same buggy, and I was solicitous lest, from the bitter things they said against each other in their speeches, they would fight on the road if they started back together. I watched with surprise and pleasure as they got into the same buggy, with no evidence of anger.

In sight of my window, at "Quakeracre," is "Castleton," now managed by Major Daingerfield of the late Confederate service. The Major now carries, in parts of his anatomy, two minie balls, property of the United States Government, which he not only declines to deliver to the rightful owner — unless the government is now barred by the statute of limitations and thirty-two years of "peaceable possession" — but also in defiance of the law against carrying concealed weapons, though the reconstructed Major is, in all other things, an exemplary, law-abiding man. The Major manages "Castleton" for his brother-in-law, James R. Keene, the Wall Street broker and multi-millionaire and turfman. In sight of my gate is a handsome granite monument over the mortal remains of "Domino," the horse that won $120,000.00 for Keene, with an epitaph that any man might emulate. At "Castleton" was born the only playmate and schoolmate that I ever had who was too lazy to play. He studied the Shorter Catechism for several years that I went to school with him. The first few pages of his book were worn out, while the pages, from there on, seemed never to have been opened. He is now one of the most attractive and influential men in Kentucky. He was a Captain in the Confederate service; he is now Brigadier-General John B. Castleman of the United States Army. I believe every man should have his most honorable title, so I still call him Captain.

Fannie Castleman was born at "Castleton." She is now the widow of Judge Eastin, of the Kentucky Court of Appeals. She is one of the handsomest women in Kentucky, with graces of heart and mind to match — Kentucky famous, worldwide, for its beautiful women, fast horses, whisky and tobacco. She was born that way and couldn't get over it. She and I were country school girls together, but when we went off to college we did not meet each other for two or three years. When I came home, one vacation, I walked across the pastures of the adjoining farms upon which we lived, to see her. I was perfectly astonished at her development, physically and intellectually, and her piano playing was exquisite. Her conversational powers were charming. When I had made a delightful call, during which she, all the time, called me "Charlie," while I had to say "Miss Fannie," I arose to go, and after several of those sweet, and apparently accidental, detentions that some bright women can so effectually compass, when they want to, she said to me, "Wait until I get my bonnet, and I will go part of the way with you." She ran out and returned, having on a common sun-bonnet that made a quaint, but cute, contrast with the balance of her handsome toilet. We walked slowly out of the immense yard and into the large and splendid woods. There was not a word of sweetheart talk in anything we said, and yet everything seemed to have a meaning that was beautiful and patent, on the surface, and then, in addition, seemed to have another far-off meaning that was not spoken. Finally, she stopped out in the middle of a large pasture; one of the most beautiful in Kentucky. It was one of those early fall days in which nature sometimes seems just to be trying her hand to see what she can do to make everything lovely and beautiful. Fannie held out her hand to say "Goodbye," and I put out mine to take it, and she turned up her pretty mouth for me to kiss, and "we kissed by chance, the usual way."

I felt that the elegant thing would be for me to go back home with her, and then I thought of the saying, "Quit while your credit's good," and I pretended to believe she was in earnest when she said she did not want me to go back with her, and now, away off here, an old gray-headed convict, I feel that college or no college, I was nothing but a common country bumpkin that I did not go back with her, even if she had come back with me a part of the way again, and we had the whole thing to do over again. In years we hardly met again, and one of the times was in the streets of Lexington. We simply clasped hands and hardly spoke. She had only lately lost the only child she ever had, a beautiful boy, and I had only lately lost our first born, a beautiful curly-headed girl.

Another locality near my home, that made its impress on my life, is Russell's Cave. At this place I got my first impressions of geology that I kept up from books, subsequently, and from personal observations in the mountains of my own State, and more especially by several visits to the Mammoth Cave, of Kentucky; and things I thus learned, in this wonderful science, got mixed up with the Mosaic cosmogony when I finally came to study theology, and the blending had much to do with my being in this prison. At this cave, at a political speaking, at which Cassius M. Clay was the orator, there occurred a most horrible fight between him, standing alone in his opposition to slavery, and Samuel Brown, the champion of the slavery cause. Brown shot Clay squarely in the body, but before he could shoot a second time Clay was on Brown with a Bowie-knife, the weapon for the handling of which Clay was famous, and Brown was fearfully cut in many places, but survived it, by the hardest, and was subsequently killed in a steamboat explosion. It was said by many of the pro-slavery enemies of Clay that he was saved from Brown's shot because he (Clay) had a coat-of-mail under his clothes, but others said at the time, as is now generally understood, that the ball which Brown fired failed to kill Clay because it struck the scabbard of Clay's Bowie-knife. That fight between Clay and Brown, and another fight in which Clay, with his Bowie-knife, killed a man at White Hall, Kentucky, both growing out of Clay's opposition to slavery, were the first skirmishes that grew larger and larger until they resulted in the war that emancipated 7,000,000 of slaves.

The leading citizens of Lexington combined in destroying the printing office of Mr. Clay in which he edited a paper against slavery. Force does not seem to succeed in its efforts to suppress the truth. Cassius M. Clay is, by large odds, the greatest hero that Kentucky ever produced, though Lincoln was born on its soil. He is living to-day, in Kentucky, a neglected man — neglected and unhonored by the Negroes for whose emancipation he took his life in one hand and his Bowie-knife in the other and dared to think and say what he thought, and to say it without mincing words. My knowledge of Clay's career taught me that, sometimes, the man who everybody says is wrong is really the only man who is right.

A little further on is the home of my distinguished and loved kinsman, the elder Carter Henry Harrison, the assassinated Mayor of Chicago. When he was a young man and I a little boy he used to visit my home, and, many a time, have I ridden behind my mother on a horse as she went to see his widowed mother. His distinction was a natural result from his breeding and rearing. I was reading his beautiful and instructive book, "A Race With The Sun," when I heard of his assassination.

I have sent the manuscript of my book home to my wife, as I have written it and cannot change it, and so I want to tell you something that I forgot to tell you when we were talking about "Cabellsdale," the old home of old Mrs. Breckinridge. In the large yard of "Cabellsdale," there was when I can first remember a log house of two rooms, that was then being used as a Negro cabin. Mrs. Breckinridge used to tell us how, in that house, she entertained Aaron Burr and Chief Justice Marshall. The latter was my grand-father Moore's "best man" when he was married. I used to hear that the names of Burr and Marshall had been written by themselves on the inner walls of that old house, but I could never find them. At that old house was the first time I ever saw "Billy" Breckinridge, since then ranking with Clay, Menifee and Tom Marshall in the galaxy of Kentucky orators. There was visiting at "Cabellsdale" a United States Army, or Navy, officer, who had been shot, in battle, through both hips so that he could not stand up, but he moved himself around in a wheel chair over the large hall and rooms and porches at "Cabellsdale." This officer, whose name I forget, unless it was Grayson, and Billy and I, little boys, were on the back porch when the officer ran the large hind wheel of his chair over the edge of the first of about six or eight steps, and was falling helplessly down them, when Billy and I at the same moment, ran under the chair, and catching it on our shoulders, only with all of our united strength succeeded in getting him back into a safe position. Thus though, in our young days, Billy and I literally put our shoulders to the wheel together, and each of us began life as a preacher, they afterward sent him to Congress, and sent me to the penitentiary. He and I have been heard of by more people than any other two living Lexingtonians.

I went to school with Billy's brothers, but only one day with Billy. He spent that day sitting straddle of a bench, reading a novel. The most brilliant conversation I remember ever to have heard between any young man and young woman was between Billy Breckinridge and Miss Rebecca Dixon, daughter of Governor Dixon of Kentucky, and now wife of Ex-Governor Brown of Kentucky. When I was the prisoner of the Christian, or Campbellite, Church, in jail, at Paris, Kentucky, and my wife seemed very liable to die, some of my friends went to Governor Brown to get him to allow me to go, under guard, for one day to the bedside of my wife, and he would not do it. I do not believe in Nemesis or anything supernatural, but a fearful affliction fell upon the Governor's family not long after that. Billy Breckinridge, now an editor, has written an editorial regarding my imprisonment here as being unjust.

The neighborhood in which I was born is the center of a strange folklore. The farm of Carter Harrison was bought by a man named Peniston, out of a part of $500,000 that he won as the highest prize in the Havana lottery. Peniston lived at the Harrison place, and I kept his bank account as a bookkeeper in the banking house of Grinstead & Bradley, Lexington, Kentucky. Peniston had been an actor. In two or three years Peniston was a bankrupt, and was a pauper inmate of a home that Ned Forest had built for indigent actors in New York. Forest began his career as an actor in a building of his own on Water street in Lexington. His plan was to have a perpetual play at that place, and all of the plays were to have horses in them, like "Mazeppa."

My wife who, as you have seen, says, "I am proud to be a convict's wife under existing circumstances —" and I, on our bridal tour, heard Forest, McCullough and Edwin Booth, all in "Othello," at Washington. I know I am "ahead of the hounds," but, please remember, that I am writing in a cell and am liable to interruption, and have to tell you some things just as I think of them.

I thought the banking house of Grinstead & Bradley was the most successful banking institution I had ever seen. Its individual ledger that I kept was the heaviest single case of bookkeeping in Lexington. The "Blue Grass Region" of Kentucky is the greatest race horse country in the world, and that banking house was the financial center of the race horse interest. Mr. Grinstead, the active member of the firm, was one of the most popular men I ever saw. He was, in many respects, so much like old "Pickwick," spectacles and all, that I asked him one day if anybody had ever told him that he was like "Pickwick." He laughed and said, "Many a time." While I was there there used to come into the bank a little foundling boy named Eddy Kissinger. He was an adept in playing the bones, and he would frequently come into the bank and play for us and go away with pay anywhere from five cents to a quarter. Mr. Grinstead died without enough to pay his funeral expenses, and Eddy, a well-to-do farmer, furnished a part of the money to bury him.

One dark night, only two or three years ago, a man who had never before been in my neighborhood, called at my yard gate in the country, not knowing whose home it was, to inquire the way to a neighboring house. I recognized the voice as that of Eddy Kissinger, though I had not seen him for years. He said that he owned two farms and that I must come to see him and see his collection of musical instruments. I do not think I was a first-class bank clerk, but I lost my position with Grinstead & Bradley unexpectedly, and when I was on the best of terms with them. I was told some years after, by an intimate friend of Mr. Grinstead, that it was because I talked against horse racing. I do not know whether this is true. I had a singular experience in the banking business which I will tell now while we are on that subject, though it is anticipating in telling this story of my life.

I will not in these instances tell the names of some parties, because I do not wish to hurt the feelings of some good people who were their friends. I had a position in the Deposit Bank of Georgetown. There was never any unpleasantness between me and any officer of the bank but once. It grew out of the fact that I claimed that I owed the bank $7.00, when the cashier said I did not owe it anything. I lost my position in that bank, as I always thought, because I talked against the Christian religion. A man who was put in my place misused the bank's money, was put in the Kentucky penitentiary for it, and was killed by a guard in attempting to escape. I applied for a position in another bank. I was beaten by one vote by a young man of splendid family. He was charged with having stolen $15,000 from the bank, was arrested and tried, and nine out of the twelve jurymen voted to send him to the penitentiary. The case, after several trials, in which juries did not agree, was finally dismissed from the courts. I tried to get a position where there was a vacancy in another bank. It was gotten by the superintendent of a Sunday school. He stole the money of the bank and ran off, deserting a pretty and lovely little wife, and has never returned. I never applied for any bank position after that. I never made but one serious mistake that I can now recall. A man came in and handed me a thousand-dollar bill and asked me to give him hundred-dollar bills for it. I gave him nine one-hundred dollar bills and a thousand-dollar bill. He took it all just to show me that I had made a mistake, and then handed it back for correction.

I was the notary of the bank, and used many postage stamps in protesting notes. The bank's postage stamps were about as free as pins, but I never took one in my life, nor did any bank ever lose a cent by me. My cell is in "Banker's Row" in the penitentiary. If novels told only what actually happens, how much more novel they would be!

Not far from "Quakeracre" General Coxey lived for a while. You remember about the unarmed army he led to Washington, and "Keep Off The Grass." Close by where Coxey lived, there resided the poorest white woman that ever dwelt in my neighborhood. She had been Miss Harrison. She was kin to the two Presidents of that name, and the elder President Harrison had visited her father's house. She was riding in a chair in a small wagon and fell out and killed herself. I will tell you one more little story about places in my neighborhood. This is a rabbit story, and has to do with James Lane Allen, now famous over the United States as a beautiful writer.

My Uncle John Moore owned a great many Negroes and a large pack of hounds, and took great pride in being good to his Negroes and to his dogs. Uncle John had a neighbor who was severe on his Negroes, and who could not bear to see even other people's Negroes idle. One day, in the Spring, there was a large gang of my Uncle's Negroes, men, women and children, all out in a corn-field, cutting corn-stalks with hoes, and the pack of hounds was with them. A rabbit jumped up, and all the dogs and all the Negroes started after him, and the clamor made by the dogs and the Negroes was immense. Just then that man who was so hard on his Negroes came riding by. The man rode up to my uncle's house and reported to him how he had seen his Negroes neglect their work to run a rabbit. My uncle heard him through and then said: "If they hadn't done it, I would have whipped every rascal of them." James Lane Allen, before he got to be famous, was a great friend to my family and myself. I got him his first position as a teacher, and afterward got him a position in Bethany College, where I was educated. He used frequently to come to "Quakeracre." He was one of the best eight talkers I ever knew. The others were, Henry Ward Beecher; Prof. W. K. Pendleton of Bethany College; W. B. Smith, Ph. D., now of Toulane University; and Judges Dick Reid and J. Harry Brent, the last two of the Court of Appeals of Kentucky; Billy Breckinridge and Ingersoll. Of course, I mean now only talking men. I have heard some women who could say things that beat all those men put together. One day Mr. Allen came to our house, and during our long conversation, said he was thinking of changing his life from teaching to writing. I told him at once, that he ought to do it. He asked me what he ought to write about, and I said: "About the Negroes in the South; that is a subject that is fast growing into great interest." He said he was not old enough to know about slavery from memory and asked me who could tell him about it. I said, "I can; almost anybody can who recollects it." I then started and told him a number of stories about slavery, showing the best sides and the worst sides of it. Among others, I told him the rabbit story about my Uncle.

Some months afterward, I went into the bookstore of Morton & Greenway, in Lexington, and picked up the last issue of Harper's Magazine. Turning the pages to look at the pictures in the magazine, I saw a full-page picture that I immediately recognized as the rabbit story of my Uncle John, and, looking further, I found other stories that I had told Mr. Allen, and found his name there, at the end of the first of the many printed articles I have seen from his pen. At that time I was a prosperous farmer, to whom a poor young man, like Mr. Allen, came for advice. Now he lives in elegant style in Washington, and I am a convict, and no word of sympathy comes from him to me.

"What is friendship but a name,
A charm that lulls to sleep?"

When I was eight years old, I went to school the first time. It was in the "Valley School House," an old log school house about two miles from my home. I had had a perfect horror of going to school. My idea of school teaching was inseparably connected with flogging, and it was, by no means, without foundation. People then said, "Spare the rod and spoil the child." They now say, "Spare the child and spoil the rod." After I got to the school I was so relieved to find it a so much better place than I had expected that I stretched myself out on a bench and went to sleep — the first thing I can remember to have done at any school. The school house was about eighteen feet square, and the oldest benches in it were made of slabs, gotten from a neighboring sawmill, the bark still being on the lower sides of some of them, while the legs were hewn out with an axe, and driven into auger holes. There were, however, some desks that were thought extra good for that day. They were made of an unpainted poplar plank by a common house carpenter, but were regarded by me as being very luxurious for a school house. In the warm weather we built what we called "the arbor." It was a kind of room made against the front wall of the school house, by the boys, by putting forks in the ground and stretching poles from one to the other, and covering the other three sides and the top with limbs of trees with leaves on them. Of course, when it rained, we just went into the house. The arbor was so romantic and attractive, and so suggestive of "Robinson Crusoe" stories that I began to hear about, that I never could study in it. In that arbor I learned the irony in the story beginning:

"How big was Alexander, Pa,
That people call him great?"

And from that day to this I have never had any admiration for military heroes. In the "Blue-back Spelling Book," in that arbor, I saw the picture of, and read the story of, the boy in the old man's apple tree, and from that day to this I have thought you could make a boy get out of an apple tree sooner by throwing rocks at him, than by throwing grass at him, and that's one of the reasons why I am writing this story where I am. It was there that I saw the first steel pens. The handles were gorgeously colored, and I thought they were very beautiful. Until that time the "goose quill," which was always a "gander quill," had been the only pen, and for a long time after it was evident that the steel pens were better than the quills, there was a journalistic superstition that any successful editorial must be written with a "gray goose quill." One of my earliest discoveries in etymology after I began Latin, was that the English pen was derived from the Latin "penna," which means a feather.

My favorite game was "Antny-over," the first word of the name, as I always supposed, being short for Anthony. It seems strange to me that school boys do not play that exciting and thrilling game, instead of the degenerate base ball and foot ball of this day. We had a "big spelling class" the last thing each evening, an occasion intrinsically exciting, apart from the fact that school was "out" as soon as it was over. To stand "head" in this class was the great honor of the school. Ed. Grimes was what Dickens would call a "carroty-pated" boy. He was small for his years, and for his ears, and he was poor and badly dressed, and he stammered and was dull. I always had such sympathy for poor Ed., that one day at "big play-time," which was for an hour, at noon, I induced Ed. to run off with me and get a good dinner at my home, a mile and a half away. We got back late, but I was not scolded at either end of the road, for, I think, all parties understood my motive.

Bob Flournoy was almost a grown young man, who rode to the school house on a horse, and was handsomely dressed, and was the son of a rich farmer. Nearly every evening there was a stay of proceedings in the "big spelling class," until it could be decided whether Ed. or Bob was "foot," each claiming that the other was — Ed., in the hardest and deepest earnest, and Bob, though apparently just as earnest as Ed., evidently doing it just to worry Ed., and to get him to stammering. Poor Ed. never seemed to understand Bob's game. The only aspiration of either of them was not to be "foot," and it finally got to be a standing joke to appeal to the class to decide which of the two was "foot," the teacher declining to umpire the case.

I was told when I was at Bethany College, that I was the only boy who had made old "Bishop" Alexander Campbell laugh. I did it by telling him about Ed. Grimes and Bob Flournoy, in spelling class, and about two incidents in the life of Bob Flournoy that occurred at the supper table, at my old home. Bob helped himself to such a large quantity of some kind of preserves that he, supposing nobody had noticed the amount, tried to eat a large piece of it at one mouthful without anyone noticing him. It proved to be a piece of race ginger, and the longer he chewed it the larger and hotter it got, and Bob, in using his napkin, managed to get the ginger into the napkin, and then into his breeches pocket. Another time at our table, Bob got fearfully choked, and managed to say, by the hardest, "I have swallowed a crumb." Just then he gave an immense cough, and nearly the half of a "beat" biscuit flew half across the table. I told that story to old Mr. Campbell at his breakfast table, and he laughed so, that, by strange coincidence, he got so choked that his daughter Virginia (afterwards Mrs. Thompson, post-mistress of Louisville, first under Garfield, and then under a Democratic administration) had to beat her father in the back. Another strange coincidence is that from the time I last saw Bob as a school boy, I have only seen him once, and that was at the house of Mrs. Virginia Thompson in Louisville. I think that, in some way, they became acquainted by the ginger and biscuit stories I told her father.

My next teacher was named Taylor, at that same school house. I have no idea where he lived. There is only one thing in connection with him that I can recall that has made any impress on me. A leather-bound copy of Josephus, with Taylor's name in it, got into my father's library, and descended to me, and is in my possession yet, and will be delivered to Taylor, if he or his heirs, or assigns, anywhere, claim it, though it is possible that Taylor sold it to my father. In that book I first saw that passage famous in theological disputation, beginning, "About that time there was a man, if it be lawful to call him a man —."

My next teacher was Samuel Balaam Barton. He taught at "Fort Hill Academy," a new school house built closer to my home, and so named from the fact that it was in the middle of a pre-historic fortification a mile in circumference, in the circular ditch of which we used to hide, in various games. The teacher was a nice and good and competent man, who was doing what was common then — teaching school to enable him to prepare himself for the Presbyterian ministry. I was the only pupil in the school that was not a Presbyterian. Half in joke, and sometimes half in meanness, some boys would call me a "Campbellite." It was my first experience as a religious martyr, and gave me just as much trouble as my present experience in the same line does. At that school, as my school-mates, were the boys that afterward became Congressman Billy Breckinridge and Judges Simrall and Robert J. Breckinridge, and Simrall, the present Mayor of Lexington, and General John B. Castleman, and Mary and Fannie Castleman, who afterward became the wives of prominent Judges, Samuel Breckinridge and Eastin.

There was an orphan boy at that school named Samuel Sloan. He was related to the Presidents Harrison. Sam was poor. He was a great oddity, and afforded me great amusement. He had a very remarkable way of licking out his tongue when he was writing, and the only clean part of his face was that which he reached with his tongue while writing. At that school Sam and I came to the front as the literary prodigies of the school. It was always expected every Friday evening that the whole school, including the teacher, would laugh when Sam and I read our "compositions." I had a large repertoire of subjects, but Sam had only two subjects. One was "The Crow," and the other was "The Hog," — pronounced "Horg." On these two subjects he wrote a series of articles that lasted through a session or two. Sam had the advantage of me in the delivery of his composition. He licked his tongue in reading it just as he did in writing it. He always brought down the house. After our school at Fort Hill my father sent to East Pembroke, New York, and employed, to teach my three sisters and myself, a lady about twenty-one years old, named Arlotta Maria Bass. It was from this lady, more than from any other being, my mother scarcely excepted, that I got the impressions that made me what I am. I was about fifteen, was large for my age, and was no slouch in personal appearance. My sister Mary was thirteen, and my other two sisters still younger. Miss Bass was not a real beauty, but she was far from being homely, with an exceedingly bright, amiable and attractive face, and a fine and graceful form. All of my memories of the stories of the "Eneid, are from sitting beside Miss Bass and reading it to her in Latin. That was in 1853. She was a devout Congregationalist, of Puritan stock I think, but without any excess of Puritanism. To come from New York to Kentucky then was very much more of an undertaking than it is now, and to entertain herself on the road she brought with her the first copy of "Uncle Tom's Cabin" that any of us had ever seen. It was only recently out and was just beginning its wonderful work on this country and on the world. It was translated into seven languages. It had more political influence than any book ever written, "Don Quixote" not excepted. We all read it aloud. Miss Bass was quite moderate in her opposition to slavery when she first came to our house, and her opposition grew less as she saw slavery in my father's family and at my uncle John's.

That book came to me just at my most impressible age, and it is one of the causes to which I can directly trace my being in the penitentiary now. I had been born and reared in the midst of slavery, and it had never occurred to me that there was any more wrong in my father owning a black man than there was in his owning a horse. I had never hated anybody in my life, except a few people who treated their slaves badly. The greatest pleasure of my young boyhood days had been to get into the very large kitchen, with a curiously constructed, immense fire place and culinary apparatus that would make a museum now, and into the Negro cabins at night, and especially by their big wood-fires in the winter time, and hear them talk and laugh. I now believe that my father's Negroes, men, women and children, were in those days the happiest people I have ever seen. Some of them still live on my farm in Kentucky and send, in my wife's letters, messages of heart-broken sympathy to "Mars Charlie."

When I presented myself for ordination to the ministry at Bethany College, Virginia, the civil war was almost on us, and slavery was being discussed everywhere. I said to the clergymen who ordained me, including the Rev. Alexander Campbell, "I will never teach the doctrine of slavery, as our Southern preachers do." The only answer made me was by one of them picking up a Bible and reading to me the first five verses of the 6th chapter of 1st Timothy. I saw plainly that it sustained the Southern view of slavery, even in the English translation, and knew that it was still stronger for slavery in the Greek original. I was ordained to the ministry, but when Rev. Dr. J. D. Pickett, now of Chicago, read me those five verses from the New Testament, he planted the first seeds of Infidelity in my brain and heart — first an intellectual conviction, and next as a moral repugnance.

My parents were not very hearty as defenders of slavery, and my grand-father Stone had freed his. My father's only apology for slavery was that the Negroes would be worse off as freemen than as slaves. He died only a few months before the election of Abraham Lincoln. He said if a Republican were elected there would be war. He owned some young Negro boys, among which was a bright little fellow named Jerry. Each of us claimed some special little darkey, and Miss Bass claimed Jerry. She trained him so that when she would ask, "Jerry, who do you belong to?" he would say, "Miss Bass;" and when she would laugh at it he would laugh, too, like he had executed an excellent piece of humor. Then some of us would ask him, "Jerry, who belongs to you?" and he would say, "Miss Bass," and would again laugh with us. Jerry and his two brothers all went into the Federal army. The other two were killed, and Jerry is living, a well-to-do man, in Covington, Ky. At intervals he has visited Lexington, and comes out, neatly dressed, in a nice carriage to see "Mars Charlie."

In order to make the school more interesting, and possibly somewhat for the profit of it, my parents took into the school as boarders from Monday to Friday evening, four exceedingly sweet and pretty girls, thirteen and fourteen years old. Two of these, Sallie Smith and Bettie Herndon, neither of whom I had seen before, made impressions on my heart almost as soon as I saw them. They were so equally attractive that I never could have decided between them had it not been that Sallie's family were Presbyterians and Bettie's family were "Campbellites," and my memory of my religious martyrdom at Fort Hill Academy turned me in favor of Bettie. Bettie had a beautiful, clear complexion, with very dark hair that hung just to her shoulders, and then curled just a little. Her eyes were large and a beautiful deep blue. She had an entrancing little blush, and a dimple in her cheek that was simply irresistible. My "beauty spot," as the girls all called it — all but Bettie — was a dimple in my cheek; there to this day, but has been hidden ever since I was nineteen years old by a beard that was never shaven — not even here in the penitentiary, as is the common rule. Our dimples showed best when we laughed, and it was a common scheme with the other girls and Miss Bass to say something funny for the expressed and alleged purpose of making us show our dimples. Really, I was proud of my dimple, but I always felt like a half idiot when thus forced to make an exhibition of myself. Bettie could manage it better than I could, and always looked as if we were both being persecuted, and would sympathize with me, and called me "Charlie" with a music in the name that I had never noticed before. Her manner was perfectly natural, and there was, about her, just such a born grace that an apron string seemed to hang from her waist as I had never seen it do from any other girl's, and the bow-knots in her shoestrings and the fit of her stockings on her ankles seemed to have some peculiar magic about them.

So long as I felt no disposition to discriminate between Sallie and Bettie, I felt no uneasiness; but as soon as I made up my mind to have a preference for Bettie I began to realize that I was having a sweetheart, and was afraid that her parents and mine would find it out, and that, on that account, they would either take her away from our school or send me off to some boys' school, because I had gotten too big to send to school with girls, especially when there was a young lady teacher who did not seem inclined to discourage any preference of the kind that I might want to show. I would take every precaution to act toward Bettie just as I would toward any of the other girls, including my sister, but, in spite of all I could do, I would have a feeling that I acted differently from what I did toward the others, and I could not disabuse my mind of the impression that others saw in my feelings toward Bettie the thing that I was trying to keep secret, and that they amused themselves by it, when they were together and away from me and Bettie. After awhile it seemed to me that they looked at Bettie and me the same way, smiled at both of us, and said nothing the same way, and I had a suspicion that Bettie was feeling about it just as I did, but that she, being a girl, knew how to hide what she thought better than I did.

If, in school or out, it came perfectly natural for me to sit right close beside Bettie, I noticed that there was a great difference between my sitting by her and by anybody else, and if her apron just happened to fall over on my knee there seemed to be a great difference between it and any other dry goods that had ever gotten on my knee; but I was careful never to sit by her unless everybody could see that it came perfectly natural for me to do so; and yet I was, all the time, under some unpleasant kind of an impression that I was acting so that others would see my preference for Bettie, and that then she would feel it her duty to be shy of me, so that great trouble would grow out of it.

We had some beautiful studies in the natural sciences, such as botany and geology, that took us wandering through the woods and by the creek, in the daytime, and astronomy that took us out at night, especially in the winter nights, with our big celestial atlases and a lantern when we wanted to refer to them, now and then. While the others were looking at the stars, and Bettie would be a little ways off from them, I would manage to find it very necessary to look over the particular big atlas that she was holding, and, in the dark, when substance and shadow blended so as to show little difference between them, I would accidentally get my cheek up very close beside hers, and finally when this accident had occurred several times, and she did not get her cheek out of the way, as I was afraid she would do, I became such a diligent student of astronomy that the stars looked wonderfully familiar to me, until the last time I saw them before coming in here. I was ready, at any time, to settle any possible doubt that we might have about the name and history of any star we saw in the heavens by referring to its counterpart in Bettie's atlas, and I was delighted that she seemed to understand that she was to hold the atlas for me, because I thought she could do it better than anyone else.

Frequently, when Friday evening came, Miss Bass, Sister Mary, Bettie, Sallie and I would, each on a horse, ride five miles to Sallie's house, spend the night there, and the next day all of us go on to Bettie's and stay there until Monday morning and then back home to school again. We all took lessons from Miss Bass on the piano, and all studied together at night. I studied physiology with those girls and learned laws of health that now, when I am past three-score years, enable me to stand imprisonment. In this way the years rolled around and the time came for Miss Bass to go home. In those days, in going from Lexington to New York, we had to go by Louisville, and my father and I went with Miss Bass as far as Louisville, he and I going on to St. Louis and further up the Mississippi. We separated for the last time that I have ever seen her, and my father kissed the pretty school teacher goodbye — I can tell it now, for he and my mother are both dead, and don't know where their boy is, and when, later, Miss Bass told me goodbye, she put her arms around me, kissed me, and said, "Remember Bettie;" and that told the whole story of what I had suspected all the time.

For a long time, long loving letters passed often between Miss Bass and all of us. Finally, the war came, and Sister Mary's and Bettie's husbands were in the Confederate army, and Sallie was dead, and a letter came from Miss Bass speaking bitterly of the South. That letter was never answered, and from that day to this I have never heard anything from, or in any way about, Miss Bass. She had married Dr. Ellinwood of New York, to whom she was engaged while she was at our house.

One night during the war there was a wedding at the house of my widowed cousin, Mrs. Sarah B. Moore, one of the truest of all the friends I ever had. My Sister Mary went to the wedding, and put on her white silk wedding dress for the first time she had ever worn it since her husband had gone into the army. By some inexplicable means while at the wedding a bright spot of blood was seen on the bosom of the dress. I saw it and heard several who were evidently talking so as to keep from

32

her mind any idea of a bad omen. Soon after her husband was shot in the breast through the heart, as he was charging on a Federal breastworks.

"Whom the gods love die young."

How strange is life! Lying beside me on my prison bed, are letters just received from my wife and men and women from different parts of the United States, mostly from parties that I have never seen. They are all full of love, sympathy and admiration. I have many times wondered how it felt to be a penitentiary convict. Now I know. I would rather have a shackled body and a free mind in a penitentiary than to have a free body and a shackled mind outside of a penitentiary. You can't imprison a man whose conscience is all right.

My next year at school was at the old Transylvania University at Lexington. That was to me a most unhappy year, caused by the fact that I could not learn mathematics easily, and had as a professor in that department one of these mathematical fanatics who think that the ability to learn mathematics is the only standard of intellectuality, and who have no sympathy for any boy who cannot easily learn mathematics, and is devoted to it. His influence on me was very bad, because he so discouraged me that I hardly had the heart to learn anything. I am sorry that I did not abandon mathematics when I only knew elementary arithmetic and some of the rudiments of geometry. Mathematics is the only one of all the sciences of which a man may know absolutely nothing and yet be a valuable, accomplished and educated gentleman. It is indispensable that somebody should know mathematics, but there are always more people who can learn it with ease and pleasure than there is any demand for in the practical application of mathematics, and these people should learn it, and people who cannot learn it easily should never waste their time upon it. Nothing can be well learned, the learning of which is not a pleasure to the learner, and that is especially true in mathematics. The greatest of all the mistakes in all of our public schools is the grading of every student by his advancement in mathematics. I have known smart men who could not learn mathematics, and smart men who could learn it and very inferior men who could learn it. The time, labor and money put upon the study of mathematics by anyone who does not learn it easily and pleasurably would be worth more to him on any science other than mathematics.

In 1856 I went to Bethany College, Virginia — now West Virginia. It was in a wild, romantic, mountainous country. At that college occurred

33

things that did much to make me what I am. My father furnished me as much money as I wanted, and I dressed handsomely. While I spent money freely I really never wasted it, and though I had all of the real pleasures of college life, I always drew the line at the immoral and never did there, or anywhere else, anything of which I was unwilling to tell my parents or would now be unwilling to tell to my wife and children. I spent two years there and graduated with about an average standing. For some time after I went to Bethany College Bettie and I corresponded, but there was never a word of love with any view to matrimony passed between us, and to this day I have no knowledge as to whether she would have married me if I had asked her. She sent me a beautiful valentine and, in New York City, where she was when the Atlantic cable was a new thing, she bought me a pretty gold-bound section of it for a watch charm. The first intimate friend I made among young ladies, at Bethany, was Miss Ellen Campbell.

(I am going to stop here long enough to give you another letter from my dear, loved and loving, precious wife. It is as follows:

RUSSELL'S CAVE, KY., February 12, 1899.
MY DEAR DADDY:
I am feeling better since I received your cheerful letter last night. I am so glad that you have found such a kind man at the helm. Give my kindest regards and thanks to Mr. Coffin, and tell him that I appreciate his kindness and consideration more than I can tell. Tell him that he has not a criminal in you to deal with, but a man whose life has been as pure as that of the purest woman who ever breathed — a man whose name is a synonym for honesty; a man who was "never caught in a lie," as President McGarvey stated from his pulpit; a man who has spent his life fighting for morals; a man whose only crime is that he will tell too much truth, and is an honest Infidel; a man who never advocated "free love" in his paper, but only answered an argument on the subject in a rather facetious way.

This is the kind of a man he has for a prisoner. I am afraid now that you fare so well that you will not want to come home if we get you pardoned. I want you to read the Warden what I have written, or let him read it for himself. I have had kind messages and love from some of the very nicest gentlemen in Lexington, including Dr. Coleman and Editor Polk, and a letter from Mr. Kaufman, that I will enclose to you, and a kind note from Major Daingerfield saying he would do all he could for you.

34

My neighbors have come and expressed sympathy and indignation. Dr. Henry Atkins came as soon as he heard of it, and seemed simply outraged and sent you his love. He could scarcely refrain from using "cuss words" about Rucker. Even Billy Breckinridge wrote an editorial expressing regret and defending you, and Leland went and thanked him.

Misses Elizabeth and Juliet came to see me, and were deeply grieved, and said their mother was sick over it, and sent you dear love from all the family.

Miss Anna Gray said they loved you like a brother. They tell me the whole of Lexington is outraged over the matter, and I hear nothing but contempt for Rucker. I really feel sorry for the creature. I had a letter from Annie Grissim expressing greatest sorrow.

Be good, be prudent, be cheerful, be brave, and take care of your health. I would so like to have a number of the little papers of the date you sent me. I want to distribute them. I am grateful to see what a good place a prison can be made, with a good man at the head of it — a humane man. Can't you send me the paper whenever it is issued? How often is that? How often will they let you write to me, and will they let you write for your paper? This is the third letter I have written tonight — I am so tired.

Good-night, dear Daddy. Brent joins me in love.

YOUR LOVING WIFE.

P.S. — MONDAY MORNING. — It is terribly cold this morning. The thermometer stood at 15° below zero, at seven o'clock, and must have been at 20° in the night. How do you sleep? Have you comfortable quarters? You said you were among the common convicts the first night. I had a letter from Sister Mary Friday night, asking about you and when you would go to Louisville. Guess she had not heard about it. It seems to me the newspapers gave a hateful account of it. It seemed to me they were afraid to say a kind word for you. Do you have a task imposed upon you, or does the Warden take it for granted you will do the best you can?

Don't fail to send me some of the little papers of the date you sent; there was such an interesting account of prison life in it. There must be great suffering among the poor. I had to give Aunt Rachel provisions.

("Aunt Rachel" is an old Negro family servant who used to belong to my father. — Author)

Is there anything you want me to send you? I will send you the

35

flannel that matches what you have on. The wrong that has been done you grows bigger and bigger in my eyes. Everybody seems to be outraged. I hear the Chamber of Commerce, in Lexington, discussed the subject. Good-bye, again, with love.

* * * * *

Inclosed in her letter is the following:

LEXINGTON, KY., February 10, 1899.

MRS. C.C. MOORE,
RUSSELL'S CAVE, KY.

MY DEAR MRS. MOORE: — I can't tell you how deeply I sympathize with you in the new trouble that has come upon you. It was very wrong that Mr. Moore did not employ attorneys to represent him. I feel, as yet, so stunned that I really don't know what is best, or what ought to be done. I have written to the "American Secular Union and Federation" in Chicago, but it seems to me that the best plan to persue is to apply to the President for a pardon. I have some influential friends in Washington who, I am sure, will aid us.

Since writing the above I have spoken to Leland, and he will explain what my views are. In the meantime believe me that you and Mr. Moore have the heart-felt sympathy of every decent man and woman in the country, and that nothing will be left undone to right the great wrong that has been perpetrated.

Your friend,   M. KAUFMAN

* * * * *

Here is another letter that was in the same envelope:

"CASTLETON," February 10, 1899.

MRS. C. C. MOORE.

MY DEAR FRIEND: — You can't know how much I have wanted to go to you in the last few sorrowful days. Only the weather kept me at home; for it seems almost dangerous to venture out. Our hearts have been with you all, our dear, sorrowful friends. Is there anything we can do to help you? There is one thing we know, and that we have done, and we trust that He, who, in answer to prayer, brought your dear boy safely home (from the army in Porto Rico. — Author) will watch over your husband, and, in His own time,

36

restore him to you.

Mr. Moore has always been such a kind neighbor — so hospitable and kindly — that he is our brother, and you know that "if one member suffers all the members suffer with it," and so we so truly enter into his sorrows and yours that you must let us express our sympathy.

Dear friend, in this dark hour, trust your Savior's love and power and believe that He will turn even this anguish into blessing, and give you consolation, and in His good time, joy also — "joy that no man taketh from us." Make Leland and Brent come over when they can. When I can I want, and hope, to go to see you. Nettie is sick in bed, and makes herself worse grieving over you. With love from us all.

Your loving friend,   ANNIE D. GRAY

P. S. — I want to write down, for you, words that have often comforted me, as, no doubt, they have you; but it is good to hold them close and plead them

"Call on me in the day of trouble. I will deliver thee, and thou shalt glorify me.

"In all their afflictions he was afflicted, and the angel of his presence saved them."

"Jesus Christ, the same yesterday, to-day and forever."

"Leave God to order all thy ways,
And Hope in Him, whate'er betide,
Thou'lt find Him, in the evil days,
An all-sufficient Strength and Guide.
Who trusts in God's unchanging love,
Builds on the Rock that none can move."

"Trust His rich promises of grace,
So it shall be fulfilled in thee,
God, never yet, forsook in need
The soul that trusted Him, indeed."

*　*　*　*　*

At the same time that I received these the Warden sent me two beautiful letters that had been written him in my behalf, by Miss Annie Gray and her brother-in-law, Major Daingerfield. I will give you one more

37

sample of the letters that I get at the rate of four or five a day. There are some prisoners here who are never allowed to write. The average prisoner can write twice a month. I can write, every day, as many letters as I want to write.

NICHOLASVILLE, KY., February 11, 1899.

DEAR BROTHER MOORE.

Hold up your head, I am proud of you. For every stripe of disgrace you bear, time will make a badge of honor, and for every hair of your bushy old head an Infidel league will spring. The only danger about such convictions as yours is that being sent to the penitentiary may become eminently respectable. We do not attach any shame or disgrace to any Russian Nihilist sent to the hell of Siberia, where hundreds of as great patriots as ever fought for liberty or light, suffer your penalty for the same cause of truth and humanity.

The Roman Catholics would send every A. P. A. where you are, if they had the power, and the A. P. A's would treat the Catholics the same way, if they had the power. I wonder that you were not crucified or burned at the stake, because you were innocent, before a prejudiced jury, who thought they were doing their duty. I thought you would make a fight, and that, if you were found guilty, you would appeal the case. The Liberals, all over the world, would have fought for you to the Supreme Court; but you took the shortest way out of it. Perhaps, in the end, you have done the best to teach the bigoted and superstitious a lesson that your new experience will fit you [for.] Your friends know that you are the friend of man, and of all that is true, beautiful and good. Jails, mobs, prisons and martyrdom cannot detract from what you are.

Your words may have been wild and whirling at times to the uninitiated, but you will be judged by your acts and deeds, and they give the lie direct to the charge under which you suffer. Men are responsible for their acts, not their words, in any court of last resort. That was the doctrine of Napoleon.

I never knew that your paper was a "free-love" paper, until I read it in the chaste Cincinnati papers. I presume you are now accustomed to your new environment, the product of Christianity and private ownership of the earth and the fullness thereof, and now you may look deeper into the social problems that breed the classes you are with, but not of. But, under far different circumstances, may not the best be made thieves and paupers under our

38

growing monopolies? Crime is a disease caused by insanity and poverty and our blind laws and customs. We are far from being civilized. The problem is yet to be solved. I see a dim torch when a man like Thomas L. Johnson, of Cleveland, Ohio, proposes to devote his life and fortune to teaching what he believes will help to think out the mad and savage scramble for existence. He is a true convert to the theory of Henry George and the single tax. The chief draw-back to this doctrine is established in beliefs and customs. George failed first to clear the world of superstition — of impossible gods, and unthinkable heavens, to correct the mistakes and the crimes of the few in authority. The Kings, priests, monks and preachers are responsible for slaves, chains, suffering and crimes. The world is divided into two classes — big and little thieves; and the first big thief was not "the Lord," but the landlord, and the first to receive the stolen property were the King and the priest.

The solution of Henry George may be a fallacy, and, if so, you may think out a true way, as you have now seen the world from every point of view. If you think it out the world will look upon that jury as the Christians look upon Judas — necessary to the salvation of the world and the works of evil.

I believe you will make a model ward, and that you will be good. Learn to set type, and keep from thinking about yourself and trouble.

"Tempus fugit." Tolstoi made shoes in prison. Prince Krapotkin is greater than the prison cell. There was Mazarin. Carl Schurtz flew here, to get away from the penitentiary, with hundreds of his comrades. The crime for which you suffer will put a halo about your memory. You are young and physically perfect, and your mind may not be impaired by your boarding-house. There is great work for you to do. If this mad world is to continue, as it is reflected by the public prints, then it would be better were the human family abolished. It would be better to give all the people on this planet a dreamless sleep.

The Hebrew conception of God once killed all but eight persons, and made the mistake of saving the ark to freight all the errors that are now our legacy.

But[,] I believe there is a good time coming. For two years, or less, you will not be kept guessing how to get a living without begging, or stealing, or sand-bagging somebody.

Yours fraternally,   LOUIS PILCHER.

* * * * *

Miss Ellen Campbell was a second cousin of "Bishop" Alexander Campbell. She was about twenty years old and I eighteen. Her widowed mother was poor and lived in a rose-embowered cottage named "Rosedale." Six or eight students boarded there. The bell would ring and we would walk into the dining room, and always find a delightful meal, but nobody else would be in there while we were in there. Miss Ellen, while not a real beauty, was pretty and exceedingly sweet in disposition and in manners, and had a voice that was strikingly sweet in talking and in singing. She had a sister, Jennie, and a brother, Tom, who was an editor, and when she told me about his being an editor I remember that I thought it must require a man of wondrous genius to be an editor. How my ideas, on that subject, have changed! She also had a brother named Archibald, who was a clown in a circus, and I afterward saw him and talked to him, in Lexington, when he was in his clown's dress and make-up, in his circus. I soon saw that the clown is not such a funny man, except in his special role. He seemed to me to be a sad man, and in thinking of him I have often thought that there was more of earnestness than is commonly supposed in what "Mr. Merryman" says when he walks into the ring, and sitting on the tub on which the elephant stands on his head, says with ennui, "Go on with the show; I've seen it all."

Miss Ellen used to sing many sweet songs for me with accompaniments on a guitar. One beautiful summer evening we started out for a walk. We went down the road to a pretty creek and then walked down the banks of the creek for a mile or more. The mountains, streams, trees and wild flowers all combined to make a beautiful scene. We strayed on, talking — she singing sometimes — until we got away out into the mountains, out of sight of any evidence of human existence, except ourselves and our belongings. We came to a beautiful little, shallow stream about ten feet wide, running down through the mountain, through the rocks, and stepping from one to the other of these, we began the ascent of this stream. We had started out rather late in the evening and the weather was so delightful and our way so shaded that neither of us had anything on our heads. She was dressed in some white gauzy material, and had on the hoops and large skirts that were then in style. Of course, if she had tried at all hard, she might have stepped from one to the other of these stones without my assistance, but we both pretended that she could walk so much better, and even that I could, if I balanced us both by taking hold of her pretty white hand. Squeezing her hand did not have to be done furtively at all; it had to be done frequently and undisguisedly, in helping her. Sometimes when we would come to the moss-covered trunk of a tree lying across the stream, I would have to get upon it first, and then take her by both hands, and pull her up. When we got tired we would find a nice place to sit down, and we would tell each other the story of "Paul and Virginia," and out of her almost endless repertoire of songs she could always find one that seemed to suit the surrounding almost as if we were on a stage and the songs had been made to suit the time and scene then and there.

We kept climbing up until we could hear a little waterfall up the mountain. We climbed up to it, and found the fall with a pretty cave behind it as large as a family room. We stayed there until it began to look like night was coming on, and we spoke of going back home, but, just then, a large black cloud rolled over the mountain, and it looked as if it was going to rain hard. It got so dark that we saw it would be dangerous to walk in the mountains, and we were under a perfect natural roof. The cloud rolled away without any rain, but there was no moon and it was dark enough to be dangerous walking then, and we determined to wait until the moon would rise, which would be about midnight. Sitting on the stone floor of the cave was not as comfortable as we wanted it, and we got out of the cave and went a little distance in search of a resting place, and waded in a bank of leaves that was knee deep. Miss Ellen sat down in them, and I laid close beside her with my head resting upon my hand, supporting myself upon my elbow, and stayed in that position, perhaps, an hour. She sang a great many songs, and I sang a second to some that we sang together. She repeated a great deal of beautiful poetry, and told many pretty stories from books and from real life. Once, while she was singing a pretty lullaby kind of a song, feeling tired of my position, I turned myself so as to lay my head upon her knee, and when she saw me starting to do this she put out her arms and, as my head came down, put her arms around my neck, and, supporting her lower arm upon her knee, hugged me up close enough for my face to feel the soft folds in the bosom of her dress. She never stopped a note in her music, singing softly and low, with her face turned up to the stars, as I could see it through the thin goods of her dress, and apparently unconscious that I had changed my position. She sang me all sorts of soothing, lullaby songs until really, though I know you hardly believe me, I was nearly, but I think not quite, asleep.

Finally, when the moon rose brightly, in front of us, I got up and raised her up, and we went back home, talking and singing as we had come. As we walked along that stream, nearly midnight, we came by a spot in the creek that was hidden in the deep shadows of the great overhanging elms, the exceedingly dramatic history of which we both knew and talked of as we came by it, and stopped for a few minutes to hear the gentle murmur of the stream, as it was in summer.

I will tell you the story as Miss Virginia, daughter of Alexander Campbell, told it to me. When Miss Virginia was a little girl, Jefferson Davis (who was afterward President of the Southern Confederacy), brought to the college a nephew of his named Stamps. One winter this young man was skating on the ice, right where the soft summer water was now murmuring. Young Stamps was telling little Virginia, who was present, about some Indians who captured a young white man about the same time they had captured the first skates they had ever seen. The Indians had seen white persons skate, but did not themselves know how to use the skates. They put them on only to get some hard falls, to the amusement of the other Indians. Finally, the Indians signalled to their white captive to put the skates on his feet and show them how to use them. The young captive was really a fine skater, but he pretended not to know how to skate. He put on the skates and purposely, fell several times, so as to deceive the Indians, and much to their amusement.

When in this way the young captive got a little distance from the Indians, he struck out in the most rapid skating, and so out-traveled the Indians that he was soon out of sight of them down the river. Stamps, in showing little Virginia how the young captive had acted, fell down several times, purposely, and finally, Stamps' head hit on a stick that was lying on the ice, and it killed him immediately. Stamps' friends were notified at once, and a grave was dug in the church yard about two hundred yards from where Stamps was killed, with the intention of burying him until his friends should come for him. Just when they had gotten to the side of the grave with the coffin, news came from Stamps' friends, directing that he should not be buried, and the coffin was set on the ground, right there; and now the strange part of it that I can hardly make appear reasonable to you, is that the coffin sat there until some students took it to Stamps' home, as they went home from college, after the next commencement, which was on the 4th of July, and that grave remained open, just as it was when ready to bury the young man, until I went there to college. I have seen the grave, over the fence, at a distance of fifty yards, a hundred times, but never went to look into it.

A book of college poems written by a student there named Baxter, has one called "Stamps' Funeral." I made repeated efforts to find how it was that that coffin had been allowed to stay there so long, and why it was that the grave had never been filled up, but never could find any explanation. Mr. Campbell was quite superstitious. Mrs. Campbell in telling me once about the "banshee," a kind of ghost that forewarned of death, as Mr. Campbell's old countrymen believed, told me, I think, with a smile, that Mr. Campbell still had some superstition about it, and I have sometimes thought the coffin and grave incident that I have given, had some kind of superstition in it. The last time I saw Mr. Campbell was after I had graduated, and had gone back to Bethany to study for the ministry, and had preached and became an Infidel and left the pulpit, and had gone to Europe and came back by Bethany as I returned.

Mr. Campbell and I were sitting together and talking on the lower of the two front porches of his house. He was talking just as intelligently as I had ever heard him do, when he began to tell me a story that greatly surprised me. He told me that once he was traveling in Syria, and that one of their party died, and they dug a grave on the roadside and were just about to bury him, when they saw some Bedouin Arabs coming and Mr. Campbell and his friends fled, leaving the coffin sitting on the side of the grave. It suggested to my mind the story of Stamps' coffin and grave. I expressed to Mr. Campbell great surprise at his story, telling him that I was astonished that I had never before heard that he had been in Syria; but he assured me that he had been, and gave me some further particulars about the grave and the Bedouins. A little after that I told Mrs. Campbell about it, and she smiled and said her husband's memory was becoming impaired, and that he had heard that read in a letter from his daughter and thought it was his own experience.

But nearly a year from the time that Miss Ellen and I looked at that water, that night, another tragedy, somewhat similar was to occur at the same place. A young man named Doniphan, son of Col. Doniphan, author of "Doniphan's Expedition," that I had read, some years before, was at college at Bethany. He took his meals at "Rosedale." He was gentlemanly, dignified and morose. He showed me a handsome pistol one day that he said his father had given him, saying, "Shoot the first damned rascal who insults you." Doniphan had, without justification, become very angry at me, and when he found out that he was wrong in having done so, was apparently making all the apology he could make without any direct allusion to what had occurred, and he was doing more little, apparently accidental, courtesies for me than I had seen him do for anyone else. I understood his purpose and most cordially acquiesced in his mode of apology, as I construed it, and liked it more than I would have done the ordinary form of apology. I was glad of an opportunity to be a friend to a boy who seemed to be sad.

One morning, in the spring, when the weather was bright and delightful, but when the water of a mountain stream was still cold, Doniphan and I and one or two other boys had arranged to go swimming in the stream, that I am telling you about, which was then deep and rapid[.] We were to go in the evening, but I found it would interfere with a class, and, when he came for me to go with him, I could not go and told him so, saying how much I regret[t]ed it. He seemed disappointed, and started away, saying but little. He had gone only about twenty yards when he turned and came back to me, and, with a serious looking air, said, "Well, I will tell you goodbye," and I advanced to meet him and we shook hands. I realized that it was an unusual procedure, but I thought it was only his peculiar way, and we separated, both looking serious, and I think both feeling so. He and Captain James R. Rogers, now of Paris, Ky., went on to the stream and began disrobing to go into the water. Doniphan undressed on the top of a large sand-stone block, such as are to be seen commonly on that stream, which in some unknown time have broken loose and come down from the mountains. Doniphan was first undressed and stood nude, and repeated the words from Shakespeare beginning:

"Darest thou, Cassius, jump in and swim with me to yonder point?" and ending, "Help me, Cassius, or I sink!"

As soon as Doniphan had finished those words he jumped into the deep, cold water, and swam for the middle of the stream where the current was very swift. As soon as he reached the swift current Doniphan assumed an upright position, his head and shoulders being above the water. He looked at Rogers perfectly calmly and said, with evident earnestness, "If you can help me, now is the time to do it," and these were the last words that any one is known ever to have heard him utter. Rogers jumped into the water and swam for Doniphan, but before Rogers could get over the comparatively still water, to the rapid current, Doniphan was so far ahead, and Rogers so nearly cramped by the cold water, that he swam to shore, and cutting his bare feet on the rocks ran down the shore until he got opposite to Doniphan, and having the same experience as he did the first time, repeated this once or twice more, when Rogers became so exhausted that he could neither run nor swim, and he had to abandon any further effort to save his companion. When he last saw Doniphan he was just turning a bend of the stream nearly a half mile away, and was still erect, with his head and shoulders above the water.

In less than five minutes Rogers had on his shoes and some of his clothing, and was running through the village exclaiming, "Doniphan is drowning." I heard it almost immediately, and, catching the situation accurately, because I knew their plans, I ran to the nearest point of the creek that circled around and came nearly back to the town, about a mile below where Doniphan was last seen. There was nothing there that I could throw in to help him or me, and I stood ready to jump into the water and swim for Doniphan so as to meet him at the right time, as I expected him every second to come around the curve of the stream into view. It was one of the most trying experiences of my life. If I had not had time to think it would not have been so hard on me; but the danger that I saw confronting me was such that I dared not to think, and I determined to swim with my clothes on, believing that they would lessen my danger of cramp. I was destined, however, not to drown there, but to have again almost exactly that same experience thousands of miles away, in a strange country.

As I watched for Doniphan, not being able to go to meet him because of the rough bank, seconds seemed like minutes and minutes seemed like hours. Night was coming on rapidly, and in less than five minutes after I stood on that bank a very black cloud rolled over the sky above me, and it grew so dark that I could not, with my excellent eyes, have seen a floating man in the middle of the stream. I never witnessed such a scene as it was when, in a minute, the news ran over the village that Doniphan was drowning. Women ran into the street and called for all who could to go to the assistance of Doniphan, and in their helplessness, wrung their hands in agony. The intense darkness shut off all effort to do anything, and when it was generally agreed that Doniphan must have drowned, I went with some friends into a student's room and we sat by the fire, and talked about the case.

Somebody suggested, after a time, that Doniphan was a peculiar fellow, and that nobody in the world would actually drown so deliberately as he appeared to be doing when last seen; that he was a fine swimmer, and had floated away with his head and shoulders out, by doing what is known among swimmers as "treading water;" that his quotation from Shakespeare was only a part of his dramatic scheme, and I remembered his strange parting from me, and for some hours that we sat there, while the night was perfectly black outside, and the lightnings crashed and the thunder roared through the mountains, there was an impression among us that Doniphan would come walking naked into that very room where we were, quoting something, perhaps from Edgar A. Poe, then a popular author among the college boys, and probably something from his "Raven," about coming in "from night's

Plutonian shore," and so daze us with the apparition that at that place, that was full of mountain superstitions, we would not know whether we saw a ghost or a real man.

We talked low and sadly. The lightning and thunder were so appalling that we got to talking about lightning, and I told a story about lightning. One of the young men who listened to me was named John Johnson Rogers, and was from Paris, Ky. I said about as follows:

When I was a boy about ten years old, my father came home one night from Lexington and told a very remarkable instance of a phenomenon in lightning in which a little boy was struck by lightning. I do not know where the boy lived, or remember what his name was. The boy was up in a barn, and, the door of the barn being open, the boy put out his hand and took hold of an iron hook to fasten it so as to keep out the rain that was just beginning to fall. Just as the boy put his hand on the hook there came a flash of lightning, and —

Just at that point in my story, J. Johnson Rogers said: "I was the boy;" and he took up the story and went on with it and finished it exactly like I remembered my father had told it to us, and just as I was going to tell it. Rogers said just as he caught hold of the iron hook there came a flash of lightning that struck a mulberry tree a considerable distance from the barn. At the same instant Rogers was greatly shocked. His brother William, who was with him, was so much frightened that, not being hurt, he ran to the house and left Johnson in the barn. One of Johnson's legs was, for the time, so paralyzed that he had great difficulty in getting down the ladder that went down into the lower room of the barn, and when he got to the house he found that mulberry leaves had been photographed all over his body. The photographed leaves on his body looked as if they had been made by pressing the mulberry leaves so hard against his flesh that they had bruised the flesh until it was blue, making pictures of the leaves. These pictures remained on his body for several days, disappearing by degrees.

The story, in itself wonderful, was made much more wonderful by the fact that under those peculiar circumstances I came to find out who the boy was who had such a strange experience. John Johnson Rogers is dead, but James R. Rogers of Paris, Ky., is living, and some newspaper man might get from him the material for a story, out of what I have here told.

For several days after Doniphan was drowned the whole college was engaged in searching for his body and gave up all hope of finding it. Just thirty days from the time he was drowned somebody saw a naked body floating out of that creek into the Ohio river, seventeen miles from where Doniphan was drowned, and the body, though much dilapidated, was identified as being that of Doniphan. The body was brought to Bethany, and I assisted in putting it in a coffin. In raising the body my finger sank into the rotten flesh of his body, while his eyes, from which the lids had rotted, stared at me.

The news of the finding of the body was telegraphed to his parents, but so far as I know, no reply was ever sent to Bethany. We supposed that some of Doniphan's friends would come for him, as soon as they could get there, and so we set the coffin on two trestles, under the floor of the back part of the church, where the floor was about four feet above the ground, there being a door, without any shutter to it, going through the rear part of the foundation of the church, which was the only one in the village. That coffin sat there exposed so that anybody could see it, until some of the students took it home as they went after commencement, the commencement being on the 4th of July, nearly three months after it was put there.

I had read the strange and frightful stories of Poe, and had from these gotten a strange infatuation for horrible situations, and I would frequently, go walking, just sauntering about, bare-headed, like "Kit North," for whom I had a fancy, in gloomy-looking places. One of my common walks in the day time was by that church. There was a carriage road that ran about fifty yards from the church, which was the shorter road and the easier and plainer one in the night, and every way the better one when the hot sun was not shining, but in the hot days in taking that walk, as I frequently did, to Mr. Campbell's house and sometimes to the mountains in that direction, I would go through that church yard near the open grave of Stamps and the exposed coffin of Doniphan sitting there, and in the day-light, thought nothing of it. One still, dark night, in the latter part of June, when the village was all quiet, I started out alone, about midnight, to take one of my rambles, and I started in the direction of the church. I knew I was going to pass that church, and knew that, at night, the carriage road was the better way, but I began to inquire of my inner self if I was afraid to go through that church yard, as I frequently did in the day time.

I thought of that open grave and the ghastly story about it, and about the rotten flesh on Doniphan's white body into which my fingers had sunk, and knew he was lying there now where we had left him, and knew that I was going right by the spot where Stamps killed himself and where Doniphan began his accidental drowning, or suicide, whatever it was, and I felt like I was just inviting a horrible experience to go through that church yard, and then I remembered that I was just walking to occupy time and for the romance of it, and I began to say to myself that if I did not go through that church yard it would be because I was afraid to do so, and I became afraid to admit, to myself, that I was afraid, and, consequently, I was afraid not to go through the church yard. So, with some difficulty, in the dark, I found the path that led through the church yard and followed it toward that place. When I got up to the gate that went into the church yard, and that was about half way between the coffin and the open grave, I saw that the gate was standing open, and right in the middle of the path through it there stood something white, the legs and body of which I could see, but no head. I knew that gate fastened by a weight on a chain, and I had never seen it standing open before. I did not believe I saw a ghost, and I was satisfied that no student was standing there to frighten me, because nobody knew that I was likely to be there, and still I was certain that so far as my eyes were to be depended upon, there was something white, that seemed, possibly, to move, standing in that gate. I had studied Abercrombie's Mental Philosophy before going to Bethany, and had studied Upham's Mental Philosophy at Bethany, and I was familiar with the phenomena of mental hallucinations and optical illusions and delusions, and I was familiar with a story that was said once to have been told there by Professor Pendleton, now living, in a mental philosophy lecture to the class, about his having plainly seen, under an hallucination, as he explained it, his wife sitting upon the steps of their house one night and walking into the house with him, some time after she had died, and though I did not believe that I really saw anything that was supernatural, I was doing what was almost as straining on my nerves — almost believing that I was under one of these hallucinations, that, it occurred to me, I had brought upon myself by indulgence in reflection upon Poe's stories, as I was then doing.

Then I heard a low, deep groan from the object in front of me, and kicking at it in a kind of combination of fright and courage, found it a cow standing facing me in the gate. Somebody asked Madame de Stael if she believed in ghosts. She said, "No; but I am afraid of them." I have never been afraid of any ghost, but sometimes, under ghostly circumstances, I have been afraid that I would be frightened, and have, more often, been still more afraid that I would frighten some one else.

I had a passion for practical jokes, that were sometimes too practical, but I always drew the line at doing anything that I would be ashamed to tell of when in after days I came to tell college stories. I could become so engaged in the details of an arrangement to take some new student "sniping," that it seemed to me like a regular part of the college cur-

48

riculum to do it. I have gone with the boys to see old man Curtis, the only restaurant-keeper of the town, to arrange with him for the cooking of the "snipes," and the old man had heard that same old joke for so many years that he and I and the new boy would arrange for the "snipe supper" with as much earnestness as we generally did, really, when the "snipe hunt" had come off and the snipes did not materialize. From this old college joke comes the expression about "leaving a man with the bag to hold." I have seen the deluded boy, away in the night, standing straddle of a small stream with a candle on either side of him, patiently holding a bag down to the surface of the water waiting for the snipes to swim into it as the others of us started up the small stream to drive the snipes down, and went on, across the mountains to the college, leaving the new boy to find out as best he could that he had been playing the leading role in a farce that had long been played at colleges.

I have eaten, and had for my friends chickens, turkeys, honey, and even milk, in luxurious abundance and into the possession of which I came quite clandestinely, in the dark; my scripture warrant being, "Eat what is set before you, asking no questions for conscience sake." I have myself been the victim of a practical joke, and have seen that it is a very easy thing to deceive a man by an ingenious combination against him. One evening Tom Allen came into my room with a distressed expression on his face, and said the faculty had expelled him for getting drunk. I told him that I had often warned him against it, and that I was deeply distressed about it. He said he did not care a damn about being expelled, except that he knew it would break the heart of Jennie Campbell, to whom he told me, in great confidence, that he was engaged, which did not greatly surprise me. He said to me that Jennie's sister Ellen and I were such good friends that he wanted me to break the news to Jennie, in the best way I could manage it, about his having been expelled. I believed the news would soon get to Jennie, so I sent my card, right away, asking to be allowed to come to see her that night. It was in June. I got, in reply, a cute and funny little note, based on the supposition that both of us recognized that I was her sister Ellen's beau, and saying she would be delighted to have me call. I went and found Miss Ellen with a beau in the parlor, and Miss Jennie came in soon after hearing that I had come. She was very bright and funny, and I felt sad that I had to tell her something that would make her sad; and, in anticipation, I looked so sad, myself, that Jennie suddenly drew her face into a sympathetic expression, and asked me in a low, tender, sweet voice, if there was anything that troubled me, and begged me to tell her all about it, and said she wanted to sympathize with me if there was no more that

49

she could do to help me.

I told her that I was sad and that I wanted to tell her about it, and suggested that we should go out upon the porch to do so. The porch was embowered in blooming roses, and the moonlight struggled through them. I began as gently as I could to tell the news about Tom to Jennie. We were walking in the porch and she had hold of my arm. When she began to suspect that I was going to say something distressing about Tom Allen, I could feel that she would shudder; and when I finally told her that Tom had been expelled, she swooned and would have fallen to the floor had I not caught her in my arms. Miss Ellen could hear that something was transpiring out on the porch and ran out to see. She was greatly alarmed at Jennie's condition, and asked me what was the cause of it. I told Miss Ellen that her sister had heard bad news and asked Miss Ellen to go to Miss Jennie's assistance in her room. When I got back to my room I found Tom and several of our intimate friends there, and Tom asked me to tell all about the meeting between Miss Jennie and myself, and I did so. Then some other friends came in and listened, with sad-looking faces, as I told the story again. The next day, and still the next day, boys came to my room and got me to tell about it. The romance of the story seemed to fascinate them, and they seemed to enjoy my style in reciting it. In about a week I found that Tom had not been expelled, and that he and Jennie and the boys had arranged to deceive me, keeping Miss Ellen in real ignorance in order the more effectually to do so.

One summer there came to Bethany, some time in June, a young lady, to stay there until after commencement. It was arranged that we were to have a fishing party of young ladies and students and I had made a most pleasant engagement for the occasion. On the day of the fishing party some of the young ladies, including the one with whom I had made the engagement for the day, said to me that the young lady whom I have mentioned was very diffident, and they told me that none of the other young men would agree to be her escort for the day, and that I must break my engagement and go with her and make her have a nice time. While I felt bitterly disappointed, I recognized that selecting me as her escort was a compliment to me. I was introduced to her and soon saw that she appeared to be a country girl, sensible enough in a very matter of fact way, but utterly unacquainted with society ways and society talk. We walked along with the other company, all of whom were having funny and delightful times. I tried all the arts of conversation that I knew anything about, and every scheme that I had ever heard of, to amuse the young lady, but she seemed as unappreciative as a Sphynx. I found a most beautiful spot on the banks of the stream, and putting some dried red herrings on our hooks I pitched them into the water, and after awhile fished mine out and ate it, in a frantic endeavor to bring a smile of interest to her face. After an hour or more I finally despaired of entertaining her, and made some very natural and common place remark, and she made some remark about what I had said that was sensible enough, but was not at all in society style. I was careful not to show my feeling of exultation that I had at least elicited an idea from her, and after awhile I said some other common place thing and she seemed again to be interested in what I had suggested and replied to that, and I endorsed some part of what she had said and objected to the other. I found that she was willing to talk about anything that required thinking. By degrees we got into a conversation that grew more interesting to me the longer she talked, and yet there was not a sentence of anything amusing or anything else other than the common place dictates of sound reason. I became very much interested in her peculiar style, and when, hours afterward, time came for us to go home, I was sorry to have to do anything that would stop her most interesting talk, that was distinguished for its marvelous maturity of thought from one so young.

We walked along home to where she was visiting, saying very little as we went, and to others appearing, doubtless, to have had a dull time; but I had enjoyed it, and, in her peculiar way, she seemed to have done the same. That was Rebecca Harding, who married Mr. Davis, and became prominent as a magazine writer, and is the mother of Richard Harding Davis, editor of Harper's Magazine, and otherwise prominent in American literature.

Chapter III

I was the most popular boy in the college. My friends were all classes of students, the President, the Professors and their families, and the people of all classes in the village. One of my most intimate friends was the wife of Prof. W. K. Pendleton. She was beautiful and had many charms of heart and brain, and had traveled extensively in Europe before her marriage; a thing that was not so common then as now. One winter, while I was at college, Mr. Campbell and Prof. Pendleton went to Kentucky and visited my home there. Prof. Pendleton was exceedingly pleased with my sister Mary, and wrote his wife to that effect, and letters from my home to me said the same. I told Mrs. Pendleton that her husband had fallen in love with my sister. She said, "I know all about it; that's all right; you and I will get even with him;" and we "got even" with him. It was magnificent sleighing that winter. "Aunt Kate," as I called Mrs. Pendleton, and I had some splendid sleigh rides; sometimes in large parties, and sometimes only two of us.

Once she and I sat together in the middle of a church where a man was lecturing to a large audience on Napoleon. I wore a black silk velvet cap. I had in this cap, on my lap, beans and a stiff piece of whalebone, about four inches long. I shot beans at the speaker. The beans hit in the globes of the chandeliers on the pulpit, and so pelted the speaker that it almost broke up the lecture. Nobody could see me shoot them. I was called before the faculty on suspicion of having shot the beans. When I came before the faculty one of them apologized to me for having suspected me, and said to the balance of the faculty and to me that he had received a note from Mrs. Pendleton saying that she sat right by

53

me through the whole lecture and never saw me shoot a bean. I never saw one myself. I didn't have to; they went too fast for anybody to see, but they got there just the same. I was acquitted on "Aunt Kate's" testimony.

There were then as now, three classes of society in Virginia. The students called them "Hoi aristoi," "Hoi barbaroi," and "Hoi phizeroi." One night there was a big party at "Aunt Kate's" — the Professor still in Kentucky. It was of the "aristoi," except that two nice young girls of the "barbaroi" were present. Oil and water [won't] mix. Neither will different social castes in Virginia. The house had a high basement story. "Aunt Kate," about midnight, whispered to me to lock all the doors going out and hide the keys, and to do it so that nobody would see me. I did so. Later on some guests arranged to go, and the doors were all found locked. The two "barbaroi" girls insisted they must go home, and I helped them down from a window about ten feet high. The balance of us spent the whole night there, and witnessed a magnificent sunrise, over the mountains, from the top of a high porch. We had a magnificent breakfast on the supper table, still standing where we left it with abundance on it the night before, with a new supply of hot oysters, hot rolls, hot coffee and chocolate.

My room-mate, who graduated the first year I was at college, was George Abbott James, then of Zanesville, Ohio. He is now a lawyer in Boston, is very rich, and his wife is a sister of Senator Lodge, the "force bill" man. He was very elegant in his manners and dress. I had gotten the worst room in the dormitory, and George had the best one, with everything most comfortably fixed, and asked me to room with him. When we separated at college we both cried and he' kissed me on the cheek, or on my black curly beard. We made many vows of eternal devotion. I have never seen him but once since. It was just at the end of the war when I had quit preaching, and he found me at work on the farm. I never hear of him now except when he orders his Blade changed from Boston to Nahant, where he has his sea-shore cottage for the summer, and then back to Boston for the balance of the year. He has enjoyed the personal acquaintance of the literati of Boston. He has never written me a line while I am in the penitentiary, his paper being paid for five years in advance. I suppose he would not now recognize "Chum," as he always called me, in my prison garb, and he probably will never again recognize me in any way.

I had joined the church when I was fifteen years old, and I was very religious when I was at college. George James was an elaborate swearer. I gave him a fine law-bound edition of Dickens' works not to swear any more till Christmas — three months off. From this start he, and six other of our most intimate friends, who were the very cream of college society, all went up one day and joined Mr. Campbell's church. George is now an Episcopalian. I will tell you more about him further on, after he fell in love with my sister. I have had some lovely moonlight walks on the banks of the Muskingum, not far from where I am now a prisoner, with his pretty sister, Miss Bessie. Another of his sisters married Bancroft, son of the historian. I could write a whole book about the family.

Miss Virginia Campbell, about whom I have already told you something — daughter of the "Bishop" — and I became very intimate friends. I was about nineteen years old, and she about twenty-one. She was rather pretty and quite handsome. She was full of life and romantic, and was well read. She was splendid company for me. She and I had one affectation in common. We both went bare-headed. I got it from "Kit North," in "Noctes Ambrosianae." Miss Virginia and I took long walks into the woods and mountains together. Sometimes we took a shotgun and shot "time about." I don't think either of us will ever have to answer for having killed anything. One time she showed me, in that same creek, where her brother had been drowned. We talked a great deal; mostly like we were of the same sex; sometimes like we were two boys, and sometimes like we were two girls; the latter being more natural to me, from my schooling with Miss Bass. I don't know what we talked about, except one time, and I don't know what we did not talk about. I went to church with her and we sang out of the same hymn book, and with very sober faces, but with signs that we understood, made fun of her father's very long and exceedingly dry sermons. She and her father were on most familiar terms, and it was through Miss Virginia that I got to know "the old Bishop" more intimately than any student that was ever at Bethany. He was grave to austerity commonly; so much so that few would dare to approach him except in the same style, but I found, after having "broken the ice," that the old gentleman thought that

> "A little folly now and then
> Is healthful for the best of men."

But there was one conversation with Miss Virginia that I shall never forget. We were sitting, one pretty May morning, side by side[,] on a little stile that came over a fence, a hundred yards from her home, into a pretty gravel foot path that wound among pretty trees and flowers, and by her father's study — a quaint kind of little house — and went on down

55

to the home. I sang, from Burns, beginning:

> "I'm sitting on the stile, Mary,
> Where we sat, side by side,
> In a bright May morning, long ago,
> When first you were my bride."

There was a pretty tree near us and I asked her what kind it was. She answered by singing a song, beginning:

> "The larches have hung their tassels forth;"

And I saw from its "tassels" that it was a larch tree. Then Miss Virginia locked her hands around one knee — hers — and, leaning back, assumed a rather serious air and tone, and said about as follows:

"Mr. Moore, I have something to tell you. You and I have been together and talked together so much that I know you as well as you know yourself. My sister, Dessie, is eighteen years old and is now at school in the East, and she will finish there this session and will be at home, at our college commencement, and you will fall dead in love with her just as soon as you see her."

She spoke like a Sybil, and it so impressed me that I did not smile, or feel like it. It sounded to me like destiny.

Since 1859 I have never spoken that name, Dessie, and have never even written it until now, for the first time, forty years afterward, while I am a penitentiary convict. Suppose Miss Virginia and I could have foreseen that, how would we have explained it? I asked Miss Virginia if she had a picture of her sister, and she said "Yes."

(Please remember that, in writing as I do, I am liable to discrepancies in dates and times.)

I asked Miss Virginia to show me the picture of her sister, and we walked together down to the house to get it. It was an ivory [type] in a blue velvet case. As soon as I opened it I was "dead in love" with the face. It was exquisitely beautiful, and I expressed my admiration in unqualified terms. Dessie afterward gave me a picture in the same style, taken after we met. After seeing the picture that Miss Virginia showed me, we were together a great deal as we had been before, and we occasionally talked about her sister's coming home, and I looked forward to it. Dessie was to have a reception the evening of the day that she got home, and I was invited to be present. On the day that she was to get home I was in a room at "Rosedale," and a student came in and said

56

that Dessie Campbell had just passed by in a carriage on her way home. I was sorry I had not seen the carriage and gotten a glimpse of her, but felt that I should see her that "night," as we say in the South — "evening," as they say in the North. George James always took care of my wardrobe for me, and saw that I was handsomely dressed for the evening. I got to Mr. Campbell's rather late, and the room was full of company when I got there. It was a large and quaint old parlor, all four walls papered with illustrations of the story of "Telemachus," some of which I had read, in French, with Miss Bass. As soon as I stepped into the parlor I was met by Miss Virginia, and she took my arm and started with me to introduce me to Dessie, who was about the middle of the room, and who, I naturally, recognized at once.

Dessie saw what her sister was preparing to do, and came to meet us and said, "Oh! I don't want to be introduced to Mr. Moore; I know him as well as you do;" and she locked her hands through my arm, and started off walking with me, and, while occasionally stopping us both to do her duties as hostess, held on to my arm, and we talked right from the beginning as if we had known each other all our lives. She was beautiful, bright, quick, witty, and was up on all popular society literature. I was "dead in love" with the girl in one minute after I saw her, and could hardly refrain from telling her so, there and then, when in the sound of many voices I knew we would not be overheard; and that I had been shown extraordinary attention by her was perfectly evident. After the reception I went to my room so happy that I could not sleep[.] I had stayed there until everybody else was gone, by an arrangement between us, and when I left she held my hand and sang "Parting is pain."

Only a night or two after that I had an engagement to see her. It was a starlight summer night, and there was no light in the parlor, but she was at the door ready to meet me, and we sat, side by side, on the door-sill of the parlor door that came out onto the porch, all clad in honeysuckles and roses, and when we had hardly said anything she sang:

"In the starry light, of a summer night,
On the banks of the blue Moselle;"

And sang it with great sweetness, as leaning on her elbows, on her knees, she looked out into the starry sky. Miss Virginia passed us and said, "Two are company; three's too many," and looked at me as if to say, "I told you so;" and Dessie said, "Yes, we will excuse you for the present." I was seraphically happy, and she seemed to be, and yet we

57

did not talk much. We didn't have to. We seemed to understand each other without talking. Under such circumstances I believe in telepathy; especially when the "pathy" is not too "tele." Hoops and large skirts can be shoved up into small space, and when Miss Virginia wanted to pass through the door in which we were sitting, neither of us got up. Dessie got over a little closer to one side of the door, and I got over closer to that same side that Dessie did, so that Miss Virginia could not pass between us, but had to go in by the opposite side of the door, and I said, "Whatsoever God hath joined together let no woman put asunder." Dessie looked at the stars most of the time and straight into my face sometimes, and I looked at her the most of the time and at the stars sometimes. After we had been sitting there an hour or more I said to her, "You have such a beautiful suit of hair; how much of it is yours?" I would not have dared to tell her that her eyes or mouth were pretty, though they were just killingly so, but somehow I felt like hair was not what the lawyers call a "fixture" and I felt like I might say what I did. She answered, "It's all mine." I said, "Yes, I suppose it's all either growing there, or paid for, but I mean how much of it is yours by nature?" She pulled out a comb and some hair-pins, and a suit of hair, all natural, and beautiful as a mermaid's fell down upon the floor. I gathered it up in my hands in great hanks, as soft as silk, and we talked on as we had been doing.

If I could remember, away across this long stretch of years, what we talked about, I would tell you exactly, but I cannot. We simply talked about anything that we thought about, and without any form or coherence more than the most natural suggestions. After commencement I went home and Dessie and I corresponded in long letters, about as fast as one could answer the other. The next session I was to see her two or three times every week. It would take a book larger than this one to give you any adequate idea of what we said and did. I will tell you of a sample night. It was in June, and the moon was about full, and the sky perfectly clear, and the balmy air was full of the fragrance of flowers and it was all still, except that we could hear the night birds and the bells of the cows and sheep out in the mountains. We walked down to that pretty creek and found a beautiful white sycamore tree that had lately fallen out onto it, and we sat together on a springy limb and talked. Some part of her dress was trimmed with beautiful large white beads that were hollow and would float, and she pulled some of these and we watched them as they floated away in the water that ran under us and shimmered in the moonlight. I thought then that it was the most romantic of all the scenes I had ever witnessed. When the end of the session came I graduated and went home. The next September Miss Virginia and Dessie came to Kentucky, and visited at different places, and at my home among the others. My sister Mary and I were with them a great part of the time, I being with them more than my sister was. I never saw any woman fall so really in love with any other woman as Miss Virginia did with my sister Mary, and when we were all together those two would pair off, and Dessie and I would pair off.

George James had graduated a year before I did, and had come home with me at vacation. We had gotten to my home and were in the parlor, and he was talking and laughing as he whirled himself around on a piano stool. He was quite handsome and was dressed in fine taste[.] My sister Mary came into the parlor and George saw her for the first time, as I introduced them. He stood looking at her like a man who was dazed, and as if, with all his society manners, he hardly knew what to do or say, and he only gained his self-possession by slow degrees. We had a triangular talk for a little while, and when she left the room George folded his hands as if in an ecstasy and said, "Oh; Chum, why didn't you tell me you had a pretty sister?" I had never thought of my own sister as being pretty. Boys generally think that of other boys' sisters; but when my sister Mary married Major Brent, and I went with them on their bridal tour, I remember that when they entered the dining room of the Cataract House, at Niagara, then the Mecca of all the most elegant bridal parties in the United States, they attracted the admiration of more elegant people than any couple I ever saw. George was, at once, desperately in love with my sister.

We made up a party of twenty persons, including our chaperons, Mr. and Mrs. B. F. Groom, of Clark County, Kentucky, to go to the Mammoth Cave. Miss Virginia, Dessie, Sister Mary, George James and I were in the party. We went through the country in two omnibuses with four fine horses to each. It was in October, and we had not only the moonlight, but a comet, that, it seems to me, must have been the grandest that was ever witnessed. I do not know the names of but three comets, from memory, as I have to write; those of Encke, Biela and Donnatti, and I do not know if the one then visible, for more than a month, was one of them; but while its head was near the zenith its tail spread clear to the horizon, over nearly a fourth of the heavens. We rode a good part of the way after night, the weather being delightful, and most of the time we were on top of the omnibuses. As we went through the mountains of Kentucky we found papaws, persimmons and chestnuts. Sometime in search of them the omnibuses would be emptied of all their passengers, and they straggled through the woods.

It took us nearly a week to go and that long to come. In going we passed over what was afterward the battle-field of Perryville, a fearful battle in which Major Brent was, and when I came across it after the war, it had long rows of trenches in which the dead had been buried. We had some exceedingly romantic and some funny experiences going.

One day Mr. Groom had arranged for us all to stop at a certain place, that he had never seen, for dinner. About dinner-time we got to a house that was unusually large and fine for that country. Our two omnibuses stopped, and the whole twenty of us rolled out and took possession of the yard and house, and the two Negro drivers took our eight horses to the stable. The women servants — it was slave times — met our party with large and hospitable grins on their faces, and told us that the Master and Mistress were at church — it was Saturday — but said they would soon be at home. Some of us were pitching horse-shoes in the yard, and some playing the piano and dancing in the parlor when the proprietor and his wife came home. We saw the lady and her force of female servants begin active preparations for a dinner, while the gentleman talked to Mr. Groom. We had a gay time and ate a splendid dinner. When the horses were put to the omnibuses and we were about ready to start, we saw Mr. and Mrs. Groom and the proprietor and his wife in what appeared to be a very embarrassing conversation, on the porch. Soon after Mr. Groom called up all of us, and we saw that he had an expression on his face that was a combination of mortification and amusement. He ordered us all to string out in a straight row before the porch, and we all obeyed, curious to know what had happened. Mr. Groom then explained to us all — the proprietor and his wife protesting all the time — that we had made a mistake; that we were not at a public house at all, but at the house of a private gentleman, who would accept no pay for his elegant entertainment of us; and Mr. Groom told us that every one had to make a personal apology to the gentleman and his wife. The apologizing was begun in hard earnest, but our host and hostess made a joke of it, and the apologizing got to be very amusing before we all got through. The gentleman and his wife had seen, from the beginning, that we were mistaken, and had tried to get Mr. and Mrs. Groom not to tell us any better.

One night we stopped at a little house that had only two sleeping rooms beside the family room, and all the ladies had to sleep in one room and all the gentlemen in another. As we went upstairs to bed I picked up a dinner-bell and a ball of yarn that were on the steps, and did it so that no one noticed it. Our party were all tired and sleepy, and were soon asleep. We had in the party a man named Gano, who was getting to be an old bachelor, and therefore more sedate than the balance of us, and we made him the victim of a good many of our jokes. I held the bell by the clapper, and managed to get it hidden in my bed, without its making any noise. Gano was sleeping on the floor. When all were asleep and still I went out in the hall between the two rooms and tied my bell under the middle of the bottom of a hickory-split chair, and, tying the yarn string to the clapper, I unwound it as I went along back to my bed and got in. I tolled my bell for a few times, but with no effect upon the sleeping household, but, finally, as I kept ringing it, occasionally I heard them begin to stir, upstairs and down. Expressions of disapprobation came from the ladies' room. After awhile I heard the proprietor get up and go to his door and call a Negro man to come to the house and go upstairs and see who was ringing the bell. I tolled it occasionally until I heard the man get to the house, and then I stopped. The old Negro man came and went around the hall and through our room, where everybody else was in deep sleep, as soon as I stopped ringing the bell, and I was, apparently, as sound asleep as any of them. The old man went down and reported that everybody was asleep and that he could not find the bell. When everything was quiet again, I commenced ringing the bell, and the baby woke up, down stairs, and began crying, and the proprietor got up, and, going to the door, called another servant to the house, and when he got there told him to go upstairs, and not come down until he found that bell. This time it was a little Negro boy. The boy came upstairs and, after taking a general survey of the situation, found the yarn string in the hall, traced it to the chair and found the bell, and then followed the yarn back into our room. I pitched the ball so that it rolled right to Gano's head, and the little Negro traced it right to him. Gano was sound asleep and snoring. The little darkey evidently thought he was awake, and that he was simply pretending to snore, and, standing at Gano's head, and looking down on him, as I could see him in the moonlight, the little Negro clenched his fists and said: "Oh! yes, confoun' you; you tend like you never wus wake." I told the story afterward, and "You tend like you never wus wake," got to be a saying through the balance of the trip.

When we got to the Mammoth Cave I undertook to amuse myself again at the expense of others, one night. The boys put me out of the room and fastened me out. I found a lot of ten-pin balls and rolled them for more than a hundred yards on the long porches of that strange old hotel, until they compromised by letting me in again.

"I have been across the ocean blue

61

And seen it in all its glory,"

I have climbed the mountains on foot, on horseback and over railways. I have swum in the Mississippi, and traveled on it in skiffs and grand steamboats, from where it is as pellucid as fine glass, to where it rolls its turgid billows below New Orleans. I have been on the great lakes when they were so dreamily beautiful that it was hard to realize that it was not "a painted ship upon a painted sea," and I have stood awe-struck as I looked out over the thundering abysses of Niagara and heard what "Paul Dombey" called "the voice of the great Creator that dwells in its mighty tone," and I looked, night after night, on the wondrous comet, such a sight as can be had only once in thousands of years, with an ineffable longing to know its story — whence it came and whither it went, dragging a fiery tail of billions of miles in length, and into the chaos of which our earth and sun and the whole solar system could have dropped and been lost as a pebble in the depths of mid-ocean, a sight that far surpassed the most weird dream of the apocalyptic seer of Patmos; but with my knowledge of geology and training in romance and poetry, and communion with beautiful scenery, at the most impressionable and susceptible period of my life, nothing so overpowered me with its inscrutable mystery and unutterable grandeur, as my first walk through the Mammoth Cave; nor do I know that my impressions have been less profound in the several visits I have since made to it, sometimes traversing its mazy labyrinth only with a guide, and sometimes with large parties. All the wonders of nature bow their heads in reverent obeisance when they come to the shores of "Echo River." Dessie was a little undersize, anyhow, and when she appeared in her bloomer costume for the walk in the cave, I thought she was the cutest looking little piece of humanity I had ever seen. Sister Mary, tall, graceful, and dignified, looked just as queenly in her bloomer of Scottish plaid, as she did, a year or two afterward, when, at her wedding, the band played "Bonnie Mary of Argyll." I had on a fancy costume of blood-red flannel, red cap and red shoes, almost trenching on the make-up of Mephistopheles in the great opera "Faust."

In all that had ever passed between Dessie and me, in writing or talking, I had never told her that I loved her, except in such action as I have described to you, but I had determined that when we got to the "Bridal Chamber," in the Mammoth Cave, I was going to tell her that I loved her, and ask her to marry me. She and I walked together, most of the time behind the others of the party, and a good part of the time we walked hand in hand. I do not recollect what we were talking about, except that I was telling her about the conjugation of Greek verbs and reduplication and the use of Nu ephelkusticon — if that's the way to spell it — in Greek euphony. We had two guides, white and black, but the Negroes were generally preferred, and we had a Negro — I forget his name — but he was second only to the dead Stephen, the Negro who had been the most famous of all the guides. I thought it proper that a guide should be guyed, and I proceeded to guy him. I was fresh and up-to-date on geological terminology, and with a pedantic concatenation of technical nomenclature, I asked him what, in smaller words, was the same as, "Why do you call those things up there above us stalactites, and these below stalagmites?" He answered without a moment's hesitation, "We call those above stalactites because if they were not tight they would not stick there. We call these below stalagmites because they might be tight; we do not know." The laugh was at my expense. To this day I have to recall that darkey's answer when I want to remember which are stalactites and which are stalagmites.

I had never told anybody, in the world, that I intended to tell Dessie I loved her when we got to the "Bridal Chamber." It is a famous place for courtships, and is the place where the girl married the man whom she had vowed to her parents she would "never marry on the face of the earth." The "Bridal Chamber" is several miles from the mouth. When we got there Dessie ran ahead of me and sat down in the "Devil's arm chair." Miss Virginia and Sister Mary, who were, as usual, together, seemed to know what I intended to do just as well as if I had told them, and managed to keep near me and Dessie, and, without saying a word, just watched us with a smile on their faces, intending to worry me, or both of us, and certainly succeeding, so far as I was concerned, and we went on by the "Bridal Chamber," and I had not told Dessie the little story of my love, and asked her that question upon the monosyllabic answer to which so much of human destiny hangs. Our whole trip to the cave, and there and back was one of as unalloyed pleasure as is ever known.

One of the young men was in love with Miss Virginia, and two of them with my sister. When we came back from the cave we visited several places together. We spent a week at the elegant home of Mr. Richard White, near Richmond, Kentucky. The weather was getting cold in the late fall, and one night in a large room where there was a bright fire, and a large group of us sitting around it, Dessie and I took our chairs and walked to the furthest corner of the room, and sat right close together, with our faces right up in the corner, and talked so that nobody else could hear us. After talking this way for half an hour, she got up and walked out of a door into a broad hall, and to the opposite side of it. Then I walked out into that same hall to meet her. The hall lamp was not very bright, and there was no one else in the hall, and Dessie came toward me and we met about the middle of the hall. I held out both my hands and she held out both of hers, and she put both of her hands on my arms and I took her by both of her arms and said: "Miss Dessie, I love you; will you marry me?" She looked me straight in the face and with great earnestness, simply said "Yes," and then quickly turned me around, and, taking my arm walked with me back into the room from which we had both come. I was so happy that I could hardly talk, and hardly slept that night[.] There was no railroad from Lexington to Richmond then, and a day or two after that, Miss Virginia[,] Sister Mary, Dessie and I all went back to Lexington in a large stage coach, there being no passengers but us four. Dessie and I sat on the back seat, and they sat with their backs to us in front of us. The day was a little dark, and it was still darker in the deep, back seat, with no windows on it where we sat, the seat on the sides and behind, all upholstered in soft Russia leather, higher than our heads, and we had the fast horses and one of the fine turnpikes for which Kentucky is famous, and forty miles ride ahead of us. I wrapped Dessie and myself all snug and warm in our fine wraps, and held her hand in mine under the wraps. After a few abortive efforts, by Miss Virginia and Sister Mary, to worry us by insinuating looks and suggestions, they quit it and fell into a spirited conversation in which they completely ignored us, and what little talking Dessie and I did was so low that our sisters could not hear.

In the early part of the winter Miss Virginia and Dessie went home, and not a great while after I went to see them, and spent about two weeks at Mr. Campbell's. Dessie and I would sit together on a divan before a big coal fire in the parlor that we had all to ourselves, and every night, about 12 o'clock, Mrs. Campbell would come in and give us a little free lecture on keeping late hours, and order Dessie off to her room and me to mine, and Dessie went with a pouting protest. On the night before I was to leave for home Dessie had said to me that when her mother came, as usual, to send us to our rooms, we must both go as usual, and then that I must come back to the parlor, and that she would steal back, too, after her mother was asleep. My room opened into the parlor, and when all was quiet I went back into the parlor and waited a long time; but Dessie did not come, and I finally concluded that she was not coming, and I went back to my room and retired. The next morning Dessie told me that she got to the parlor soon after I had gone to my room the second time, and that she waited there for me until daylight.

We corresponded after I went home by long letters in which we recognized each other as prospective husband and wife, but we never set any time when we were to be married, and I said to her that though she knew it was the great hope of my life, we were both young enough to wait, and that I would wait, as patiently as I could, for her to name the time when she was to become my wife.

The next commencement my Sister Mary and I went to Bethany, and without effort on her part she won the hearts of everybody. The next fall Miss Virginia and Dessie went to St. Louis. It was commonly known that Dessie and I were engaged, and a lady got the news to me that Dessie was receiving such attentions from young gentlemen as no affianced girl ought to do. I never knew whether it was true or false, but it seemed to crush every hope in my heart, and I wrote Dessie a letter upbraiding her. She was, all the time, wearing a very handsome diamond ring that I had given her, on the inside of which was the date of our engagement. Dessie wrote me in answer to my letter, a sweet and affectionate letter, but in which she asked me to let her break her engagement to marry me. With a crushed heart and a brain that was aflame in agony, I answered at once my willingness for her to break the engagement, and I never again even hinted one word of love to her. I was fond of walking, and on the day that I got her letter asking me to break her engagement I looked at the lunatic asylum as I walked by it on my way home, eight miles in the country, and thought it possible that, before long, I would be a patient in that institution. The world all turned dark to me, and remained so for the six years that should have been the happiest and most important of my life. The inherited spirit of my preacher, grand-father came upon me, and, to bury my sorrow, I determined to devote my whole life to preaching. I went back to Bethany to study theology. The war was almost on us, and military companies were organizing. I was ordained to the ministry, Mr. Campbell being the leading minister on the occasion. Dessie was present, but I never spoke to her until the day that I was to go home. I went to see her and we walked out into a beautiful mountain overlooking that stream of which I have told you, she leaning on my arm. We sat in a beautiful place, and both of us cried like we were both heartbroken. We sat there for an hour, and we scarcely said a word, except that when I raised her up to go back to her home I said "Goodbye," the last word I ever spoke or wrote to her, and, as I believe I have told you, I have never spoken her name to this day, and have never written it even once, until I have written it here in this book while I am a penitentiary convict. When she had married Dr. J. Judson Barclay, United States Envoy to Palestine,

Dessie wrote me a long letter from Cyprus, telling me of her little girl that had lately been born, her first child, and saying it was "as pretty as Miss Venus herself just out of the sea," an expression she had often used to me, and that now seemed strangely applicable when she was born of the sea. Fifteen years after that I saw her the only time I have ever seen her since we parted at the door of her home in Bethany after our last walk on the mountain. Dessie was about the middle of ten thousand spectators at the Lexington fair, in the grand amphitheater, and I was out in the ring in front, two hundred feet away, among newspaper reporters and editors. She could easily see me. I picked up a splendid pair of field glasses and turned them over that great crowd, and finally found her and recognized her at once, and I saw plainly that she had a pair of large opera glasses and was looking at me. I took down my glasses and that was the last I ever saw her, and we did not, in any way, communicate.

I believe I will start the story of my preaching with a new chapter, which is

Chapter IV

The idea of making any money by preaching had never entered my head. My only purpose was to drown my sorrow in doing good, as I thought, for my fellow-men, and I never, in all my life, took a cent for preaching. My father had died and I was appointed administrator on his estate, which was worth nearly $100,000. He owed about $6,000, and I paid about $3,000 of this out of personalty of his estate, and it would have been necessary for me to sell enough Negroes to pay the other $3,000, but rather than to do that I incurred my first debt and borrowed, individually, $3,000 to pay the balance. I thought they would be emancipated in the war, and I wanted them all to go free from the old home. The romantic was still dominant in my nature, though my whole life was changed from gladness to sorrow.

I had a suit of black cloth made, that I wore all the time. The coat was very long and was the conventional style of the clergy, straight breast, and buttoned with only one button at the throat, my vest being also of the clerical style. I wore a broad, black soft hat, with low crown, and I had a beautiful patent-leather knapsack, in which I carried my books and underclothing. I had thick-soled walking shoes. I had in my knapsack a flute. Thus equipped, I started for the mountains of Kentucky to preach whenever and wherever I found opportunity. Beyond Richmond I passed right by the house where Dessie said "Yes." Life in this cell is a paradise compared with what I then felt with the first blue outlines of the mountains marked dimly on the sky far away, and I was, apparently, the freest of the free. There were three brothers, named Azbill, who lived in the mountains, and who were all preachers in my church, and a fourth brother of the family who, I was told, desired to preach. His first name was Overton. I found him in a very wild place in the mountains, making a speech to the worst looking body of men I ever saw to induce them to volunteer as soldiers in the Federal army. We had never met before, and he had never heard of me. I walked right up to him while he was making a very excited speech to the men, nearly all of whom had rough home-made fighting-knives sticking in their belts, and told him that I wanted him to come, right then, and go with me to preach. He left the crowd without one word of explanation to them, and went with me. I was the officiating preacher in his ordination, next day, and he preached with me, much of the time; quit his preaching when I did, and was killed by a fall from a horse, years afterward, when he was practicing medicine. As we walked from the place where we first met, he showed me a picture of a witch that one of his neighbors had cut on a beech tree and shot with a silver bullet, because the witch, a woman living near there, had bewitched his cows and made them give bloody milk. The first shot had missed the figure, and I could see the hole it had made, but the next one had struck it in a fatal place, and the cows had gotten all right. It was hard to get silver bullets, as they were always made of coin, and there was no silver in circulation. Azbill showed me the picture and the shots as an instance of superstition that he did not believe in, but he did not ridicule it. My peculiar dress, and traveling on foot and preaching, at a time when war and fighting were the only things that anybody was talking about, excited some curiosity to see me and hear me talk and preach.

I went, that night, to the home of James Azbill, the eldest of the preacher brothers. His home was an exceedingly poor one. When we had family prayers, that night, the light which they furnished me to read from was a stove leg in the hollow of which bacon grease had been poured, and into this was put a cotton rag, twisted into a string, and lighted. We arranged that I was to go with him, the next day, which was Sunday, and that I should preach, and before we started, Sunday morning, he shod his horse, I blowing the bellows for him. The meeting was in a log house that was used for a church and school house, too. I preached there twice a day for a week, and baptized some persons who joined the church.

I there saw, for the first time, one of the strange religious demonstrations that are mentioned in the history of my grand-father's preaching. My preaching was nearly all just in a conversational tone. During one of these talks an unmarried woman about twenty-one years old, began to shout, and kept it up so long and with such vigor that she finally had to be carried out of the house by some of the other women, and was, afterward, brought in with her head tied up like one suffering from headache. The same thing occurred with a married woman in maturer years, once after that when I was sitting and talking, in ordinary conversational style, about religious matters, in a private family circle. Those were the only two instances of the kind I ever witnessed. Many cases of that kind, though in greater degree, are reported in connection with my grand-father's preaching, and occur, at intervals, in Kentucky, to this day. My mother has told me that my grand-father never encouraged or condemned it. In my own experience I was surprised to see how little of excitement, as I regarded it, in what I was saying, produced such marked results in those who were influenced by it. I was an indifferent orator, especially as they count oratory in the pulpit in the mountains. I preached in the open air, or court house, or school house, or private house, or church, just as the occasion suggested. I rarely had large audiences, but every day of the week, two or three times a day, I would have small audiences, the people making all the arrangements as to where I was to preach. It was always arranged by the others where I was to stay, and there was nearly always a company invited to stay with me wherever I was. Sometimes I was taken to the very best houses in the country and sometimes to the poorest. The people who heard me talk in the family circle seemed to enjoy it very much.

I was fresh from college and loved the natural sciences, and they listened with great interest to what I told them about botany, zoology, astronomy, and especially about geology, their country abounding in most wonderful geological phenomena. It was geology in these mountains that had much to do with my subsequent abandonment of the ministry. I was wonderfully impressed by the conglomerate that I found on the tops of the mountains. Here were great masses of pebbles, as hard as flint, that had evidently been rolled in the sand and water for ages until they were polished into the shape of almonds, and then the sand had been packed down between them and the whole mass had become so hard that old millstones made of that conglomerate stone are now found in Kentucky. Of course it indicated to me that the tops of those mountains had once been the bed of the sea, and what Hugh Miller called "the testimony of the rocks" as to the age of earth, seemed to me in hopeless conflict with the chronology of the Bible, as interpreted by its highest accepted authority, Bishop Usher.

One of the most [inexplicable] things that the mountaineers showed me in their country was the "gnawed pine." In the midst of pine forests, where there was no difference in the nature of the pines that the mountaineers or I could see, and at intervals of ten or twenty miles apart, there would be a pine tree to which the bears would come, for miles, and they would gnaw every particle of the dermoid membrane — the rough bark — down to what we may call the cutis vera, from the very ground up as far on every branch of that tree as it would bear the weight of a bear — a sort of bear and forbear. Such was the eagerness of the bears to gnaw on one of these trees that the hunters watched the trees to kill bears, as they did salt licks to kill deer. I have never been able to find any explanation of this phenomenon. So little did these mountaineers know of the world, that when the government, for war purposes, put up, about that time, a telegraph through their country, many of them went miles to see it.

During the several days that I would preach at one place there would nearly always be some persons who would "join the church," and I would baptize them. Generally they were young people, and most of them young women, some of them fine specimens of mountain beauty. Some of the baptismal scenes were very romantic. There were places in the streams that were beautiful enough for the homes of water nymphs and naiads. The mountaineers would furnish me some of their rough clothes for baptismal purposes, and I would stand at the edge of the water and deliver a short discourse, explanatory of the ordinance and then, after a prayer, I would lead the candidates, one at a time, into the water, and baptize them while the singing from the audience, or spectators, who stood on the shore, was very impressive. The people would follow me from one place to another as I went to preach, most of them riding on horses, and some walking with me, but all of us going along together. On one of these walks we stopped at a most beautiful place where a stream ran along beside our road; and I baptized eighteen young men. I preached a good deal at McKee, in Jackson County. The only vehicle of any description that I ever saw come into that town was a wagon driven by a girl, and drawn by one ox that had gear made of hickory bark. Long before I got to the home of Frederick Lynx some persons had expressed a desire to see us together and hear us talk. "Old Brother Lynx," as everybody called him, was a German, about 70 years old, when I first saw him. He was below medium height, but otherwise was tremendously strong in his build. When he was a young man his passage to this country had been paid by General Garrard, and Brother Lynx had begun to work for Gen. Garrard to pay his passage, and had continued to work for him for years. Gen. Garrard, was, all his life, an infidel, and Brother Lynx had been an infidel until only a few years before I first saw him, when he had become a most enthusiastic Christian of the denomination to which I belonged. When I got to the home of Brother Lynx, only Overton Azbill was with me. Brother Lynx was unusually active for one of his age, and was enthusiastic on meeting me. He was an enthusiastic "Union" man, and at once expressed a hope that I was the same. I told him that I took no part in politics, and was merely a private soldier under a flag with a cross on it, and the old man never, afterwards, said anything to me about politics. His German brogue was very funny. As we walked up on the path to his house, which was considerably better than the average mountain home, he stopped me and said he wanted to warn me before I went into his house about mentioning the subject of religion to his wife. He said she was an infidel, and would be very kind to me if I said nothing about religion to her, but that if I ever said anything to her in favor of religion she would give me a tongue lashing that I would never forget. I received a great deal of hospitality at that home, and "Sister Lynx," as I called her, did all she could for my comfort and happiness, but no word about religion ever passed between us. They had a family of unmarried daughters who lived with their parents, and two married sons, who were well-to-do and respected, who lived at their homes near by. The daughters were religious like the father. The wives of the sons were religious also, but the sons combined the father and mother in their views. They would go to church, but would never become members of the church. It seemed to be thought, and hoped, especially by old Brother Lynx, that I would convert his sons to the Christian religion, but I never could do it, though I made a special effort to do so. The sons would follow me to hear me preach, but more than this in a religious line they would never do.

Old Sister Lynx never put her foot inside of any church. When we would have family worship, at night, the girls would hand hymn books to everybody but the mother, and she would light her pipe and sit by the fire-place and smoke through the whole service. And yet, when her husband and daughters would be getting ready to follow me a long distance from their home, Sister Lynx would cheerfully do all she could to assist them. Brother Lynx always called me "Brudder Mo." He was famous as a story teller, all of which were of his personal experiences, and they were made funnier by his brogue. He was grave but had a high sense of the ridiculous, though I never heard him laugh. He would only tell his stories when specially asked to do so, and, though he rather protested against it, Overton Azbill made him tell me a number of them. I am a poor story teller under favorable circumstances even, and of course, do not feel very jovial where I am. I will, therefore, simply give you an outline of the facts in Brother Lynx's "salt-house key" story.

General Garrard lived near Manchester, Ky., and made a fine fortune by making salt at the Goose creek salt works. He was so much pleased with "Fred," as he always called old Brother Lynx, that soon after Fred got to the General's place, he made Fred his foreman, and Fred always carried the key of the big salt warehouse in his pocket. In those days, and only somewhat less when I was there, in every neighborhood there was a bully who, it was generally conceded, could whip anybody, and who wore the distinction with the same pride that a prize fighter now wears the champion's belt. In those days it was an individual affair and was fought to a finish with fists. In these days it has grown into the feuds and Winchester rifle killings, for which the mountains of Kentucky are famous. In the young days of Brother Lynx every man who came into that country had to acknowledge a fealty to the reigning local bully, or get whipped by him — a sort of a remnant of English feudalism. Brother Lynx was an unusually quiet and inoffensive man, naturally, but he was unwilling to recognize this peculiar custom of his mountain country. He was invited to a "corn shucking." The corn with the "shucks" on it was put up in piles of equal size, and a gallon of whiskey was given to the man who first shucked out his pile. The neighborhood bully had been seeking an excuse to get into a fight with Brother Lynx, and, so, took a pile next to that of Brother Lynx. At a given signal all commenced shucking, and in a minute the bully threw an unshucked ear off his own pile onto the pile of Brother Lynx. Brother Lynx saw it, but said nothing. In another minute the bully threw another unshucked ear from his own pile onto Brother Lynx's pile. Brother Lynx said "Don't yer do dot no mo." Then the bully threw another unshucked ear on Brother Lynx's pile, and Brother Lynx started to get up. The bully was on the alert and was on his feet before Brother Lynx was, and knocked Brother Lynx down before he was fairly on his feet, and jumped on top of him and so beat him in the face and head that Brother Lynx thought the man would kill him. By the laws of that country when a man hollered "Nuff, nuff," the man who was whipping him had to quit. Brother Lynx wanted to holler "Nuff," but in his scant acquaintance with the English language he forgot the word, and, by mistake, hollered "Hurra, hurra." The man who was beating him thought it meant defiance, and the crowd thought it meant pluck. Brother Lynx could not explain, and the man was still beating him unmercifully. Brother Lynx got his hand into his breeches pocket and got his thumb through the ring of the salt-house key, closing the balance of the key in his fist, so that the point of the key stuck out through one side of his fist. Brother Lynx got his fist out of his pocket with the key in his fist, and he said, "Brudder Mo, efry time I hit dot man in the face de blood jes fly, and he holler 'Nuff, nuff," and de udder boys dey stop me, but none uv em effer did know I git dot salt-house key, and Brudder Mo, I neffer forgit dot wurt, Nuff, no mo."

Another of his funny stories was his curing of a man who for years had been reported to be insane, and who, for years had never been known to speak a word. He was a big, strong man, and Brother Lynx thought he was affecting insanity to get rid of working. Brother Lynx caught the man and told him he was going to whip him if he did not talk, and the man did talk, and promised Brother Lynx that he would go to work[,] and did so, and was healed of his years of "insanity." Brother Lynx's admiration of Gen. Garrard amounted almost to adoration, and he was very anxious that I should convert Gen. Garrard to Christianity. Old Sister Lynx was the first person I ever met who was said to be an infidel, except one student at Bethany who was the son of a preacher. I had never mentioned the subject to that student. He was a boy of strong mind, but was morose, it seemed to me, and did not affiliate with me. Brother Lynx and several others went with me to see Gen. Garrard. He was, in all respects, by far the most influential man in his country. His sympathies and his talk were all for the Confederates, while everybody around him were ultra Union people, but the old man had so many children and grand-children who reverenced him that the authorities did not dare to arrest him. His son had been Treasurer of Kentucky, and was then a Colonel in the Federal army. In a community where everybody else dressed in plain, rough style and had the ordinary manners of mountaineers, old Gen. Garrard dressed in elegant taste, and was an elegant gentleman. He was just the soul of hospitality to me. He never said anything about his infidel views until someone expressed a desire to hear them, and then he gave them very firmly and tersely and clearly and very modestly. I was all the more anxious to hear him talk on the subject, and repeatedly induced him to do so. His reasoning made its impression upon me. Ingersoll then had never been heard of, and I found, only a very little to my surprise, and a great deal to my gratification, that an infidel was not necessarily the repulsive kind of a character that I had been taught to believe he was. I had seen that old Sister Lynx was a kind-hearted, self-sacrificing woman, but she was ignorant and smoked a pipe, and she did not so favorably impress me with infidelity as old Gen. Garrard did. In my political views I was opposed to slavery, but old Gen. Garrard discovered, without my telling him so, that my sympathies and prejudices were with the South. He soon became much attached to me. I would preach in the court house in Manchester, and the old General would not only come to hear me every time, but he would bring a chair and sit right by my side while I was preaching, and listen in a manner of the deepest respect from the first to the last of my sermon. I could see that old Brother Lynx, who, with his daughters, had followed me that distance from their home, would anxiously watch the old General all the time to see what effect my sermons were having upon him.

One day I asked the old General why it was that, with his religious views, he so often came to hear me preach when I passed through his town. He said: "I always enjoy hearing any man reason, on any important subject." The old General, not long before I first saw him, had married, as his second wife, a lady about 30 years old, who was one of the most magnificent looking women I ever saw, and a more devoted couple I never saw, in the stately old-school dignity that I had seen in my father toward my mother. I supposed that Mrs. Garrard was of the same religious opinions as her husband; but one day, as I was preaching in the courthouse, she and others arose from the audience and came forward to signify their desire to become members of the church. The baptismal scene, when I baptized them at a beautiful place in a most beautiful stream, was the prettiest one I ever witnessed. Mrs. Garrard was tall and the personification of grace, and when she came down to the edge of the water, gracefully dressed for the occasion, the old General led her as gallantly and gracefully as he led her to the marriage altar, and so received her again when I led her to the bank of the stream. Old Brother Lynx was a great singer and was always the leader of the singing when he was with me, and on this occasion he sang like one inspired, and as their voices blended and rang through the mountain gorges and over the bright and shaded surface of the pretty water, there was in that music something more nearly seraphic than anything I have ever heard from the paid choirs and thundering organs of great city churches and cathedrals.

One day as I was walking up to the court house door, in Manchester, to preach, I saw one of the most beautiful creatures I have ever seen. To me beautiful women are the most beautiful of all nature's handiwork, and sometimes there are female faces that appear beautiful to me not so much from their own symmetry as from qualities of head or heart that I know their owners to possess. I frequently think of Burns' lines,

> "He tried on man his 'prentice hand,
> And then he made the lassies, O;"

and of Ingersoll's suggestion that "When God made woman out [of] a bone, considering the raw material that he had, it was the best job he ever did."

That girl I saw at Manchester was about 18 years old, and I was about 22. She was walking bare-headed, and she was coming in a narrow footpath, so that she would cross at right angles, a path of the same kind in which I was walking, just about the time we would get to the intersection of the paths. She wore a common calico dress. She was enchantingly beautiful. She was more like Bettie Herndon than any girl I had ever seen, but the difference was, that, while Bettie's beauty appealed to your appreciation, this mountain girl's beauty commanded your admiration. It was a case of "beauty unadorned." She could not have expected to impress any man in so artless a costume, but to my eye, trained to love nature, there was in her simple dress suggestions of grace that are not to be found in any of the artifices of the modiste. She was so rapturously beautiful that, in a second, I had almost determined to apologize for stopping her, and asking her name, and asking if I might call to see her; and then I thought that she was possibly not educated up to the standard that I would want in a woman, and thought even if I could induce her to marry me, it would conflict with my resolution to devote my life exclusively to religion, and then I remembered all the suffering that I was still enduring from one love affair, and though the beautiful girl and I would necessarily come within a few feet of each other, as we followed our crossing paths, and I wanted to see her face at the shortest possible distance, when I was very close to her, I never looked at her, and have never known any more about her than what I have told you.

One of the best friends I had was a woman who had two pretty, unmarried daughters about 18 and 20 years old. I do not remember their name, and, though you may think it strange, I cannot remember whether there were any male persons who stayed in the house. The house was in a secluded place in the mountain wilderness. I got to it one night a little before supper time, when it was very dark and pouring down rain, and I was thoroughly wet. There was only one room to the house, but the woods were full of pine knots, and there was, soon, roaring for me, such a fire as only pine knots can make, and beside which coal and gas, natural or artificial, "pale their ineffectual fires[.]" If there was any man on the premises I do not now recollect it. It was in the fall and the nights were very long. There was an immense fireplace, half as broad as one side of the house. They were all engaged in cooking our supper of very simple and very few materials, but when

75

they set it on the table it was one of the most delicious meals that I have ever eaten, and I have eaten at Delmonico's in New York, and paid $5.00 in gold for a single meal in Europe.

In all cases like that I always got the wood and did anything I could to help. I had done a good deal of surreptitious cooking at Bethany, and was not so utterly ignorant of the art as was King Alfred in the neatherd's cottage.

"We may live without friends; we may live without books;
But the civilized man cannot live without cooks."

At Bethany I remembered the principle of the ancient spits in old Mrs. Breckinridge's kitchen, and hanging a dressed turkey, by a string before my hot coal fire, in the little cottage that I had, my last college year, all to myself, I could cook it literally "to a turn," as it turned itself on a string. While those mountain lassies knew but little in books, and less of the great fashionable world, they all had strong natural minds, kind hearts, and healthy bodies, and as I sat there and they and I watched the steam rise from my wet clothes, and the smell from the boiling and frying and baking of our supper whetted our appetites, and we talked about funny things and religious things, all together, and laughed and sang hymns alternately, and then, at late bedtime, all kneeled together before that grand fire, and while I prayed for us all, it seemed to me that, somehow, a strange Providence that

"Moves in a mysterious way his wonders to perform,"

had for some strange purpose, led me through the mazes of only an outline of which I have been able to give you to bring me to such happiness as I now felt that seemed to me, in some senses, greater than any I had ever experienced. There were only two beds in the room, and we all had to sleep in that one room. When the time came, in which, without any special mention of the matter, it came to be understood that we were all to go to bed, the ladies left the room by going out of doors, after having told me that the better of the two beds was for me, and I undressed at my leisure and was in bed and soon asleep, and absolutely unconscious that I was living, until I awoke next morning and saw that the other bed was all nicely made up, and breakfast was nearly ready. When they saw that I was awake, they all went out of the room again, and came in when I had dressed, and by the time I could go down to the branch and wash my face and [hands], and come back, breakfast

76

was ready.

I learned once that away across the mountains, about ten miles from where I was, there was a man of whom it was said that he did not believe the Bible was true. I had a great curiosity to see him, and know about him, and I got all the information that I could about him. They said he was a good citizen and an industrious man, and that, although he was poor, he had quite a library. I determined to go to see him, and arranged to take a day or two off, in my preaching, in order to do so. I came up to a little shop that he had in front of his house just as his wife called him to dinner. I told him my name and that I was a preacher, and he gave me a most hospitable invitation to dinner, which I accepted. I found him making cedar buckets, and I expressed to him my surprise that such pretty work could be done with such simple appliances. I said that I was sorry I had not gotten there in time to see him make one before we went to dinner. He said he would make me one right then, and in about fifteen minutes he made a pretty cedar bucket. He was a nice looking man of about 30 years age, and he introduced me to his wife and his two little tots of children. The house had but one room. The wife had evidently seen, from her house, that she was going to have company for dinner, and she was all sweetly dressed in her plain, but neat, best dress, and there were preserves on the table that had the general appearance of being held in reservation for company. He showed me his library, and I found it to be well selected. Everything about the little cabin was neat and clean, and my stay there was the greatest intellectual feast that I have ever had in the mountains. His wife was a sweet little woman and seemed happy that somebody had come along who could appreciate her husband. I had heard much of "love in a cottage," and it seemed to me that here was the most beautiful instance of it I had ever seen. The man and his wife seemed to think they were naturally cut off from the society of their neighbors, by reason of their difference in religious views, and he was there making his living by a nice, clean work that seemed no harder to him than whittling a nice cedar stick with a sharp knife.

Many of the people of that country made the better part of their livings by hunting ginseng that grows wild in the mountains. They call it "sang," and going out to hunt ginseng they all call "goin' out a sangin'." They were very anxious to know of me what was done with it, as they did not use it for anything, and all that I could tell them about it was that it was sent to China. The greater part of all this time the war was going on, and there were spies and deep-laid schemes for aiding and abetting the opposing sides by their respective friends. There were some who thought that my whole preaching and traveling and living as I was, was all a part of a plan by which I was conveying intelligence to the Confederate army, and one day I was arrested at Barboursville, Kentucky, by the Federal authorities and sent out of the mountains under the escort of a cavalry soldier. I soon returned to my preaching in the mountains, however. One day, during my preaching, my audience and I could hear a battle going on, seven miles from us. We heard the incessant rattle of musketry and regular boom of cannon during the whole service, but it never interrupted my audience or me. We were on the north side of the road running from Cumberland Gap, in the eastern extremity of the state, west, to Lexington, and I knew that the Federal troops had marched from Lexington to meet the Confederates, who were marching from Cumberland Gap toward Lexington, and I knew that they must have met where we could hear the battle going on. I knew that the Confederates were regularly driving the Federals back, because, although the firing was kept up continuously, I could hear that it was regularly going west, which was toward Lexington, and that, therefore, the Federals were retreating and the Confederates were following them. I knew that the Confederates were going on to Lexington, and believing that my widowed mother would be uneasy about me, I started my march for home. By that time I had spent two and a half years in preaching, marching afoot through summer's heat and winter's cold and snow, and having such experiences as I have given you samples of. I followed along behind the two armies. They had fought all along through Richmond, and all along the road where Dessie and I and our sisters had ridden in the stage, and when I got to Lexington the town was flooded with Confederate soldiers, and they were lying asleep and resting from their fight, almost everywhere that they could drop down on the ground, and the people were bringing them hot coffee and food. The University building that is now standing, and another University building, that stood at the corner of North Broadway and Second Street, which was soon after burned by the soldiers, were both converted into hospitals.

Kirby Smith, the Confederate General commanding, was an Episcopalian, and conducted the Episcopal service in what is now the Episcopal cathedral. When I got to my home, eight miles from Lexington, I found there a Confederate soldier named William J. Hatch. He was about 22 years old, and had been cut off from his command, which was defeated in a battle at Pea Ridge, Arkansas, and he had come to Kentucky to go into the Confederate army again. He was my distant kinsman, though I had never heard of him before. His father was the

President of the University of Missouri at Canton. Young Hatch was at that time by far the most scholarly young man with whom I had ever met. He looked through my library and got, among other books, Plato's "Gorgias," in its original Greek, as a part of his literary entertainment. Though he did not show much disposition to ventilate his religious opinions, my experiences with infidels made me anxious to know what so learned a young man thought about religion. I soon found that he was skeptical. I had never heard or read any argument against the Christian religion. Once in my preaching in the mountains I had noticed, as I have told you, that when the people listened to me talk about history and science, in their families, they listened with an interest that seemed greater and more natural than when they listened to my sermons in which I made such arguments for Christianity as we have in "Butler's Analogy" and "Paley's Evidences;" and it seemed to me that if I would just collate all the evidences of the truth of the Christian religion that were to be found outside of the Bible and deliver them to the people in my sermons, just as I did science and history in my family circle talks, I would attract a new interest in the Christian religion, and, in order to prepare myself for argument of this kind, I quit my preaching long enough to go home, and, from my books, get all the information I could in this line. I devoted probably two weeks to this research, and found so little evidence of the truth of the Bible from what are called the "external" evidences, that I was surprised and greatly impressed by the fact. I determined to embody all I had learned in this way, in a sermon, and did so. I delivered the sermon, but the people who listened to me did not seem to feel the force of my arguments, and I felt that I could not blame them for not doing so, because they seemed to me to be open to many objections, and I never again attempted any argument on that line. This experience had so impressed me that when I found out the views of young Hatch I proposed to him that we should supply ourselves with books for and against the Christian religion, and study them together carefully. We began the investigation, and, for six weeks, ten or twelve hours a day, out under the shade trees at my home, we studied, from both sides, the question of religion. The first book we read, which was then new, was by Colenso, Bishop of the English church at Natal, in Africa. It was against the authenticity and genuineness of the Pentateuch. It made, in a very dignified and learned way, all the arguments that Ingersoll has since made in a ridiculous and funny way, in his, "Mistakes of Moses," and it is almost certain that Ingersoll got the suggestion for the most famous of all his lectures from this book of Bishop Colenso, though all of the Colenso-Ingersoll "Mistakes of

Moses" are just such as occur to anyone who reads the Pentateuch carefully and intelligently and free from religious bias. Colenso repudiated the Old Testament and still held his position as Bishop, preaching the New Testament.

Hatch and I then read, in the same way, a number of learned orthodox replies to Colenso. Of these replies five were written by English clergymen, under the special auspices of the English church. At the end of six weeks I went into a long and dangerous spell of fever, as my two physicians called it then. I suppose it would now be called "nervous prostration," superinduced by long and close study, with what then appeared to me would be disastrous consequences. I lay in bed for weeks, not sick, as far as I could see, except that I could not sleep, and was so weak, consequently, that I could not walk. Hatch and I never discussed what effect the investigation had upon us, but so far as I was concerned, it had overthrown my faith in the inerrancy of the Old Testament, and I determined to do as Colenso had done — discard the Old Testament and preach only the New Testament. My mother was afraid for me to go back to the mountains and wanted me to stay near her, and I accepted a position as the regular pastor of a church at Versailles, Ky., about twenty miles from where I lived. I went to that church, and with what occurred there I will begin

Chapter V

Versailles was then a pretty town of four or five thousand people, twelve miles west of Lexington, and in one of the finest parts of the famous "Blue Grass Region," and to which there ran from Lexington one of the most beautiful of the famous Kentucky turnpikes. It then had no railroads, as it has now. Versailles was and is the home of Thomas F. Marshall and Senator J. C. S. Blackburn. All of the prominent churches were represented in the town, and the one of which I had charge was the largest. I had the largest congregation of any church there, having beside my regular congregation, which was larger than any of the others, as the regular attendants of my church, a fine female college of as beautiful girls as the world ever saw. Of my younger two sisters, of whom I have told you, Alice was at that college at Versailles, and died when I was in Europe, and Jennie graduated, with the first honor, at Daughters' College, Harrodsburg, Ky., married Lieutenant-Governor of Kentucky James E. Cantrill, and died young. Her husband had been a Captain in the Confederate army.

At Versailles, though I was the poorest of the preacher orators in the town, I was the most popular preacher. I made some interesting acquaintances there. William J. Hatch, the young Infidel Confederate soldier, with whom I had examined the evidences of Christianity, came frequently to hear me preach. One day we went out into the woods and discussed religion, and I advised him to become a Christian. He joined my church and I baptized him. He died a few years afterward, then employed by the Government as an engineer of Mississippi levees. As soon as I got to Versailles I was met by a young man who was afterward

81

Judge Dick Reid of the Court of Appeals of the State of Kentucky. He met me as if he knew me familiarly, and expected me to know him, but I did not. He said he knew about me every way, and, among others, through a Bethany College magazine, and through his brother, who was my college companion. I remembered, after awhile, that I had heard of Dick Reid as the first-honor man at Georgetown College. He said he wanted me to room with him, and that he had the nicest place in town to room. I accepted his proposition and we roomed together as long as I lived in Versailles. Dick Reid was one of the most interesting characters that I ever knew. He was then about my age — 24. He was quite handsome, of fine, large figure, and of perfect health. He had a fine fortune, and was of a fine family, and was, theoretically and practically, one of the purest moralists I had ever known. He had won the honors at his college, and was then beginning the practice of law. He was devoutly pious, and every night, he and I, in our room, had a Bible reading and prayer. He was very jovial and was a fine talker, with an acute sense of the ridiculous. He was always ready to take any part that I would assign him, in the services at the church, only asking that I would notify him the day before of my purpose to call on him. His memory was the most remarkable I ever knew. He wrote very rapidly and very beautifully. He would write every word of what he intended to say in church, throw away the manuscript after having scarcely read it once, and then when I called on him he would repeat, without a second's hesitation, exactly what he had written, but with no genius in his delivery, and with such embarrassment that unwiped drops of sweat would stand on his face, at any season. But what he said was splendid. Over the whole of Dick Reid's life hung perpetually a kind of autumnal halo of sadness. This was the result of the fact that he had gone to Missouri to marry Miss Linda Jameson, and when he got to her home found her in her coffin, in the elegant bridal robes in which she was to have married him. Dick and I talked much, in our room alone, on every subject bearing upon morals. He and I thoroughly harmonized on every question that we ever discussed. Both of us wanted to go into the Confederate army, but he would not go because his conscience would not allow him to fight, and I did not go for that reason, and because I was opposed to slavery. One day my Southern sympathies got the better of me. I could hear the cannon toward Frankfort and knew that a little battle was going on, about fifteen miles away, between Gen. John H. Morgan, of the Confederates, and some body of Federal forces. I said nothing about it to anybody, but I made up my mind to go into the Confederate army, and have it appear, so far as possible to others, and to myself, that it was accidental. I knew that the forces engaged were cavalry. I determined to get me a fine horse, so that the owner would only suppose I had gone for a ride, and drop an order for him to be paid for, in the post office, and then start toward the battle so that Morgan's scouts and pickets would capture me, and when I was taken to him, as I knew I would be, I intended to tell him that I wanted to be a combination of chaplain, hospital nurse and soldier with a gun. I went to the livery stable of Mr. Thornton, who I knew was such a Rebel that he would give me a horse if I asked it for the purpose for which I really wanted it. I ordered a good horse, as if I were merely going out for a ride, but he said he had, early that morning, sent all of his horses away, because he was afraid the soldiers would be in town that day, and steal all of his horses. I went away without betraying any special disappointment and spent some time walking and thinking about it, and especially about my obligation to my widowed mother, I being the only male member of her family, and I finally made up my mind not to go then. I subsequently went into two such places, hoping I would be captured and pressed into the service by the Confederates, who would see that that was what I wanted to be, but I only acted as chaplain and nurse in the hospitals.

Dick Reid afterward married the widowed sister of Miss Jameson, a Mrs. Rogers, who was and is, a most beautiful, elegant and accomplished woman. I visited them at their beautiful home in the suburbs of Mt. Sterling, Ky. It was a perfect picture of domestic happiness. Dick was one of the Judges of the Court of Appeals, and was very popular. He was the leading man in the church of that town. This was about the year 1885. A lawyer of Mt. Sterling, named Cornelison, who was an elder in Reid's church, had a case in the Court of Appeals that was decided against him. Cornelison accused Reid of having, for personal motives, influenced the decision against him. Reid denied the charge to the entire satisfaction of the public. Cornelison went into Reid's law office, and with a heavy cane, beat Reid almost to death, Reid making no resistance, because he was morally opposed to fighting, even in his own self-defense. So great was the sympathy for Reid and the indignation against Cornelison, that from the State press, solidly, there was a demand that Reid should kill Cornelison. I was employed as editor and reporter on a daily paper, and did all I could to convince the public that the way they were treating the case was not the way to encourage Reid, who had done, as he had, as an example to his countrymen. Some papers insinuated that it would be cowardice if Reid did not kill Cornelison. One day Reid went into his office, wrote a neat little card to his wife, bidding her goodbye, and, putting a pistol to his temple, blew his brains out. Cornelison was put in jail, spent three years there, came out a physical wreck, and died soon after[.] A beautiful biography of Judge Reid, written by his wife, has in it a contribution from my pen, which she did me the honor to ask.

Another interesting acquaintance that I made in Versailles was a young man, several years younger than myself, named Clarence Greathouse. His family consisted of his widowed mother, his exceedingly beautiful and every way attractive sister, about 18 years old, and himself. The mother and sisters were members of my church, when I went there, and [Clarence] joined after I went there. He did not want to be baptized in a baptistry, so we went, accompanied by a large crowd of people, some miles out into the country, and I baptized him in a large pond. I frequently visited at his home, and he and I spent much time walking and talking together. He was studying law, and soon after I left Versailles he went to San Francisco, California, to practice his profession. He rose rapidly in his profession. In a few years he did something that so favorably attracted the attention of the Emperor of China that the Emperor offered him a position as lawyer in his court. Young Greathouse went to China and soon so established himself in the Emperor's favor that he became wealthy, and his sister having died, he sent for his mother, and the two have lived in China for twenty-five years, and are so delighted with the people and the country, that when they have come back here on visits, they have said they could not be induced to live in America again. In his success he seems to have forgotten me, and has never communicated with me.

Among the clergy in Versailles, Bishop Kavanaugh, of the Methodist church was one of my friends, and sometimes preached for me in my pulpit. Rev. Venerable, of the Episcopalian church, was also my friend. He was a very attractive character, was a beautiful orator, and was delightful in conversation. The other preachers of the town I did not like. One of my friends was Ex-Lieutenant-Governor Thomas Payne Porter. He sometimes came to hear me preach — his wife was a member of my congregation — but he was said to hold the views of the man for whom he had been named. One of the few times I ever saw Tom Marshall was then, in Versailles. The war had been going on for three years, and Tom, then the greatest orator in America, and his brother Ed. had on cheap hats that they had bought before the war, and said they would never buy another until the Confederacy was free. One day a Federal Colonel, finely dressed, was standing at the head of his regiment in the streets of Versailles. Tom Marshall, in very dilapidated apparel, was standing on the curb-stone looking at the regiment. Somebody told the Federal Colonel that that was Tom Marshall, and the Colonel started toward Marshall, and touching his hat as if to a superior officer, said to Marshall, "I believe I have the honor to address the Honorable Thomas F. Marshall." Tom was, as usual, loaded with the liquid staple of Kentucky, and said to the Colonel, "Yes, you have the honor to address the Honorable Thomas F. Marshall, and I've got more sense than you and all your regiment put together." While I was in Versailles Mr. Marshall died with scarcely the comforts of life around him, and almost alone, except his wife, and it is one of the regrets of my life that, by an accident, I was not with him when he died. I believe he would have given me his dying testimony about religion.

Ed. Marshall was almost as great an orator as Tom Marshall. The hardest laugh I ever had in Versailles was in Dick Reid's office, listening to Ed. Marshall give a ridiculous description of his own farming. Ed. Marshall, a Democrat, was at the Presidential convention in which Ingersoll nominated Blaine. Marshall threw up his hat and acted almost like a wild man, when Ingersoll had finished. Marshall said, "I would rather have made that speech than be President of the United States."

The female college, which was under my pastoral care, was a place of great interest to me, and to it I had unrestricted access. At this college I first saw Miss Josie Williamson. She was a music teacher and was so young that she seemed to me like one of the school girls. She was pretty, and sweet in her manners and full of good spirits. I suppose she was about 19 years old. She was an Episcopalian, and I cannot remember whether she ever came to my church, but I think it probable that she sometimes did. When the war was over she married Captain William Henry, of the Confederate army, and she now ranks as high as any writer and speaker in the infidel cause in America. She has been one of my earliest literary patrons and supporters ever since I began in infidel journalism. Her husband established a splendid school immediately after the war, and made a great success of it in every sense. They have a beautiful home at Versailles, and entertain with royal hospitality. Of all the things that have ever been said about me outside of my own family, I prize most what has been said by Mrs. Henry. I regard her as the person who, of all who have lived in Kentucky, has made the most valuable impress upon that State. During my imprisonment her letters to my wife and to me have been one of the highest sources of encouragement to us. While Mrs. Henry has attained by far the greatest prominence ever attained by any Kentucky woman, I cannot recall that there was in her, so far as I could see, anything more upon which to forecast such distinction than upon quite a number of other bright girls in the school.

One of the most elegant homes at which I was ever entertained was that of Mr. Joseph S. Woolfolk, who was a member of my church in Versailles, though he lived in the country, quite a distance from the town. The family were my most devoted friends. He had a niece, a Miss Harris, who was at his home when I was there. She was a member of my congregation, and was one of the greatest beauties I ever saw. She and I got up early one morning and took a buggy ride before breakfast, down a beautiful turnpike that ran into the magnificent scenery that begins the descent toward the Kentucky river. Miss Harris was exquisitely dressed, and except that I had determined to devote my life to preaching, I would have asked her that morning to become my wife. Mr. Woolfolk moved to Lexington, and was the foreman of the grand-jury that indicted me for blasphemy.

In the church in which I was a preacher each congregation elects its minister, by vote of its members, each year. A month or so before my year was to expire, I had been investigating the question of the truth of the New Testament, just as I had, with Hatch, investigated the Old Testament, and the conviction began to dawn on me that someday I would be compelled to abandon the New Testament, just as I had done the Old. I made up my mind that at the end of the year I would quit preaching, and, of course, I made no effort to be elected again. A young preacher, Rev. John S. Shouse, who became very popular, and commanded a fine salary, wanted the place I had at Versailles, and offered his name for the position. I did not authorize anybody to offer my name as a candidate for the position, but my name was offered, and I got every vote in the congregation, including the aunt and nieces of Mr. Shouse, except that of one of my most intimate supporters and church workers, named Duvall, who voted against me because, he said, I was a Rebel. He was an intense Union man.

My conviction of the inaccuracy of the New Testament grew upon me so that I began to see that I could not honestly fill my position in the church until the end of the year. I felt inclined to preach sermons of morals merely, but I could not conscientiously conduct any of the church sacraments. So one day I went into the pulpit and preached a sermon, and at its close, with no explanation to anybody, closed the Bible, picked up my hat and walked down the pulpit steps and up a side aisle and out the front door of the church. That evening I called the officers of my church together and explained to them that I had quit preaching because I had become skeptical as to the truth of the Bible.

They treated me with great kindness and seemed not to have any doubt of my sincerity, and while they regretted it, seemed to think it was all I could do under the circumstances. I had not a single infidel acquaintance in the whole world, except those I have told you of in the mountains. I had never read any infidel book or infidel newspaper, and the name of Ingersoll had never been heard of. One day as I passed along by a little hotel, I heard one man say to others, "There's a preacher who went crazy about a woman."

The world all seemed very dark to me, and especially as my leaving the pulpit, under the circumstances, was almost breaking the heart of my mother. She seemed to suffer great agony, and I tried to explain to her that there were reasons for my doing as I did, but she had never heard anything but one side of the argument about religion, and I could not comfort her. In abandoning the Christian religion, I felt that it would subject me to numerous disadvantages, but all the time there was a consciousness that I was living up to my honest convictions and a strong belief that the time would come when many intelligent and good people would honor me for my courage, and these sustained me in my new departure. Had I then known that three times in my life I would be a prisoner for my religious opinions I do not know that I would have dared to let my sentiments be known, but the example of John Brown, who had given his life for his fellow-men, in defiance of the plain Bible teaching that slavery was right, had so aroused my admiration for him that I now believe I would then have given my life in attestation of my sincerity. How it would be if I had fallen into cruel hands, as a convict, I do not know, but as it is now, I congratulate myself that I have had the courage so to stand by my convictions that I am now in a penitentiary cell, and I am assured that my being here will make me friends and will honor my family and will do good to the world. It is highly probable that I may not live to the end of my sentence, and the longing for my home is something awful, and yet if it were possible for me to step out of this prison a freeman, merely by recanting or saying I was sorry for what I have done and written, I would remain a prisoner here.

Chapter VI

D uring my stay at Versailles I had, in the capacity of a chaplain and nurse, in Confederate hospitals, my only experience in war. There had been a battle at Cynthiana, Ky., between Confederate General John H. Morgan and Federal General Hopson. The Confederates were defeated, and Confederate Surgeon Kellar, now of Lexington, was left in charge of the wounded. An old church had been converted into a hospital simply by taking the benches out. Nearly everybody about there was in sympathy with the Confederates. One would hardly suppose there could be any romance and fun in a military hospital, especially in one so without the comforts and necessaries of such a place as a Confederate hospital at that time, must necessarily have been, but there was much to entertain both the wounded soldiers and their attendants. It was in a highly cultivated and wealthy community, and nearly every soldier had his sweetheart, who came daily to spend the day with him, from the beautiful women that abounded in that vicinity. Most of the wounded were from among the cream of Kentucky society, and their lady friends were from the same class of society. Each young woman, I soon saw, could be relied upon to do all that was possible to be done for the particular soldier in which she was interested, but further than this she would not go, and all of us soon recognized that that was the best way. Each girl would sit close by her special patient and read to him, or talk to him, or feed him, or give him medicine, and the pretty girl would often bend down so low over the wounded soldier that sometimes their faces would be almost together for a long time, and they would talk low together, almost like they were husband and wife, as some of them subsequently were, and they did it without any embarrassment, all recognizing that it was all right, and some fearfully wounded poor fellows were viewed with actual jealousy, while the girls with combs, brushes, perfumed soap and towels tenderly manipulated the hair, beard, faces and hands of the brave young fellows. Among the wounded there was one fellow who furnished continual amusement for the whole hospital, by antics and queer talk. He had been struck right in the center of the breast by a minie ball that passed straight through him and came out close beside his backbone; a wound that one would suppose would kill him instantly, but he not only lived with that hole through him, but had an exhaustless supply of spirits. He was not like the others were, from the highest rank of society, and he had as his sweetheart, who was devoted to him, a lady of his own class of society who was getting along to the "old maid" stage. She had a quaint-looking yellow sun-bonnet, which her patient insisted on wearing most of the time. In his half dress he would go running about the hospital and perform capers that were in perfect consonance with the Darwinian theory of the consanguinity of man and monkey. From the loss of blood and hospital confinement he was very pale. Every day or two the Federal surgeons would come to our hospital, and would examine the wounded and send off all they thought could stand the trip to Camp Chase, in two miles of where I am now a prisoner. We would keep somebody on the watch-out for the coming of these Federal surgeons, so that the sick and wounded might prepare to look as bad as possible, to keep from being sent to prison, which they all dreaded; and we would give a signal when any of them would be seen coming. The funny fellow, with the hole through him, would throw away his yellow sun-bonnet and run and jump into his bed, and stretch himself out flat on his back, and look so that the Federal surgeons would evidently think that it was only a matter of a few more days before they could send him out to sleep the eternal sleep beside some of his companions in arms. One would hardly have thought his nurse, who owned the yellow sun-bonnet, capable of playing her role so perfectly, but the doleful and despairing air with which she looked into the faces of the Federal surgeons to catch any possible hope that her charge might possibly live a few days longer, would have made any of us laugh, except for the fatal consequences to the funny fellow, whose services to cheer the other wounded were simply invaluable. But when the surgeons were gone and that woman again gave up her recovered sun-bonnet to her patient, with no appearance of any appreciation of the grotesqueness of the whole thing, I could but give away to the heartiest laughs that I had had at anything, not even excepting Brother Lynx's "salt house" key story, since my love affair had brought its gloom over my life. The saddest case in the hospital was that of a boy fifteen years old who had run away from his parents and gone into the army and got shot three times in his first day's experience. He was shot in the chest, through the arm and through the knee. He said he did not care for the first two, but seemed to think the shot through the knee would kill him, as it did, after most excruciating suffering.

I had a singular experience with a handsome young soldier named Longmore, who afterward became clerk of the Court of Appeals of Kentucky. I think he was a Captain, and he was lying with his head at the foot of the cot upon which was Captain Stone, who has since been a very prominent character in Kentucky politics. Stone and Longmore were shot in almost the same way, each having a thigh bone broken by a minie ball, and after the time of which I speak each had his leg amputated at the hip. On the morning of which I speak, the beautiful young woman that he afterward married, and who is now his widow, was sitting by him when I came to her and told her that we would excuse her while I dressed Captain Longmore's wound. When she had gone I turned back the cover and saw a row of mushrooms growing from under the bandage on his leg, from the hip clear down to his heel. The largest was about as big around as a dollar, and they diminished regularly in size down to his heel, the smallest of them — about twenty-five in all — being about the size of a ten-cent piece. The bed was nice, clean and dry, and there were no mushrooms there when I left him late the night before. They grew on the outer side of the wounded leg, and came from between the bandage and the sheet, their roots spreading out under his leg until they were so thin that I could not see where they started. I expressed great surprise, and showed some of the mushrooms to Captain Longmore, who was lying on his back, unable to move, and smoking a cigar. He said nothing when I showed them to him.

After that I went to the Confederate hospital that was established on the battle-field of Green River Bridge, in Kentucky, at which battle my brother-in-law, Major Thomas Y. Brent, had been killed. A ball struck him in the breast and as he was strangling with the blood that was gushing out of his mouth he simply said, "Turn me over," and these were the only words he uttered. The Federals were on the inside of a "horse-shoe bend" of Green river, the banks being very precipitous. Across the narrow place from one to the other point of the "horse-shoe" the Federals had fine breast-works, and back of them were large trees cut so that they lapped into each other, and still back of these was a very strong stockade fort. The Confederates — Morgan's cavalry — had to come for half a mile over a perfectly clear, level and open old field, right up to the front of these breast-works, but they had done this and had driven the Federals from them, and the Federals had fallen back into the felled trees. Major Brent was leading his men through the top of an immense fallen tree when the ball struck him that killed him.

The Federals remained in possession of the field, and their dead were all nicely buried. The private Confederate soldiers that were killed were piled into one great hole, one on the other, and the dirt was piled over them, but Colonel Chenault and Major Brent had been buried by Confederate soldiers, each in a home-made poplar box, in a pretty place off from the others. I exhumed Major Brent's remains and took them to my old home, where they are now buried, my Sister Mary, his widow, still owning the old home. Considerable delay was necessary in order to get a coffin to carry the remains home, and during that time I waited on the wounded at the Confederate hospital, which was an old deserted house in the wilderness. Here the conditions were all different from what they had been at Cynthiana, the chief difference being that there was not a woman there, and scarcely the necessities of life. There was no one to help the wounded and dying, except the Confederate soldiers who had been left in charge, and they were so exhausted that they were very inefficient nurses, and seemed to be so hardened by the cruelties and horrors of war that they had lost all natural sympathy for each other. I worked with them day and night until I was so overcome from the want of sleep that I determined that I would have to harden my heart as the others were doing, and go to sleep, and I laid down for that purpose. But, awfully drowsy as I was, I could not sleep for the groans of the wounded.

(I find here that I cannot recall whether this was while I was at Versailles, or afterward, and situated as I am, I have no way of telling.)

The weather was intensely hot, and it was about midnight of an intensely dark and perfectly still night. There was a splendid young man shot right through the chest, almost exactly like the funny fellow I have told you about at Cynthiana, but the one at Green River Bridge was suffering the pangs that killed him a few days later. Unable to sleep, I went to this man who I heard begging for "just one cold drink of water before I die," and all around him were sound asleep. There was no good water that I knew of anywhere, and I could only find an old dirty bucket and a tin cup to get any. I roused a sleeping soldier who had been detailed as a nurse, and getting him a stool that I thought he would fall off of if he went to sleep, so as to wake him, I made him promise to sit and watch the man with the hole through his breast until I got back. As

I went out of the door with my bucket, I could see in the little light from the house a poor fellow lying on an old bench, and resting his head on an old board split out to cover a house, one end of which was against the house, who had been shot a little in front of and a little below the ear, and the ball had passed clear through his head and come out in the corresponding place on the other side. His jaws were so broken that his chin fell back against his throat, and the sight was ghastly, and his groans, while he was asleep, were piteous; though, while he was awake he never uttered a groan, and had said to me if I would fill his tin pan with water for him, once each day, that would be all the waiting on that he would ask. I walked by the spot where Major Brent had lain dead on the ground, and where another officer had shown me, on his own feet, the cavalry boots that he had pulled off of the feet of the dead Major Brent. I went out into the road, on the side of which, near by, lay in a hole the piled dead bodies of the Confederates. I was almost exhausted physically, and weighed down mentally from the horrors with which I was surrounded. The country was very wild and rugged, and in front of me was a deep and dark ravine, filled with great rocks and trees, fallen and standing, and undergrowth and vines. I knew enough about such topographies to suppose that in the bottom of that ravine there would probably be running a stream of water, but how to get there, and whether I was liable to fall over a precipice and kill myself, or step on a rattle-snake, or copperhead, I did not know. I had heard Hatch give a most realistic description of his walking up on a dead soldier, lying on his back, with his eyes wide open, one night, and he said the sensation was far more horrible than anything he had ever experienced in any battle, and he had described to me how once when the command to which he belonged was retreating from the pursuing Federals, through a wilderness, he had been one of a company that was ordered to conceal themselves and ambush the vanguard of the Federals. The Rebels were hidden behind a little hill, just high enough to conceal them, near the edge of a little stream that was almost as deep as they could ford on horses, and they knew the Yankees were following them, and would cross at that place. The Rebels were ordered to lie flat behind that bank until a certain man was to fire his gun at the Yankees as a signal for the others to rise and fire.

The Rebels could finally hear the Yankees riding into the stream on the opposite side, and could hear their horses drinking, and could hear the men talking about how deep the water was. He could hear his own heart beating with the fearful excitement. Finally the signal rifle was fired and jumping up instantly they found the stream full of Federal cavalry, so near and so thick that it was hardly possible for any shot of the Rebels to fail of some deadly effect. They all fired at once; the stream was full of dead and dying men and horses, and before the Yankees could train their cannon upon the Rebels, the latter were on their horses, and scouring away, while bombs and solid shot could only cut the tops of the trees above them. And yet Hatch had said that going up on a dead man in the dark had frightened him more than that ambush, and more than a long engagement, in which the opposing lines were stretched for miles, and in which the command in which Hatch was[,] had been defeated. I did not feel like I was a coward. As I was coming to that battlefield with my peculiar clerical dress on and on a horse with cavalry trappings on him, a drunken Federal cavalryman had met me, he being greatly enraged by the defeat of his command near there only a few days before, and cocking his gun had looked at me — nobody but us two out in the lonely wilderness — and had said to me: "If I thought you were a damned Rebel I would kill you right here." He seemed to assume that I would lie to him if I were a Rebel, if he should ask me, so that he did not ask me, and I never told him. I felt relieved when the fellow rode on, and felt some little apprehension that he might shoot me in the back as I rode off, for he was a much worse looking man than a fair representative man of either side, and was drunk beside, and I carefully examined my own state of mind and felt that I was not frightened, though I had intended telling him the exact truth if he had asked me.

But in the exhausted state of mind that I was that dark night that I started down into that great gorge after water, the thought came over me that somewhere, there in the dark, I might come upon the body of some poor soldier who had died there and not been found, and though I have, several times in my life, looked death in the face at pretty short range, my search for that water had in it more that was horrible than all the other experiences of my life. I climbed down the mountain side, over fallen trees and rocks, until I thought I could hear water in the distance, and was finally assured that I could hear it ripple in the perfect stillness, and I thought about the possibility of getting that poor dying soldier the drink of water that seemed to be the last gift that he asked of earth, and my whole excitement was turned into the fear that I might not get back with the water. I finally got down to where I stooped and felt the cool water on my hand and took a drink of it out of the cup. I filled my bucket, cupfull at a time, and then found, to my gratification, that I could get back up the hill, or small mountain, faster, and, of course, safer, as I was not then liable to fall over anything, than I had done coming down, and under the feeling that I had conquered my fear, and with the hope of getting to the sufferer while the water was so cool, I clambered up in less than half the time I had taken to come down. When I got to the wounded man I found him nearly dead because the soldier that I had set to watch him had gone to sleep and had fallen right across the wound in the breast of his fellow soldier, and was so sound asleep that he was apparently unconscious of the fact that I dragged him off and away to a corner of the room where he continued to sleep. The poor wounded man, as soon as he could speak, simply said: "Just to think that my own fellow soldier could treat me in that way, in the fix that I am;" and a vision came into my mind of how the two bosom friends, possibly, had left their homes in the Sunny South and gone to "seek the bubble, reputation, at the cannon's mouth," and this was what they found. I gave the wounded man a drink of that cool water, and when I remember the eagerness with which he swallowed it, as if every drop of it was giving him an hour more of life, I think about that "cup of cold water" that is told about in the New Testament, and wonder if any man of kind heart and sound brain, anywhere, can say that the fact that I could not believe the marvelous stories of the Bible would rob me of the blessing promised for such an act, even should the Christian religion prove to be true. In a day or two more that poor wounded, bleeding heart stopped beating and the young soldier was at rest. One splendid young fellow, in dying, made it, among his last requests, that his parents should never be informed of his fate, giving as his reason, that his father was a bitter Union man and had opposed his going into the Confederate army. When he was dead I cut a curl off his forehead and sent it in a letter to them, telling them all the circumstances, and asking them to write me, but I never heard from them. Did I do right? I helped to a dig a grave for him in the corner of an old rail fence, the nicest place we could find, and we buried him.

Chapter VII

My old home stood in the middle of a yard, of about seven acres, that was full of large trees, some indigenous and some imported. In the back of this yard which began the slope down toward Elkhorn creek, was a spring over which was a large two-story spring-house, such as was to be found at some of the most aristocratic old mansions, built before cisterns were in this country. In the top room of that springhouse there was a large pile of shingles, and one of my amusements was to make little ships out of them and sail them on Elkhorn creek. History is the greatest of all the studies, and with it should be taught geography, the handmaiden of history. I knew the stories of the Bible before I knew geography, and I made a geography to suit those stories, and such an impress did my own home-made geography make upon my mind that, in after years, when I came to read the Apocryphal New Testament, I still mixed the Bible stories with the scenes in which I had located them in reading about them in my childhood; and to-day, were I a freeman, I could go to the very spot on Elkhorn creek where Jesus and his school-mates went at "big play-time," to play in the mud, and, while the other boys made mud pies, Jesus made two little white doves out of mud and held them up on his hand and they flew away.

Further up the stream, near my present home, "Quakeracre," on my part of the old farm, there now lies the immense trunk of a sycamore tree. This is the tree that Zacheus climbed, because he wanted to see Jesus, and was so small that he could not see him when he was down on the ground in the crowd. It is also the same tree upon the roots of which there is a sad little family tradition that Major Brent addressed my sister Mary. That one stream, the only one with which I was familiar, in my childish mind, stood for the lake of Gennesaret, or sea of Tiberias and the river Jordan. To this day there is plainly before my mind the very spot, in Elkhorn creek, where Jesus and John, waded out into the deep water for Jesus "to be baptized of John in Jordan," so as to be sure that the baptism was by immersion and not by the sprinkling that all of my preachers taught me was rank heresy. Further up the stream was where Jesus met James and John, and caught so many fishes; and it seems to me, somehow, now here, in the penitentiary that I am, that away back there, somewhere, I had noticed how people told large stories about fishing, and I read in one place about the net breaking and in another place that it didn't break, and then about the men pulling in so many fish that they sank the ship, and I recollected that there was nothing like that when my father would stop the Negro men, on Saturday evening, and all have a frolic seining, while he walked along on the bank, like Jesus did; and I loved to read true stories and history more than I did fairy stories, and sometimes, in spite of all I could do, it seemed to me that the interest of those stories was somewhat destroyed by the faintest suspicion that somehow those stories about fishing were not told just exactly like they had occurred.

I have wondered, a thousand times, if there was anybody in the world who had faith enough to pray that the big sycamore tree would just pull itself up by the roots and hurl itself into Elkhorn creek, as I read about in the New Testament, and I could, if free now, go to the very spot on the edge of Elkhorn to which I walked one morning after reading about Jesus walking on the water, to see if the Lord would give me faith to walk on the water; but I did not try it. I learned to swim when I was quite young. I spent once a good deal of time for several days digging a hole with my hands in the mud. In my imagination this hole was a large and beautiful well, and I could imagine how Jesus sat on the edge of it and talked to the woman of Samaria, as at Jacob's well. Right in the bottom of that "well," which was about two and a half feet deep, my middle finger stuck into something that I would have thought a shell, or an acorn cup, if the conditions had allowed it. I held to it and cleaned the mud off of it and out of it, and found it to be a silver thimble. It had on it the initials A. W. B. I showed it to my mother and she said it was the thimble of her sister, Amanda W. Bowen, of Hannibal, Missouri, and that she had lost it while fishing there twenty years before. The chances were scarcely more than one in a million that that thimble would ever be found, and yet I could write a whole book full of just such unexpected things as that which have occurred in my life, showing that "it is the unexpected that happens."

Aunt Amanda knew Mark Twain when he was a boy, at Hannibal, and used to tell me about him. Long before Mark became famous I had gone swimming at the same places in the Mississippi river at Hannibal that Mark did, and had gone into McDowell's cave as Mark describes in "Tom Sawyer," and I wrote Mark a letter about it, and got one from him identifying the places mentioned in "Tom Sawyer" with those where, by accident, I had had almost his same experiences, showing that Mark's jokes were based on history. Some time, away back in the days when I was sailing shingle ships on Elkhorn that went across to China loaded with missionaries and swapped them off for cargoes of tea and firecrackers, there came into my head all the dreams induced by such passages as these: "They who go down to the sea in ships and do business in great waters, these see the wonders of the Lord, and his works in the mighty deep;"

"A life on the ocean's wave, a home on the rolling deep;"
"Rocked in the cradle of the deep;"
"The boy stood on the burning deck;" and

"On Long Island's sea-girt shore,
Many an hour I've whiled away,
List'ning to the breakers' roar
That washed the beach at Rockaway."

Since then, at the home of my friend, Dr. E. B. Foote, Sr., on the Sound, at Larchmont, I have stood and watched the roll of the ocean, all so beautiful and dream-like, that it was hard for me to separate the reality from my boyhood daydreams on Elkhorn. Distracted by my religious troubles I determined to try to relieve my mind and, at the same time, gain information upon the great subject of religion, by crossing the ocean and walking all the way to Palestine; and in the early part of the first Spring after the war, I sailed, or rather steamed, from New York for Liverpool. To write of a sea voyage or of travel would only be doing what so many others, and especially Mark Twain, have done better than I could do, and would not be in the line of my present purpose, and I will only give you some incidents and salient features that are specially germane to my case. For seasickness I refer you to Horace [Greeley]. For days I saw fire-works that were not "nominated in the bond" when I paid my passage, that rolled in scintillations and corruscations, and constellations and iridescent [gyrations] with an elaborateness and regardlessness of expense, before my eyes, open or shut, such as Paine, the pyrotechnist, and Dante, the poet of the "Inferno," never dreamed of in their philosophies. I saw seven whales, but they did not do as they were billed to do in McGuffey's school readers and on the circus bills. It's true that we did not stop to go and fool with them, for they seemed to be attending strictly to their own business and wanted us to do the same, on the "live and let live" principle; but they didn't look like fishes — if such we may call these legless beasts that suckle their twin babies at the breast, like a woman — that wanted to flirt up boats with their tails and let all the men fall on their heads, on the whales' backs, as Mr. McGuffey had led me to believe. On the other hand, once, when the sea was so calm that the Nautilus, called, familiarly, the "Portuguese sailor," had come up from down where the mermaids live and had spread his sails of coral tracery that discounted the deftness of the artist's chisel in the Taj Mahal, I saw these great "leviathans" lying so lubberly and blubberly out on the water that had I had at my disposal a good skiff and fine oars I would not have hesitated to row out to one of them and take him by the "flipper" and greet him as a jolly old boy, and perhaps go aboard of him for a ride, like you see the Triton son of Poseidon and Amphitrite, on a sugar dolphin on a bride's cake at a wedding.

While a man, already in the penitentiary for being "too fly" in the expression of his theological convictions, ought not to say anything that might stick a year or two more onto his sentence, still, apropos of sugar dolphins, I must be so [candid] as to say, in justice to the whales that I saw, that I think the one that swallowed Jonah — if he did it maliciously, and not in kindness, because he regarded Jonah as a stranger and took him in out of the wet — was a kind of a heathen whale, born in a foreign land — or water rather — and naturally thought a missionary was something to eat, and threw up his contract when he found Jonah a tough citizen.

One day after I had "gotten my sea legs," I was standing at the bow talking to a sailor when he hushed suddenly, put his hand above his eyes and gazed with a picturesque intenseness for several minutes in one direction, then turning to the "man on the bridge," put his two hands around his mouth and shouted, "Land; ho!" I thought I had as good eyes as any man ever born; I could find a squirrel and shoot him with a rifle as only the Kentuckian to the manor — or manner; suit yourself in that mooted question — born, is supposed to do, but after exhausting all my natural endowments in vision, backed by what I had learned at college from Comstock's — no kin to Anthony — Philosophy, I could no more

100

see any land where that sailor said it was than you can now look up into the sky and literally see the new Jerusalem. But after looking for half an hour in the direction that the ship was going under wind and steam, I saw, where the sea and sky came together, a little blue — not green — streak that upon the word of that sailor I agreed was Ireland — Erin Mavourneen, Erin gobrah; the place where the "harp once hung in Tarah's hall."

"'Tis believed that this harp which I now wake for thee,
  Was a Siren of old, who lived under the sea,
And who often, at midnight, through the dark billows roved,
  To meet, on the green shore, a youth whom she loved.

But she loved him in vain, for he left her to weep,
  And, in tears, all the night, her gold ringlets to steep,
'Till heaven looked with pity on true love so warm,
  And changed to the soft harp the sea maiden's form.

And her hair, shedding dew-drops from all its bright rings,
  Fell over her white arms to make the gold strings."

Finally the little sail-boat, with the special pilot, came alongside, and we took him aboard with a rope ladder longer and stronger than that which "Juliet" throws to "Romeo" in the play, and when that pilot stepped aboard and strode the deck so much like a Neptune just out of the sea, that I almost looked for the tines of his trident sticking out from under the tail of his big gum coat, the captain of that ship who had until then seemed to us like a demi-god,

"Monarch of all he surveyed
While his right there was done to dispute,"

Doffed his gold laced cap to the supplanting demi-god and was as docile as Mary's lamb; and while we went up in the mouth of the river, at Liverpool, I, watching that pilot, thought of Tom Hood's lines,

"That Mersey I to others show
That Mersey show to me."

The average tourist elaborates the "docks of Liverpool" — no kin to the burdocks of Kentucky — but the thing that most interested me in

101

all of Liverpool was a life-sized bronze statue of Godiva as she rode "clothed on with chastity," on her horse through Coventry; and as I afterwards walked through Coventry, and saw where "Peeping Tom" had lived, I could not keep from feeling that possibly the day would be when Tom would have a monument to his memory as being the most gallant man who ever lived in the town. A fellow prisoner here with me, lived in Coventry, and he told me with a touching zest the story of Tom and Godiva. Poor fellow; he is further from home than I am! I spent two or three days of the time I was at Liverpool writing a letter of seventy foolscap pages to my mother. I believe I have told you that I was still dressed in the black broad cloth suit that was a combination of a clergyman's dress and a pedestrian tourist's garb; the nicely fitting gaiters, from the knees down, giving a pretty shapely outline to my nether limbs.

One day I walked into a gorgeous building, on the main portal of which was a beautiful sign that simply said "Bazaar." I had no idea what it meant, but when I got into it there swarmed over me flocks, bevies, coteries, squads and platoons of young women, who were selected because they were the most beautiful in England. Liverpool, London and Paris are places of many strange and often unique costumes, but those young women did not seem to have ever before gone up against anything exactly like my get-up. Whether they took me for some strange cleric, or young lord in disguise, or some nondescript incog curio of the genus homo, I don[']t know, but they came to me like steel filings to a big horse-shoe magnet. It seemed to me like I was dreaming and had gone into some

> "Bank whereon the wild thyme blows,
> Where ox-lips and the nodding violet grows,
> Where sleeps the fairy queen,"

And that these were her legions armed with smiles and caresses more potent on man than the bows and arrows of the Amazons. It proved to be a church fair.

Another day I was walking in a handsome place on a street in Liverpool, where there were not a great many people passing, when I met one of the most beautiful and exquisitely formed women I had ever seen, dressed in faultless taste that was a little matronly, she being apparently about thirty years old. When she was in ten feet of me her handsome eyes took me in from head to foot, and she said, most charmingly, "You have a handsome leg, sir." I glanced down at my right

102

leg and said, "Very good, madame, for practical purposes," and I never stopped.

And still I don[']t believe that story about Joseph and Mrs. Potiphar occurred just as we have it on record. It may be because I know some Jews. They are not built that way. One day in Liverpool a pretty woman accidentally jabbed me with her parasol, and blushingly and beautifully apologized. I relieved her embarrassment as gallantly as I could. It was not long before just such another parasol accident occurred. I was surprised at the repetition of the accident, but was equal to the occasion and accepted the apology gracefully. When it occurred the third time, with the same pretty apology, I began to calculate some on the laws of chances, and an element of doubt entered my mind. The fourth, fifth and sixth occurrences of the parasol accident with the same accompanying phenomena, eliminated all element of chance from my calculation, and, after that, whenever I saw an unusually pretty woman coming with a parasol in her hand, I walked clear around her, like you would an open coal hole in the pavement.

As I walked out of Liverpool, one charming May morning, and took the road toward London, I thought about "Turn back, Whittington," and Mother Goose's boy, where

"The rats and the mice kept such a strife,
That he had to go to London, to buy him a wife,"

and all the strange things that I knew in history and story that had occurred on the road to London.

I have to this day two dreams that I am liable to have any time I go to sleep troubled. One is that I am at college and do not know my lesson and can't learn well, and then I remember that I have, once before, been at college and have graduated, and I conclude to go home; and the other is that I am walking into London, and that after I thought I was in the suburbs of the great city, I walked all day without being able to find the city, as actually occurred.

All along the wonderful turnpike from Liverpool to London there are most charming inns, at which I would stop every night. In nearly all of these there would be each night a club meeting of some gentlemen, all in their dress attire, occupying a parlor and smoking pipes and drinking beer, stout and ale. They were exceedingly orderly, and without any effort on my part, I would, two or three times a week, be invited into these clubs with such earnestness that it almost required that I should be rude to decline them. Pipes and tobacco were in abundance for all

103

on a table in the center, the pipes being those with the long and graceful stem that you see "Uncle Toby" poise on his knee as he looks for the mote in the widow's eye in the statuary in Dusseldorf gallery. I smoked there, but never drank anything, except when, occasionally, after having declined all the regular card of drinks, they would find I would drink cider, and get me some. Every time, at these club rooms they would lionize me and make me the center of attraction telling about things in my country. The hospitality and cordiality that were shown me clear across England were remarkable, and especially as I had nothing to introduce me to anybody.

One evening I stopped at a pretty inn, in the country, about six o'clock, and had fixed myself to rest in a chair that I had taken out into the grounds. Off at a distance of fifty yards there was a gay and happy looking party of about twenty young people, about equally representing each sex, all laughing and talking. I had not been there more than fifteen minutes before three beautiful girls and three nice young men escorts got up from where they were sitting on the grass and started so that I could see plainly that they were coming to see me. When they got to me one of the young ladies told me, with exquisite grace and modesty, that their party had chartered a car — "carriage," they called it — and would be glad to have me go, as their guest, with them that night on the railway a distance of about twenty miles to hear a nightingale sing. She did this without any possible clue to my identity. I excused myself, to their evident disappointment, by telling them that I was traveling as a pedestrian and had determined not to ride in any way. I gave them a little introductory sketch of my personality and then asked them to give me the particulars of their going to hear a nightingale sing that they said was loose in the forest, and which, therefore, did not seem to me certain to carry out this part of the program. They explained to me that though nightingales were common in Southern Europe, and more common in Southern England, they were very rare where we were, and that when they came to any part of the country there, the people would take great pains to hear them; that the habit of each nightingale singer was to come to a certain tree each year and that he would sit in that same tree and sing from night to night, while the young people danced to music under the tree.

One day, about the middle of the evening, I came to one of the several palaces of the Duke of Sutherland. The Duke was not there and the palace was closed. The grounds attached to the palace were so extensive that I could see no kind of a wall, fence, hedge or dike in any direction, and they were marvelously beautified with trees, flowers and fruits, the last being in all stages, from bloom to luscious maturity, under glass. Through the grounds were fountains, lakes, statuary, deer and swans. In the grounds, about a hundred yards from the palace, there was an exquisite cottage of six or seven rooms, the only occupant of which was a young man about my age — twenty-five — who lived there in charge of all that vast estate. I gave him an outline of my plans, and he listened with a most rapt interest. He said he lived there alone, and he so felt that he would enjoy my companionship that he would be delighted to give me a home there in his house and supply me with every comfort without any cost to me, and that sometime, in the future, if I still cared to do so, I might make my tour [of] Palestine. He had a nice meal prepared for me, showed me what a lovely room he would give me, told me I could have unlimited access to the Duke's library and private galleries when the Duke was away, which was a great part of the time, and he begged me like a child to stay with him. I told him I was walking and had determined to reach a certain town by a certain time. He said to me if I felt that I was under any vow to do just that, that I might go on, on foot, as I was, and that if, when I got there, I would drop him a note he would come for me on a train and bring me back; but I declined this because I was not going to ride on a train. I cannot see, any plainer than you can, why he should be so infatuated with the idea of having me to live with him, but such seemed to be the case. He gave up his time to showing me the features of interest about the place, and seemed deeply disappointed when I bade him good-bye.

One time I had intended from what someone told me to stop at an inn called the "Prince's Feathers," in a small town the name of which I forget. When I got there, about six o'clock, in the evening, the proprietor told me his house was so full of soldiers that he could not entertain me, and I found that every inn in the town was full of soldiers. I walked on out of the town, and soon learned that there was a nice inn on the road about three miles from the town, and I intended to stop there. When I was within a half mile of the inn I came to the porter's lodge at the entrance of the spacious and elegant grounds of one of the magnificent homes in which the aristocracy live, and I noticed what I had never seen before, that the great gate was standing open and that there was nobody in sight that was in charge. As quick as a flash I determined to try to stay through the night at that elegant establishment as the guest of the people whose names I did not know, and without slackening my pace, I marched like a soldier, right through that gate and turned up the elegant broad roadway that meandered beautifully to the house. I expected every second to be ordered to halt, but did not intend to stop, and no one interrupted me. I walked to the main front door and was met by a handsomely dressed and personally handsome female domestic, instead of a liveried man as I had expected to see. I was sufficiently self-possessed not to suppose the handsome woman was a member of the family, and, on that supposition, said I wanted to see the proprietor. She involuntarily scanned me in an instant from head to foot, including my knapsack and somewhat dusty gaiters, and said: "The master is in the garden; I will call him." I left the door, walked out in front of the house about twenty steps, and stood waiting for him. In five minutes he came sauntering around an end of the house, bare-headed, and in a luxurious looking robe of handsome bright colored material. I told him my name, and that I was an American, and related the circumstances to him just as I have done to you, and told him that I had come to ask to be his guest through the night. He looked at me with a combination of earnestness and quizzicality, but with a reasonable amount of kindness, but as if he was put to it to know just what to say; but he finally said: "But I don't know you," and I said: "And I don't know you either." He then said: "But you might cut my throat;" and I said: "And you might cut my throat; but I am willing to take the chances." He hesitated, and I turned around slowly and walked very slowly back toward the gate. He followed me like a man who was unpleasantly hesitating as to what he should say or do. I said to him: "I know the circumstances are peculiar, but I am assuming that you are a man of sufficient intelligence to understand that I am not a fraud, and I am only asking you to do for me what I would gladly do for you in my country, were the circumstances reversed. But you need give yourself no further trouble; I am going to unstrap this shawl from my knapsack, wrap it around me and sleep under the hedge on the public road, opposite your house, and during the night you may think of this." At the close of these words I politely bade him "good-night" and started, in my regular marching gait for the gate. I had not gone more than twenty steps before he called to me and said: "Wait a minute; let me go and talk to my wife about it." I stopped; turned toward him and waited, while he went back rather hurriedly to the house. He came back in a few minutes, with a pleasant expression on his face, and I went to meet him. He said that he and his wife would be glad to entertain me, and he gave me a most cordial invitation into his house. They had just finished their meal as I came, and they had a nice one set for me, on a beautiful round table in an elegant room. He left me to eat alone, but when I had finished my meal, he invited me into another room and introduced me to his wife and daughter, the wife apparently about thirty-five years old and the

106

daughter about seventeen, both very handsome and very elegant. The twilights there are very much longer than in Kentucky. When we had all talked together some time, the daughter invited me to walk out into the garden with her, and we went together and spent the time in that garden, a hundred yards from the house, walking, sitting and talking until twelve o'clock at night. In American politics the gentleman was such a rabid Federalist that he and I could not discuss the matter pleasantly, and he dismissed it by saying that in the morning at breakfast he would have with us his wife's brother, who was an officer in Her Majesty's army, and that he and I would agree in politics. I met him, at breakfast, magnificently dressed in full uniform, and he and I were thoroughly congenial in politics. When I announced that I was ready to start, the gentleman, whose name I have forgotten, though he gave me his card, asked me to wait a few minutes longer, until he gave me a letter of introduction that would insure my cordial reception at the homes of a list of friends whose addresses it contained, and who lived along my route to London. He made me promise that I would write to him, but I lost his address and have never done so. I was curious to see if his letter would do for me what he had said it would, and presented it only one time, at a very handsome establishment. It gave me a most hospitable reception without a moment's hesitancy. Can it be possible that, some-day, when this appears in a book, a copy of it may stray to somebody who will recall this incident, and somebody will write me whether that pretty girl died years ago, or is now a living grand-mother?

In Oxford I had been walking all the morning looking at that city of colleges. I had been through the Bodleyan Library with its 1,500,000 volumes, and I had stood a good while at the crossed stones in the street that marked the spot where Christians had burned at the stake, for heresy, Rogers, Latimer and Ridley, who were Christian preachers. Suppose somebody then had told me that I would live to be put in prison three times for my religious convictions, in my own country, the Constitution of which says: "Congress shall make no law respecting an establishment of religion, or forbidding the free exercise thereof," could I have imagined how it would come about?

I went into the parlor of a beautiful inn, and, no one else being present, I stretched myself full length on a Russia leather covered sofa and put my broad-brimmed hat over my face to take a nap. A couple of people, who proved to be a gentleman and his wife, apparently respectively about forty and thirty-five years old, came in and took seats at a table and called for bitter ale. Their talk aroused me, but I lay still and could see them from under my hat. They seemed to talk as if they were on some kind of an outing, and Oxford was on their route, and as there were only us there in the room I became interested in their conversation. They were handsomely dressed, everything indicating that they were people of wealth, and they were each handsome and splendid specimens of English health. They talked just as if they thought I was asleep. Finally the man said, evidently alluding to me, "I will wager that that man there is an American, and from the Southern States." They talked on a few minutes longer, and I got up and, bowing to the two, told them that I had heard what he said about me, and that I was curious to know how he could tell that I came from the Southern States of the United States. He said he knew by the broad-brimmed hat I wore. He motioned to me to sit down to the table with them and I did so, and he at once called the waiter and asked what I would drink. I declined all kinds of ordinary drinks, and that seemed to surprise him. He went over the whole list of drinks that he could think of, and finally when he came to "cider," I said, "Yes, if I had some cider I would drink it." He said he did not know whether they had it there, but he would go out and see if it could be gotten. He soon came back with some delicious cider, and, thanking him, I sat with them and drank it. They were an exceedingly interesting couple of people and were evidently taking a most remarkable interest in me. After awhile they began to talk to each other so that I could hear perfectly plainly all that they were saying, but I could not understand its purport, as it alluded to matters between themselves of which I had no knowledge. They talked that way, quite earnestly, for about five minutes, ignoring my presence, and seeming to agree heartily in the matter they were discussing. When they had evidently agreed about the matter they were discussing, the man turned to me and said about as follows: "My wife and I are wealthy people and we have no children, and it is not my fault that we have none," and the lady said: "And I'm sure that it's not my fault;" and just then he went into the office to pay the bill. It would have been embarrassing to me, except that their manner seemed to indicate that they were merely talking candidly and plainly. In a few minutes the man came back and resumed his talk about as follows; "We have everything in the world to make us enjoy life, except that we have no children, and for several years we have been on the lookout for some young man who seemed to be our ideal, and we wanted to adopt him as our son. We have met you here as you see, never having known anything about you before. We are traveling with a horse and trap, just in search of adventures, and are ready to go anywhere, at any time. We have agreed that you are the young man we are looking for, and we are willing to risk our judgments, and we want you to come and live with us at our home, near Newstead Abbey, where Byron, for whom you express such admiration, is buried, and you can go to his grave every day if you want to. I will put at your disposal horses, guns, and hunting and fishing privileges, and I don't want you to do anything in the world except to be happy yourself and try to make us so by talking to us, just as you have done here, and otherwise as your judgment may suggest. You have expressed a desire to see Stonehenge, in the southern part of England, and we want you to have lunch with us here, and all at our own expense, and we want you then, this afternoon, to get in our trap with us, and we will start to Stonehenge, and then we will travel all over England just the same way, and we will not go back to our home until you say so, and I will order you a whole barrel of cider from here, and then order another one as soon as you drink that up."

The lady was evidently just as earnest in the request as the man was, and by her appearance, and an occasional sentence, sanctioned all that he said. Their proposition was so unusual that it was hard for me to divest myself of the suggestion that there must be some sinister scheme back of it all. They seemed to realize that I would naturally suspect that and they evidently courted investigation. I felt grateful and complimented if they were true people, and, of course, indignant if they were frauds; but I could not see why they should have any designs on me. I did not attempt to hide my perplexity, and, getting up, rather abruptly, I went to the proprietor of the eminently respectable house that we were in and gave him an outline of what had just occurred in one of his parlors, and he gave me every assurance that the people were just what they professed to be. So far from being disconcerted by my suspicions, the man and his wife seemed to give me credit for my precaution, and said they would stay right there, in Oxford, until I had had all the time and opportunity that I asked to assure myself about them. Finally, however, after thanking them for a kindness that I had concluded was genuine, I explained to them why it would be impossible for me to accept their offer, and when they shook hands with me, in parting, they both looked like people who had undergone disappointment.

I had a little adventure at Kennilworth Castle. I had inherited my father's admiration for Sir Walter Scott, and his "Kennilworth" was deeply impressed upon my mind. It had been my expectation to get to the village, in the edge of which Kennilworth is, after dark, and not to see the castle until the next day, but when I found I would get there a little before night, I became very anxious to get a glance at it before I went to bed. I hurried to the gate in the wall around the ruins of the castle and asked for admission, but was told that I was too late, and could not get in until next day. I saw through the open gate a gentleman and lady walking along slowly toward the gate to come out, and upon my assuring the porter that I would only go so far as to meet them and come out with them he allowed me to do so. But the few minutes that I had to stay in there only increased my desire to see more of it that night. I ate my supper and began to walk around the outside of the walls and the ditch which is outside the walls. The ditch had been filled until it looked like the ancient "fortification" that I have told you of at my Kentucky home. Grass and even large trees were growing in the bottom of it. I came to a place where a tree, that seemed easy to climb, grew close to the wall, and I climbed the tree up as high as the top of the wall, which was about twenty-five feet, so that I might look over into the grounds. The tree was so small that it bent slightly by my weight toward the wall, I not noticing that it was bending. When I got to the top of the wall I carefully got off onto the top of it, and the tree sprang back to its natural position so that I could not reach it. The stones were loose on top of the wall, and there was great danger of their falling if I moved much, so that I sat astride of the top of the wall and began to consider whether I should stay there for the night, or call for help. Soon I heard what I recognized as being the sound of a hoe, with which someone was digging inside of the enclosure, and, dark, as it was, the man was working in a garden. I thought of what S. S. Prentiss had said about the Tarpeian rock being a cabbage garden. I called, and the man with the hoe answered me, and came to the part of the wall where I was. I told him my story and he went and got a ladder and put it up to me, and I got down on the inside of the castle grounds, and he led me to the gate and let me out.

Next day was spent mostly among the ruins of the castle. There were holes in its walls that had been made by the very primitive cannon of Oliver Cromwell. There were sheep in the grounds, and a number of them started and ran out of a large fire-place, in front of which I supposed that once Queen Elizabeth, called "good Queen Bess," because she was so bad, had sat with Shakespeare and Leicester, and probably sighed in sympathy when the "Bard of Avon" read "Romeo and Juliet" and "Anthony and Cleopatra," or laughed at the stories of Falstaff and Bardolf and the doings of the "Merry Wives of Windsor."

The two things that I now remember plainest about Kennilworth castle are a winding stairway, all in stone, and across which there was so large a crack that it took a special effort to step over it, and on the next step, as you go up, so many people had stepped through the long years, all having to step just in one place, that there was a deep impression of a shoe in the rather soft rock; and the other thing was the largest ivy I have ever seen. It grew to the highest part of the castle wall, and was so large that I could only reach about two-thirds of the distance around the body of it. Kennilworth is so in ruins that there is but little to be seen there.

One day I came to Bardolf castle, pronounced Biddell, in keeping with the English disposition to pronounce all the names of their places wrong. In the town near Bardolf castle I met a nice looking young policeman and asked him how to get to the castle and some other questions about it, and he said I must wait a few minutes until his duties for the day would be over, and that he would put on his citizen's clothes and go with me to the castle. During the quarter of an hour that I talked with him I found that the girl who was the guide to the strangers who visited the castle was his sweetheart, and that he was glad of any opportunity to go there. When he had donned his citizen's dress we walked to the castle, about a mile away, and his best girl came to meet us as guide. She was quite pretty and bright, and I was introduced to her. The fact that her beau was with me gave me advantages over the ordinary tourist. I told her that I had been to a lot of old castles where men and old women had told me about them, and that I was tired of that kind of talk and didn't want to know anything about the history of that one and would rather hear her talk about something unprofessional. She was glad enough to vary her routine duties and we had a good deal of fun there. Old Oliver Cromwell, who was either a grand old patriot and broad-minded, advanced and conscientious thinker, or one of the biggest old religious hypocrites and villains that ever was born, I never could decide which, had never brought his famous old cannon, "Black Betsy," to bear upon the walls of Bardolf castle, and it was in a good state of preservation.

There was in one room, in which Queen Elizabeth had slept, when she used to visit there, an interesting collection of relics, including the quaint bedstead in which "good Queen Bess" had slept. There was, hanging on the wall of this room, the armor of Edward, the Black Prince. I remembered the pictures in history of Edward riding along by the side of the French King, Henry, that he had captured, and that Edward looked like a little boy riding with his large and imposing looking father, and yet, though I was only a little under six feet, there was Edward's reputed armor that seemed to be large enough for me. I pushed a table, three or four hundred years old, up to the wall under Edward's armor, and got the whole outfit down, sword, spurs and all, piece at a time, and proceeded to put them on, the young fellow and the girl laughing, but helping me, as always had to be done for the original owners of those iron uniforms. I knew that they were often so heavy and thick that unhorsed and fallen knights frequently had to be helped up and lifted upon their chargers, and I thought of "Don Quixote," "Rosinante," "Sancho [Panza]," Flodden Field, and Agincourt, Joan of Arc and Rheims all mixed up together; but I was, after all, astonished at the weight of this armor. When I had gotten into it all, finishing my toilet by putting on the helmet and pulling the visor down before my face, and started to walk, my steps sounded like those of the "Galatea" you have seen and heard on the stage, before the marble had fully warmed into life under the chisel of Pygmalion.

There was such a suffocating feeling about it, and the chains and hinges about the thing clanked and screeched so, and there was something so weird and ghostly about my general get-up that I felt almost frightened at my own appearance. I told the girl that I wanted to stay at that castle that night and sleep on the bedstead of Queen Elizabeth. She laughed and said there was no bed-clothing for it, and seemed to think I was joking. I told her that I was in earnest and that I would pay extra for the privilege, and that I would use my knapsack and traveling blanket for bed-clothes. After I persuaded her that I was very much in earnest in my desire to sleep in, or on, Queen Elizabeth's bed that night, she seemed to sympathize with me in my romantic idea, and said if we would wait there she would go and bring her mother and that she would tell me about it. She ran off and in ten minutes came back with her mother. After a little persuasion the mother agreed to let me sleep in that bed. I then began to tell her why I wanted to do so. I told her that I had a fancy for ghosts and that I thought that was a good place to meet them, and that some-day I thought I would write a book and I wanted to tell how I had slept in Queen Elizabeth's bed — calling attention to the fact, of course, that Queen Elizabeth had died some years before I did so, and that consequently there would be no possibility of any royal scandal growing out of my publication.

As soon as I mentioned that I was liable to publish the incident the mother seemed alarmed at the contemplation of the danger she had escaped. She said: "Why, if you were to print that you had slept on that bed it would be as much as our living is worth; we should be discharged from the keeping of the castle." She said, however, that so long as she had promised to let me sleep there, if I would promise never to tell anybody of it, she would still allow me to do so; but I told her I would not give a penny to sleep on it, except for the privilege of writing about it; and she would not let me stay there. I suppose that if she had known that I would not write anything about it until thirty-five years after, when I would be a penitentiary convict in America, she would not have urged that objection.

One day I came to Banbury Cross. Where the cross now stands there was, when Julius Caesar invaded Britain, a Druid altar; their religion, as their name signifies, requiring that they should worship only under oak trees. Human beings had probably been offered in sacrifice upon that altar. When Christianity was introduced into Britain and they quit offering human sacrifices — on stone altars and on so small a scale — they destroyed the Druid altar and put a Christian cross in its place. Two of these crosses had been destroyed by the tooth of time and the cross that I saw there was the third one that had stood there. It was apparently not more than twenty-five years old, and was a beautiful thing in white marble that probably cost $5,000. The base of it formed a seat upon which I sat and ate a noon lunch. As I was eating, a man, of the middle class, apparently, came along by me and I asked him to give me a little history of the cross. He said: "Oh, I can't tell you anything about it. Do you see that man walking across the square, yonder? If there's anybody here that can tell you anything about it, he can." I looked in the direction that he pointed, and saw a man whose dress indicated that he was a clergyman of the established church. I walked fast enough to overtake the clergyman, told him that I was a traveler and that I had been directed to him as a man who would tell me the story of the Banbury Cross. He said: "We do not know any more about it than you do. We only know that that cross is the place where an old woman got on a white horse, and every ten years there is an old woman who goes to that cross and gets on a white horse, and a company of young men and young women, all riding white horses, follow her over the town distributing Banbury buns to the poor." I have always regretted that I did not ask that preacher if the old woman had "rings on her fingers and bells on her toes," and he didn't say.

One of my earliest recollections of my life is seeing my father cross one leg over the other and putting my sister Mary on his foot and holding her by both hands while he rode her and said:

"Ride the horse to Banbury Cross,
To see the old woman get upon her horse,
With rings on her fingers and bells on her toes,
Making sweet music wherever she goes,"

I was astonished in several instances, to find that intelligent English people regarded some of their legends with a kind of religious reverence. On one occasion, at one of my talks to the people at the inns, of which I have told you, I alluded to the story of St. George and the Dragon, just as we, in America, would allude to St. Patrick and the snakes, but I saw, immediately, that the levity with which I regarded the story was not responded to by them.

The Avon river and Stratford-on-Avon were places that I longed to see. I am bound to confess that, since that time, Ignatius Donnelly has, in my judgment, destroyed some of the mystery that formerly attached to the name of Shakespeare, though once, when I heard Ingersoll on Shakespeare, I asked him if he felt no doubt about the accuracy of Donnelly's Baconian theory of Shakespeare, and he laughed and said Donnelly was ridiculous. If the commonly accepted history of Shakespeare be the true one, he and Homer have come nearer the miraculous in writing than any writers, sacred or profane, known to me. The mere mechanical preservation of Homer is more marvelous than the pyramids, and the brain of Shakespeare, the "coney catcher," who wrote rhymes with chalk on the gate of "Lord Lousy," is that to which generations have gone, as to the Coliseum and Cheops, to get ready-cut stones from which, like Sir Christopher Wren and Michael Angelo, they have built what has made them famous.

I came to the Avon near Windsor Castle, and followed down the banks of the stream to Stratford. So many people have described the home of Shakespeare that I found nothing new to say about it. I spent most of my time there on the Avon river. There is much about the Avon that is calculated to develop such a genius as Burns, but, as was said of Washington, it is true of Shakespeare that "no age can claim, no country can appropriate him," and while Avon is an idyl; the dream of a lotus eater, in its beauty, there is nothing about it at all adequate to account for the impressions that were on the mind of its famous bard. The stream, at Stratford, is not more than seventy feet wide, but is very deep and not rapid. Its banks are almost level down to the water and beautiful grass grows right to the water's edge. I am fond of rowing; claim to be an expert as an oarsman, and the most beautiful light row boats that I have ever seen were at Stratford. I hired one of these pretty enough for a mermaid queen to ride in, and rowed, sometimes rapidly and sometimes leisurely, under the trees that hung over and so beautifully shaded the water. I had gotten a package of cakes and was eating some of them. Beautiful droves of swans followed me, and when I stopped would reach over into my boat, evidently wanting some of my cakes. They seemed to be a kind of pirates who, from long experience with visitors there, had learned, like human beggars, that they could extort this kind of a tariff from those who came to ride upon their fairy-like stream, and I divided liberally with them. Sometimes I would run into so large quantities of water lilies as to stop my boat.

I awoke one beautiful morning realizing that that day I was to see London. In walking to London the houses get so gradually thicker and merge from elegant country residences into a city, that I could not tell within twenty miles of where the city began. As I think I have intimated to you — I send my manuscript home every day or two, and cannot always recollect what I have written — it was during that walk into London that something made a singularly vivid impression on my mind that I did not at the time appreciate, and to this day I am liable to dream any night that I am in the suburbs of London and cannot find my way into the city, though I walked many hours and many miles in trying to do so. The British Museum and the Temple, Buckingham Palace, Trafalgar Square, the tunnel under the Thames, the House of Parliament, Westminster Abbey, the Strand, the London Bridge, the Black Friars and the eternally ebbing and flowing sea of human beings in this, the largest city in the world, have been seen, or read about, by so many people, that I only care to give my own experiences, and I will just give them as they come to my memory.

The first place I saw in London that I had ever heard of was Day & Martin's shoe blacking manufactory. It is mentioned in one of Saxe's poems. Blacking was being handled in great hogsheads that would hold a thousand pounds each, and it looked as if enough was made there to supply the world; but when you get fully into London it would seem impossible that any one establishment could supply that city with shoe blacking. It is practically impossible for any decently dressed man to walk the streets of London whose shoes are not polished to perfection. You may have thought that your shoes were well blacked, but if something has injured the polish on one of them a boy runs with his blacking outfit to the first place that you can stop, kneels on the pavement before you and with his brush points to your shoes as you go by. If you do not notice him, he runs to another place ahead of you and again kneels and waits for you. If you never notice him he finally quits to have another boy take up the same thing where he left off. If you have any distance to walk you will soon get tired of seeing this, or of being seen thus besieged and of being suspected of being moneyless or stingy, and you will let the boy black your shoes; and, after one or two experiences, you will learn to stop when the first boy kneels before you.

The next place I saw that I had heard of was Bow street church, within the sound of which a man has to be born in order to be a Cockney, the man who says "'am and heggs," and singularly puts his h's where they ought not to be and fails to put them where they ought to be — who says to that relic of the Greek aspirate, "Get hout of my 'ouse, you 'orrid creature, and go to Hamerica, where they love you so."

Speaking of churches reminds me that I had forgotten to tell you of an incident in theology at Oxford. One of the men who had replied to Colenso's book against the Pentateuch, was connected with the University at Oxford, and was to preach there one Sunday when I was there. I forget his name, but his reputation was that of one of the most learned of English theologians. I congratulated myself that I would have a chance to hear him preach if I could get a seat in what I supposed would be the crowded large church in which he would preach. I went to the place where he was to preach, found it a very costly but small room, and with about half as many people in it as I had had at Wednesday night prayer meetings at Versailles. The famous theologian finally appeared and conducted the regulation service and preached a sermon. The language was, of course, well chosen, but the sermon was no more interesting than the average elder's prayer meeting talk in the churches in Kentucky, and if the people were listening, at all, it was from a sense of duty rather than from actual interest in what he was saying. If I had preached such a sermon I would have regarded it as a failure, even for me. He was a young and boyish-looking fellow. When the sermon was over I went to see the janitor and told him I wanted to see the clergyman, and was told that I could see him by waiting at the door until he came out of the vestry room. When he came out I told him that I had been a preacher and was then an infidel and that I wanted to talk with him about the Bible. He was very affable, gave me the number of his room and directions how to get there, and asked me to meet him that night at 12 o'clock; that, in some way, seemed a more natural hour for an engagement there than it would do here. At the appointed minute I was on hand, and he was about one minute late. He lived in almost palatial style, and told me that the suite of rooms into which he received me were those that had been occupied by Wesley and Whitfield when they were students.

He drew up a handsome table and set on it a nice lunch and wine, and putting two chairs to the table asked me to take one. I declined with thanks, telling him that I had had my supper. While he was eating we had a desultory conversation in which he did not seem extraordinary. When he had finished his repast he signified his readiness to discuss the

116

special matter that I had made the engagement for, and I selected what I regarded as some of the strongest arguments against the Bible, and presented them with all the force that I could. He heard me patiently, and, when I was through, added one or two points to my side of the argument that were new to me, and then proceeded to answer them all. In doing so he frequently read from several large books, on which he showed me his name as author of them. In all the experience I have ever had that was the only man who has ever come near to converting me to Christianity again. I have never been able to recall the arguments that he made, and now think he was a very learned man and an ingenious logician, and that some of his arguments were misleading, and that things that he gave me as facts could not be sustained; but he so defeated me in the discussion that it made me waver the only time I have ever done so in my infidel views. I have never since then found any man, or any book, that seemed to me so strong a defense of the Christian religion as that man was; but I was then merely a beginner in the study of the infidel side of the argument, and suppose now that I could show the fallacy of his replies to my objections to the Bible.

St. Paul's, in London, is simply a great gallery of fine arts and architecture, the part devoted to preaching being quite inconsiderable. I noticed that everybody in it went with their hats off, when I could see no reason why they should do so any more than in any other art gallery. I concluded that I would put my hat on, and when some guard came to me about it pretend that I did not understand and ask him why I had to keep my hat off. I had not had my hat on more than a minute or two before a fellow came to me and asked me to take it off, and when I turned to him for the purpose of asking him about it, I saw that he was such a blank and unappreciative perfunctory that I thought I could get no information out of him, and I bared my head in regular idolators' reverence of the canvas and marble misconceptions of their famous authors.

In the "whispering gallery" in the dome of St. Paul's, I essayed to get a little more information out of that marvel in acoustics than I had paid the guide for, who stations you at one point while he goes off quite a distance and in ordinary voice gives his professional outline of the history of St. Paul's and of the phenomenon which we are at the time experiencing. I saw a young fellow and his summer girl that seemed to be having one of those talks where a third party is too many. While my experience had just taught me that I could hear the professional exhibitor, as I did, it was hard for me to realize that I could hear, at that distance, anybody else in the same way. So under the pretense of

117

accidentally sauntering there, I walked toward the focus where the voices of the two young people would concentrate. I didn't hear them say a word, but whether I had miscalculated the place, or whether they were watching what I was doing and wanted to rebuke me, I never knew, but I walked on feeling like I had been caught eavesdropping, at long range, and it was hard for me to persuade myself that it was solely in the interest of science.

In "Poet's Corner," in Westminster Abbey I thought of Byron's having been denied sepulture there, because he was a heretic, and near by saw a tablet to Major Andre. It depends upon who are judge and jury as to whether a man goes to the Pantheon or the penitentiary. A man who greatly admired two distinguished men longed to see how they looked in the privacy of their studies. He went in upon them unexpectedly and found them balancing peacock feathers on their noses. I had supposed the wigs and gowns in the House of Parliament would be imposing. The first members I saw were eating cherries and spitting the seeds out so like ordinary men, that they, in their wigs and gowns, reminded me of Esop's ass that masqueraded as a lion. If I were asked to say what was the most wonderful thing I saw in London it would be hard for me to decide between the British Museum and the miles and miles of silk "stove-pipe" hats that I saw on the heads of many men riding on the tops of omnibuses.

If a man who wanted a "lodge in some vast wilderness" was really sighing to experience the feeling of desolation he would have to go alone to London. Robinson Crusoe, even before the advent of his man Friday, was "lord of all he surveyed," and felt his individuality, but a stranger alone in the throngs of London feels like we might imagine a single tear dropped in mid-ocean might feel if endowed with reason. There was to me a feeling of littleness as I floated, a drop in that great human tide, that was akin to that we feel when, with some knowledge of astronomy, we gaze into the depths of the star-lit skies.

When the day came upon which I began my march toward the Channel and France, I stopped on London bridge and going out into one of the beautiful seated balconies that jut out over the water like opera boxes — by the way, I forgot to tell you about seeing the Prince of Wales and Gladstone at Covent Garden Theater — stood there, and was looking down at the water, and wondering if I would ever see that bridge again, and if I would not die alone somewhere, and nobody know what ever become of me, and my poor mother and sisters at home wonder all their lives what ever became of me. A nice looking, neatly dressed man came up by me and looked over the balcony as I was doing.

I asked him something about a peculiar boat that we saw, and he said he did not know about it; that though he was born in London he had lived for years in Australia, and was just in London then on a visit. We soon got to talking and he showed great interest in me. I had thought that among all the men who showed such interest in me I would probably come across one sometime who was an impostor, and I determined just for my own information that I would study this man even if I had to incur some risk in doing so. He asked me where I was going, and I told him that I was walking to Palestine, and that my next stop would be in Paris, France. He asked me where I was going to stop there, and I told him that I did not know. He said he was going to Paris before a great while and that he would like to meet me there. He asked me how I managed my money matters, and I told him that I had gold buckled around me in a belt under my outer clothes. He seemed to think me a remarkable character, and when I finally said I must bid him goodbye and march on, he said he was just walking at leisure, and asked me if he might not walk some distance with me through the city. I said yes, and he walked along with me. In about a half mile from the end of the bridge we came to a very elegant building up into which there was a flight of ten or twelve long and handsome steps, a beautiful open door being at their top.

The man said to me, "Let's go up here and see what is in here." I went up with him and we went through the door into a very large and very handsome room in which there was nobody. He threw himself into a large and luxurious cushioned armchair, and I stretched myself full length on an elegant divan. We talked for a quarter of an hour, nobody else appearing. He then pointed toward the wall and said, "Pull that thing." There was a broad, heavy silk band with a beautiful large ring in the end of it that I could see, from the fixtures up near the ceiling, was a bell-cord. I put my hand in the ring and pulled it, without getting up. A man came in who was dressed as elegantly, in full dress suit, as clothes could make him, but a napkin on his left arm signified that he was a waiter. My companion told him to bring in a couple of bottles of champagne. I said to him immediately, that if he was ordering wine for me I would decline it, and that I never drank it. My companion, whom, for convenience, I will call Gray, because he was dressed in a gray suit, seemed quite disappointed and urged me to drink wine with him with an earnestness that seemed to me was perhaps a little greater than of any ordinary interest. When he found that I would not drink with him, he countermanded the order, saying he was glad I would not, because his physician had ordered him to quit wine. He then asked me if I would

119

not smoke, and when I said that I would he ordered pipes and tobacco — I saw nobody smoking cigars — and the waiter brought in a beautiful casket of tobacco and an ornamental rack containing probably as many as two dozen pipes, all as white as snow. Each of us filled one and resumed our positions and were smoking and talking when a short fat man, very elegantly dressed, came up the steps into the room and, bowing to both of us, as to strangers, began to tell us in an excited manner a bit of his very recent experience which in substance was as follows: He had recently had a rich uncle to die and leave him a large fortune in the country, and he had come "to town," as they call London, to see something of the world. Only an hour or so before that he had given an order to a cab driver to wait for him at a certain place, telling him he would be back there in fifteen minutes. The driver had asked him to give him some assurance that he would come back, and he had handed the driver his watch, and when he came back the damned rascal was gone with his watch. I noticed that the man had a fine watch chain that went into his pocket with the appearance of having a watch on the end of it. I thought of suggesting that it had not taken him long to buy another one, and that a little episode like that was nothing for a man of means to be worrying himself about; but I was afraid it might arouse in him a suspicion that I did not believe his story, and thus defeat my desire to see if he was playing a game in which Gray was his partner and the near a thousand dollars in gold belted around my waist was the stake.

Gray joined with me in rigging the little fat man for his verdancy and consequent discomfiture. When we had finally gotten him pacified and had prevailed on him to have a seat, he asked me to pull that bell-cord, just as Gray had asked me to do, and on the appearance of the same waiter ordered champagne for three. I declined, as I had done before, and the little fat man was disappointed, and Gray explained to him that neither of us drank. The fat man took a pipe with us and began to tell that there was going to be a fine target practice that day of Her Majesty's soldiers, down at Sydenham, and that he could beat anybody shooting that would be there, and he made some marvelous statements about his marksmanship which I told him I did not believe. He said he would bet me he could do it, and that if I would bet him he would call a carriage and pay all expenses for all of us, there and back. I told him that I did not bet and that I had been to Sydenham to see the crystal palace there, and did not care to go again. He said he did not want to bet money, but just a basket of champagne or a box of kid gloves or any nominal thing, and that having doubted his statement I was under an obligation to him, as a gentleman, to give him an opportunity to prove what he said.

I finally agreed that I would go with him to a place in the city, of which he said he knew, where he could do rifle shooting. He went out and soon had a fine carriage at the door, and all three of us got in. I had a revolver in my right hip pocket, and I took the seat on the right hand side of the carriage, behind, so that I could easily get my hand on my pistol. We drove for miles through the city, until we began to get in a part of it where the streets were narrow and the houses of the poorest class I had seen in London. We finally stopped before a small house of not prepossessing appearance, and we all got out and went in. We were met in the first room by an old man who asked us to have seats, and when we were seated the little fat man ordered drinks, pipes, and tobacco, just as he had done for all three of us at the elegant establishment we had left. I declined all drinks, but took a pipe, carefully watching the flavor of the tobacco to detect any possible foreign drug that might be in it. When we were through smoking we all walked through a back door into a long skittle alley that was in the rear of the house. The old man, in answer to questions from the little fat man, said he had once had a shooting gallery there but he had changed it into a skittle alley.

The little fat man seemed nonplused. He picked up a large arbor vitae ball and said he would bet that he could hold it at arm's length longer than any of us. Nobody proposed to bet him. He held the ball out and Gray pulled out his watch and timed him, calling the seconds when the little fat man dropped it on the sawdust. The fat man then went with the old man out into the back yard, and while Gray and I were talking in the skittle alley, I picked up the ball that the fat man had dropped and held it out at arm's length as long as I could, and then dropped it on the sawdust. When Gray saw what I was going to do he took out his watch and timed me. When the fat man came in again Gray said to him, "I will bet you that there is a man here that can hold that ball out longer than you can." The fat man said, "I will take the bet." Gray then said, "I timed you and my friend here, and my friend has already held it out longer than you did."

The fat man said it was not right to do it in his absence, but that we were all gentlemen together and that he would be as good as his word, and would pay his bets. He ran his hand down in his pants pocket and pulled out a handful of gold and silver coin and slapped it down on a bench before Gray and a similar handful on the part of the same bench that was near me. I suppose there was an amount equal to a hundred dollars in American money in each pile. Gray hesitated to take his pile and watched me to see if I would take mine. I moved away from the pile

121

that had been put down for me, said that I had not made any bet and did not claim it, and talking carelessly as if I suspected nothing, I sauntered, by degrees, toward the door at which we had come in, and turning to the two men said, "Goodbye, gentlemen," opened the door pretty quickly, went out through the front room, and swung on my knapsack that lay on a table in that room, and was soon in the street making my way, as best I could guess, toward London bridge again, that I noticed we had crossed in the carriage. I never saw or heard anything more of the men. Of course I do not know, but I suspected almost from the first minute that I saw Gray that it was a plan to rob me, and in order to see how they would manage it, I went just as far as I thought I could go with safety. I think they were pals and that their plan was to get me under the influence of liquor and rob me, but I don[']t know.

Much of the country from London to New Haven on the Channel is nothing but solid chalk, with barely enough soil on top for the heather to grow in. It was of great geological interest to me.

The first thing I saw when I landed in France that interested me, after having noticed that even the horses understood French, was a parrot. I walked up to him with some possible misgivings that I was not approaching him in his own language, and remarked with the proper rising inflection, "Polly want a cracker?" but he seemed to regard me as something outre. I ventilated some of my French, much after the style prescribed in "Ollendorf's Method," and asked a man standing by what that parrot could say. He said the parrot could say "J'ai besoin de pomme de terre" — not the exact equivalent of our American "Polly's" selection from the menu, but still, like a parrot, wanting something to eat. I tried to get him to say it for me, but he seemed to detest the foreigner in my accent and was stolidly reticent.

The most striking contrast between the appearance of the country in England and in France is that while the first is all enclosed with walls, hedges and ditches, there are none of these in France, and all along my road toward Paris there was one unbroken expanse of beautiful country with nothing that I could see to indicate the boundaries between estates — no enclosures of any kind, and all the stock kept by shepherds and herdsmen. My marching through a strange country, accoutered as I was, had been a day dream of my boyhood, and I suppose of thousands of other boys, and as I walked then a large part of my journey along the banks of the Seine, it still seemed like a dream to me. While in this there was some pleasant food for thought, and though, now that it is all over and incorporated into my past life, I am glad it all happened just as it did, I can now remember that I realized then, for the first time, the meaning of the words

"'Mid pleasures and palaces though we may roam,
Be it ever so humble there's no place like home."

And I realized all that is meant by the Horatian saying, "Coelum, non animum mutant qui trans mare currunt."

So different are the conditions of our lives that it is hard for one properly to advise another, but if any man has a home, as a general thing it is a good place to live. Rouen was the first place on my route that I can now recall as having been of great interest to me. Of course one of the great attractions there is the cathedral, elaborately carved in alabaster from bottom to top, many of the representations being very grotesque. Among some of the first that attracted my attention was the story of St. Dunstan, the patron saint of all the blacksmiths, and the Devil, the patron saint of pretty much everybody else. St. Dunstan had the Devil by the nose with his red-hot blacksmith tongs — a kind of "fighting the Devil with fire" — and the contortions and gymnastics that the Devil was going through did not seem to me well calculated to inspire the feeling of solemnity in church going people. Such conceptions as that in old statuary and paintings of religious things are not unusual in Europe, and whether they are the serious conceptions of their authors or little underhanded jokes on religion, I could never determine.

Inside of the cathedral one of the curiosities is an immense wax candle some hundreds of years old that is decked with jewels and only lighted on some rare occasions, and costing a nice fortune. This in connection with the St. Dunstan sculpture naturally suggested that line from Saxe, Hood, or somebody,

"Making light of cereous things
Is truly a wicked profession"

There in the floor was the place where the heart of Richard Coeur de Lion was buried, and high up in the groined ceiling was a rope on which were strung a collection of red hats of defunct cardinals, a conception scarcely less grotesque than that of St. Dunstan. When I was tired of wondering and wandering around in the cathedral I started out in search of new adventures and soon found quite an interesting one. I was going along a narrow street in which there was not very much travel, and that was principally of persons on foot. The carriage way of the street was so smooth and nice and the pavements were so narrow

123

that fully half of the people, including myself, were walking in the middle of the street. I saw coming and meeting me, though they were on the foot pavement, a pretty girl, apparently about 18 years old, with an elderly gentleman who proved to be her father. I saw the girl step off the pavement, on which she left her father standing, and start toward me as if she were coming to meet me, and she spoke to me in French, of course, telling me that she and her father were on their way to the cathedral, and that they were strangers there, and she asked me to direct her how to get there. This much I gathered, with some difficulty, was the trend of what she was saying.

My resources for making other people understand in French were even more limited than those I had for understanding them; but allured by the idea of a perfectly legitimate detention of that girl until I could get a good look at her pretty face, I launched out into a ventilation of my French that really was intended to be a more elaborate answer to her question than the circumstances actually demanded. I was soon in a labyrinth of lingual intricacies that would have embarrassed Perseus that time he went to assist Andromeda. If the girl had laughed at me it would have relieved me some, but "these things to hear did Desdemona seriously incline," and she listened with the politeness for which the French are famous. When through a long struggle I had done my best to make myself understood and had finally come to a period, she turned toward her father and, in beautiful English, told him what she had understood, and guessed, that I said.

Smarting under a feeling of mingled indignation and disgust that I had conspired with her to make a fool of myself, I said to her, "If you had spoken to me in that kind of language I would have told you long ago," and I marched off like one who felt that he had been injured. I went down to the monument erected to Joan of Arc, on the spot where the English burnt her at the stake. I didn't feel inclined to take my hat off in St. Paul's, where the regulation demanded that I should do so, but at the foot of the monument to Joan of Arc, where everybody else was passing, just as they would by the monument of John C. Breckinridge, on Cheapside, in Lexington, I took off my hat in reverence. I stood there a long time and tried to realize what had once occurred there, but it seemed like a dream. Even assuming the story of Calvary to be all true, there it was a man who suffered; here it was a woman. England to-day, like "Miss Flora McFlimsey," is

"proud of her pride,
And proud of a thousand things beside,"

But it seems to me that the story of Joan of Arc should forever be a thorn in the flesh of Britain.

My walk toward Paris was right up the banks of the Seine. I had long had an idea that I could walk a hundred miles in a day of twenty-four hours, and intended someday to try it. One morning at 9:30 o'clock I started out from Pont de l'arch, which was seventy-five miles from Paris. When I had been walking an hour I pulled out my watch and noticing a kilometer post saw that I was making fine speed. I felt very fresh and strong, the road was almost perfect, giving me the choice of walking on the hard and smooth macadam or on the beautiful grass plot that was trimmed and kept in perfect order all the way; the temperature was just right and there was a slight breeze at my back. It was only seventy-five miles to Paris, but so sure was I that I could walk a hundred miles that day that I intended to walk right on through Paris until I had completed my hundred miles. I increased my speed almost to a run, and stopped for the first time thirty miles from where I started. I sat down on the roadside and played a tune on my flute, intending to stay there fifteen minutes. Right across the road from me was a church, and a couple were going in to get married. I intended to go in and see the wedding, but it was over so quickly that when I got to the door the bridal party was coming out. I ate only a few cakes for my dinner, as I sat there on the roadside. By the time night came on I was disappointed by seeing that I had gone only fifty miles, but I did not feel tired. I stopped only half an hour, and took some coffee and bread at a restaurant on the side of the road. I started out to walk, and by midnight I was very tired and had made only sixty-five miles. I had given up all thought of walking a hundred miles in a day and was beginning to doubt whether I could walk to Paris that day. When I had walked seventy miles I was suffering great pain from the leaders in my legs and knew that in a few minutes after I stopped I would not be able to walk at all, and determined to walk until I could walk no longer, without stopping any more. At half after six o'clock I was in the edge of Paris, seventy-five miles from where I had started twenty-one and a half hours before. I could barely walk at all, and dropping down on a grass plot I put my knapsack under my head and tried to sleep, but could not. In five minutes I was so stiff that I could hardly get up. I managed to get to a hotel about 9 o'clock in the morning and went to a room and got in bed to go to sleep, but between the fatigue and the excitement of being in Paris, I could not sleep. I got up and sat by a window and looked out on the street. But I could not see to suit me there, so I went down stairs to the front part of the hotel and tried to rest there. I soon wanted to see other things that were a little beyond where I could see from the hotel, so I hobbled along like an old man and spent the whole day walking the streets of Paris when I was barely able to walk.

My most vivid impressions of Paris are those made by the picture galleries in the Louvre. Many of the most beautiful pictures are on the ceilings and in the days I spent looking through these galleries I would look at the ceilings until I suffered with pain in the back of my neck and yet I could not resist the temptation to do so.

The French Revolution had long been to me a most interesting event, and I went and saw among the first places I visited the column that marks the spot where the [Bastille] stood. The impress of the influence of the first Napoleon upon that great city is wonderful, and when I stood in his gorgeous mausoleum and looked down upon the casket that contains his remains it was hard to realize that there was all that was left of that matchless genius that had commanded the French armies from the snowcovered ruins of Moscow to where, at the foot of the pyramids, he said to his men, "The eyes of the world are upon you."

The little story that I am going to tell you now is one to which I suppose some prudes may object. I am going to tell it just as far as it is printable and leave you to imagine the rest, and I am going to do this in the interest of morals and history and general information, and I want it to be remembered when I tell it that I am in this prison under the charge of having said things about the relation of the sexes that were demoralizing. I have told you in this connection, and now repeat it, that never, in all my life, have I done anything that I would now be ashamed to tell my wife or my dear old mother, were she living, or that I would now be ashamed to have my wife tell our only daughter, an unmarried girl eighteen years old, now at school in Washington City, about me. I believe that the Government of the United States, that has me here as a prisoner, for expressing what could scarcely be called an opinion, on the sexual relation, is making a fundamental mistake in leaving the adjudication of this great question to judges, juries and attorneys who have no reputations either as moralists or scientists in this department, instead of selecting men of the highest special qualifications for the work, to inform the people, through the Government publications, that are to go freely to the old and young, of both sexes, about an appetite that is as natural and indispensable for the happiness and well-being — yea, the very existence of our race — as is the appetite for food and the desire for sleep, or bathing, or exercise.

People who read Byron's "Don Juan," or Boccaccio's "Decameron," or "Tom Jones" — Fielding or Laurence Sterne, I forget which — are supposedly forewarned and forearmed, and purposely read that which they antecedently reasonably know was simply intended to appeal to this passion without any moral quality or valuable information in the discussion.

I have, as I previously suggested, more than an ordinary reason to be interested in the literary welfare of James Lane Allen, and have more than once cited the strong resemblance, personally and as a literary man, between Mr. Allen and Washington Irving, who was one of my ideals of a man. And yet, in the matter of the relation between the sexes, I regard Mr. Allen's "Choir Invisible," a perfect gem of English, as being the most demoralizing book ever printed in America. This is because the story is told by a man of the highest moral character personally, while the thought of illicit relation between the sexes is so deftly and charmingly told that the purest young woman in the world would not hesitate to sit down and devour it, line at a time, in the presence of her parents or young friends of either sex. It is a book the rapid editions of which have carried all the evil of the discussion of this question into thousands of the homes of the very nicest and best of people where any book that is commonly suspected of having any taint of impurity in it would never have come. And yet Mr. Allen's book leaves its readers in no sense advanced, morally or intellectually, by it.

The censors of the press of the United States, who are generally self-appointed and have forced themselves upon the attention of the Government, and are possibly sincere in some instances, are rarely, if ever, experts in this matter, and the very best of them simply have a "zeal not according to knowledge," and the result is that the great masses of the people, and especially of intelligent people, are profoundly ignorant of a subject, for information regarding which the United States Government should have a special bureau of information.

There is in America what is properly designated a "mock modesty" that is not so common in Europe. A most elegant lady in London to whom I had carried a letter of introduction from an elegant lady in America, in arranging for my comfort, at the home of her husband and herself, said things to me that actually embarrassed me, and that her friend in America would never have thought of saying to me; and yet they were plainly only what true kindness and hospitality suggested. When Dessie Campbell and I were walking together in Mammoth Cave, we were once just behind our two sisters when Miss Virginia Campbell lost, right in the path before us, a beautiful silk garter. I picked it up and handed it to her, saying, "Honi soit qui mal y pense," and I believe I did just what a true "Knight of the Garter" should have done. She smiled an acknowledgment, turned around and put her foot up on a stone and we all heard it go on with a snap as plain as that of "Miss Betsy Trotwood's" reticule.

At the hotel where I stayed there was a young Frenchman who spoke English scarcely better than I spoke French, and we pooled our lingual resources in communicating with each other, and mixed the two languages. One night he took a young German and me with him to a jardin opera, and each of the three spoke the language of either of the others with about the same fluency. We then put the three languages together and came nearer talking volapuk than anything I have ever heard.

You have seen, already, that I had some striking instances of friendship shown me, but my French friend, at that hotel, went further in one direction, in the line of hospitality, than anybody had yet done. We have heard much about French morals, but I believe what I am now going to tell — partly by words and partly by suggestion — illustrates one feature of their morals better than you commonly find in books. My French friend was a man about twenty-five years old, and seemed to have fine health and buoyant spirits. He was fairly good looking. He lived at that hotel and if he had any business it was only such as he could leave any day to go walking with me, as he frequently did. His room was next door to mine, and besides his door that opened out on the same hall that mine did, there was a door between our two rooms, which latter one I never saw opened but once.

This man had two women, both of whom seemed to be regarded as his wives, both by himself and the proprietor of the hotel. They ate at the table with him and occupied the same room with him, with no appearance of any purpose, of anybody, to conceal the fact. They acted toward him in public just as any lady-like wife acts toward her husband, and they were a happy looking trio. Both he and I alluded to the two ladies as being his wives, but one day when I alluded to him as being a married man he said he had never been married. I asked him if he did not think it was wrong to live with his women, or wives, as he was doing, without having been married to them, and he seemed utterly incapable of understanding how there could be anything wrong in it.

I never asked him anything about his religious opinions except incidentally one day. We were together in Notre Dame cathedral when there was a very grand procession of priests marching around in the cathedral in some very gorgeous religious ceremony. I then asked him what was his opinion about all that, and he said it was merely a super-

stition, but was all well enough as a means of amusement and entertainment for a large class of people. His two wives were apparently each
about twenty-one years old. One was a brunette, with dark eyes and
dark hair, was of fine figure, medium height, and while not a real beauty,
was a very handsome, healthy looking woman. Neither of them knew
any English. The other one was a blonde, and was very beautiful. She
had beautiful blue eyes and a wealth of light colored hair, pink and white
complexion, a beautiful form and exquisite hands and arms, and was
perhaps a little under size. She was dressed in exquisite taste.

One day I was sitting in my room playing the flute. I never played at
all handsomely, but only simple airs and some snatches from popular
operas. I was, by no means, an Orpheus — not even a Pan. As an artist
in that line there was nothing in my playing to excite the admiration of
any one who had opportunity to hear the music of Paris. I had heard
all of those stories about it being unlawful to play the Marselaise in Paris,
always doubted the story, and played it just to assure myself that there
was nothing in the story. While I was playing the flute the door that was
between my room and that of my friend was opened, without any
premonitory knocking, and the pretty blonde woman came in and
fastened the door behind her, and greeted me with a pretty smile and
bow, saying that she had come in to hear me play the flute. I thanked
her for the compliment, and rating my musical attainment at its par
value, offered her one of the several chairs with which my room was
supplied. She declined the chair and went and sat down on my bed. She
leaned her cheek upon her hand and her elbow upon a pillow, and was
as beautiful as a Mussulman's dream of houris in a Mohammedan heav-
en.

I felt that it was a time when my strength lay in my flute, as Sampson's
did in his hair — from hair to air is an easy transition — and I as thoroughly put my soul into that flute as ever "Dick Swiveller" did into his,
with the "Marcioness" for an audience. I played all that part of my
repertoire that was from Burns' songs; "Ye Banks and Braes o' Bonny
Doon," "What's a' the Steer Kimmer?" "Down the Burn, Davy Love,"
"The Ingleside for Me," "Coming thro' the Rye," "Mary of Argyle,"
"John Anderson, My Jo," and then from opera, "I Dreamed that I Dwelt
in Marble Halls," and "When the Swallows Homeward Fly," altogether
occupying an hour. During all this time the pretty blonde sat, or leaned,
on my bed, her Cinderella feet and pretty ankles — and scrupulously
no more — showing from under the bottom of her beautiful white skirts
that were spread out on my bed. I felt all safe so long as I was playing,
but I was afraid to stop playing. I finally did so, however, and thanked

her for the compliment she had done me, and she thanked me for the music, each of us supplementing with smiles, bows and blushes, the inadequacy of our linguistic powers, and she went back to her room.

The next day I met her husband. He said to me in our combination language what would be the equivalent in English to "Didn't my wife go into your room yesterday?" I said "Yes." He said, "What did you do?" I said, "I played the flute for her, and she sat on the bed and listened." From that point on it is not proper to put into a book what he said, but he said a good deal and he said it emphatically. It was to the effect that he and his two wives all liked me, that I was evidently an interesting gentleman stranger in their country, and that between us there had existed a friendship for some time, that they were all inclined to show me every mark of hospitality and kindness, and that for some stupid conception of morals that I had that were utterly inconsistent with my other evidences of good sense, I had impolitely declined one of the highest courtesies in a manner that lowered me in the estimation of all three of them; that some views about morals that I entertained might do for a new country like America, but were not up to the standard of Europe.

Of course he did not say it all in exactly that language, for he could not speak that much English, but that is partly what he said in French, partly in English, partly in gestures with his arms and hands, partly in the proverbial French shrug of the shoulders and partly in facial grimaces, and all translated into current conventional English by me. I was then about twenty-five years old, unmarried, and never expecting to be married, in perfect health, in a strange country, an infidel, had all the money I wanted, and every guarantee of impunity that any man could have, and with nothing but a rational conscience to control my action. Now I am a man over sixty-one years old, with a devoted wife and devoted children of both sexes, and I am in the penitentiary charged with having written that which tended to induce lewdness between men and women.

I went to the can-can in Paris, and a pretty girl came up to me and taking me by the hand fixed herself and waited for me to put my arm around her waist and dance with her, but I told her I could not dance, which was true, and in all that I saw there, saw nothing that was such an appeal to the passion of a man as I have seen in Christian women, who were leaders in church and society, in a ballroom in Lexington, to which I had gone as a newspaper reporter.

One day my French friend and I were out at Bois de Boulogne, in the suburbs of Paris. We had been walking up the banks of the Seine for a mile or two. He said we were far enough away from any house to undress and go in swimming and he had begged me to do so, but I had declined. I do not now know why, for I was fond of swimming. While we were talking, I saw up the river, two hundred yards ahead of us, and out in the river a considerable distance from the shore, a man's head come up out of the water, and though I heard him make a scream, it was so unlike any American signal of distress that I had ever heard that I did not recognize it as such, but I saw the head so quickly disappear under the water again that I thought the man could not be diving just for amusement, and as it flashed over my mind that the man was drowning I determined to run and swim for him. I know enough of the phenomena of mental philosophy to know that after an exciting incident of that kind we are frequently left under the impression that there was some strange premonition about it, and that there was a sort of a super-natural train of events that led up to the incident. These are recognized facts in works on the phenomena of the mind, and yet it seems to me that I can now recollect distinctly that while that man was under the water the following reflections passed through my mind: I have always believed that I was destined to save some drowning man. I narrowly escaped drowning in the middle of the Mississippi river. I have always regretted that I did not have a chance to save Doniphan from drowning. I believe he suicided, partly in sorrow for what he had said to me. Some strange power from behind, that I cannot understand, has brought me across the ocean to save that man drowning yonder, who I never saw or heard of before. I am home sick and if I save him I will think my mission here has been fulfilled and I will go home. If I drown in trying to save him, I will die like a hero, and I am only a poor heartbroken man, anyway, and I will take the chances; but if I stop to think of the danger my courage will fail me. All of this passed through my mind in a second and while I was running as fast as I could the two hundred yards to the point nearest the drowning man. While I was running he came up and screamed again. I had not time to pull off any part of my clothing, and had a considerable weight of gold belted around me under my clothes. The whole bank of the river was held by a wall ten feet high. I did not have time to climb down it, and ran right over it, at full speed, and fell on a narrow margin of the soft ground below.

Out in the river where I had last seen the man there was not even a movement of the water to show where the man had gone down, and I had to calculate distances and take ranges of objects to tell where to swim for the man, and all of this had to be done quick enough to save the life of a man who was under water, if I was to save him[.] There was, near by where I fell on the ground, an awkward, clumsy flat-bottomed boat, with no oars in it. It was about fifteen feet long, and six feet wide, and its gunwales stood nearly three feet above the water. It was fastened by a chain that was twenty feet long, which was wrapped around a post a dozen times. The post was eight inches in diameter and stood four feet above the ground. I knew I would not have time to unwind the chain. It would take me five seconds to do it and I could not afford to use more than two seconds on that boat. The ground seemed soft and I determined to try to pull up the post. I stooped and caught my arms around it about half way down; found that I could shake it, and, pulling as if to save my own life, I pulled that post up from two feet in the ground, threw it and the chain into the boat, gave the boat a shove with my foot, and jumped into it at the same time. It went toward where I last saw the man, but was going too slowly to get to him in time, and the boat would evidently not go half way to him.

I ran to the end of the boat nearest the man and jumped into the river and swam toward the man. People who swim nude or in bathing suits have but little idea of what swimming in a full suit of clothes means. Of course I was tired even before I struck the water. I swam to where I thought the man ought to be. I thought of the saying, "A drowning man will catch at a straw," and I thought that man would catch me by the feet under the water. My French friend had not yet gotten to the river, and it seemed to me that I would drown there and that my friends at home would never know what became of me, but I did not take time to look at the world, for what seemed to me would be the last time, before going, in one more minute — for I was so exhausted that under the water I would be dead in a half minute — into an eternal sleep.

One beautiful clear day I had been lying on my back on the slightly sloping lead roof of Notre Dame cathedral, looking in vain to see, if I could, in any direction, beyond the limits of the great city into the country. I had seen, at a great distance, a continuous stream of people going into a low, but handsomely built house. I was so curious to know the nature of that house and what it could be that took that incessant stream of people into it, that I carefully counted all squares in one direction and then in another, on the streets that led to that house, and went down and followed the streets, counting the squares, and, sure enough, came up to the low building and stream of people that I had seen. I followed the crowd in and found it to be the Morgue. There were, lying under glass, with jets of cold water falling over them, the naked dead bodies of men and women who had been found dead in the city, and had been carried there for identification, their clothes hung up near them and a written account of the circumstances under which they had been found. There were bruises, gashes and wounds on some of the bodies, some seeming to indicate that they had been murdered, and some that they had been hurt accidentally. Some had been taken out of the river; some appearing to have been drowned accidentally and some by suicide. Some of those taken out of the river had lain in the water so long that they were greatly swollen. I recollect distinctly, to this day, that I am here a prisoner, the appearance of one of these men taken out of the river that I thought I would look like, if I drowned and my body was ever recovered.

All of this passed through my brain in a second, while I was swimming with my head as high as possible above the water, in order to see the man if he should come up again. I knew it was useless for me to dive for him, both because I did not know where he was, and because I did not have the breath to allow me to do so. I had all the time been calculating the time that that man could stay under the water and still be alive. When I thought his last second must be gone, I saw just the hair on the top of the man's head almost right in my face. The man was evidently upright in the water, just as Doniphan had been. There was not a single movement in the man that I could see, and I thought he was either dead or so near it that nothing but the most expert resuscitation could save him, even if I could get him ashore. I caught him right in the top of the head, by his pretty long hair, with my left hand, and was gratified to see that I could easily raise his head above the water, and, of course, I did so. I started to swim with him, holding him off at arm's length, because I thought he would catch me and drown both of us; but seeing that he did not struggle, I drew him up to my body and held his head above the water under my left arm and swam only with my right arm. It was easier to swim with him and hold his head above the water than I thought it would be, but even then I saw that every stroke that I made was not only a life and death struggle, but a struggle for two lives or two deaths. But the thought that I could leave that man and swim only for my own life never occurred to me, and I thought I might as well die from a struggle that would break a blood vessel as to drown, and I saw that drowning was certain unless I used every ounce of power that was still in my muscles. I had come near drowning when we were hunting for Doniphan. I remembered how, under the water, I had seen the light through my closed eye-lids and had seen and heard the bubbles that went up, and I wondered how long it would be, if I went down, before I lost consciousness. But though I was only deistic then — not agnostic and then atheistic as I afterward became — there never came into my mind the thought that after that one minute that my head would be under the water there would ever again be any consciousness in my brain. During all this, and at the same time unseen to me, that boat had gotten back to shore, and my French friend had gotten in it and had given it a shove out into the river, but having no oars could do no more, and was silently watching my struggle with the man. I swam to that boat and by a last great effort managed to get my hand up over the edge of the boat. I cannot recollect whether my French friend was still in it, but if he was he did not help me at all. I swung on to that boat in that way for a quarter of a minute to gain the breath that I knew I must have to raise myself and the man into the boat. I finally began to draw up myself and the man, who proved to be as large as I was, with my one arm. I got over the gunwale and into the boat, and as near gone as I was, I had the strength and presence of mind to pull the man in after me feet foremost; and with his head down, as I pulled him over the edge of the boat the water poured out of his mouth as if out of a jug.

When I had gotten him into the boat he dropped limp on the bottom like a dead man, and I thought he was dead, and sat for a few seconds on a seat of the boat to get my breath. I felt greatly disappointed, but determined still to work with the man. I picked him up and set him on a seat of the boat and sat by him. His head fell over on my shoulder and I sat there for five minutes, I suppose, thinking the man was dead. Finally, the man, without moving, said, in a low voice, "Merci, merci, mille fois merci," and I knew that I had saved my man. Sometime during all this, in some way that I cannot now recall, even if I knew then, the young man who had started out with me had gotten into that boat. I do not remember that he said a word at any time during my life and death struggle. There seemed to be no way that he could help me except to swim to my assistance, and that probably would not have helped me, even if he had been willing, and able, to do it. His first words to me were strange. He said, "I asked you to undress and go in swimming with me and you would not do it, and now you have gone in swimming with your clothes on." I saw from the despondent look of the man that I had saved and from the fact that he had laid his hat, vest and cravat on the shore, as if to tell what had become of him, that his purpose had been to suicide, and that, unable to swim, he had jumped into the water and struggled out into the river.

We sat there until we had gotten our breath, and then I got his hat, vest and cravat for him, and he put them on and he took my arm, and I walked with him to his home, a mile or more away. When we got to his home, which was also his place of business, I saw a sign above his door which said, "Marchand de Gaunterie;" and when I had gone inside with him I found that he only had kid gloves for sale. We walked through the store and into the residence part of the house, and his wife came to meet us. She was a good looking and healthy looking woman about forty years old. She showed no excitement, and not a word passed between her and her husband, and he went and sat with his head down in a corner of the room, behind the door that came in from the store. They seemed to have quarreled. She, seeing me wet, and evidently taking in the situation, brought me some wine, which I declined, and bidding them both goodbye I left them, and at this place I will begin

Chapter VIII

I had left my home feeling very sad, and was still sad and home-sick. I had, whenever I found an opportunity, tried to get any information on the subject of religion that I could, but none of it had been satisfactory. In England religion was so much a part of the government that nobody seemed to regard it as a thing to be investigated upon its own merits, and to say anything against it seemed to be regarded by the people as talking treasonably against the government. In France I saw nobody that seemed to regard religion otherwise than as, in America, we regard the story of Santa Claus, at Christmas — a thing that by intellectual people was not supposed to be true, but which had so long obtained in the country, and so long afforded a certain entertainment to some people that nobody felt inclined to dispel the illusion.

I was not entirely free from the influence of my religious rearing. I wanted to abandon my purpose of going to Palestine, and while I felt the reproach that attaches to him who puts his hand to the plow and looks back, I tried to persuade myself that in some way some kind of a Providence that presides over the destinies of men had sent me all the way there to save the life of that man, and that, now that I had done this, my mission in that direction had been accomplished, and that I ought to go home. I pondered over the matter for several days and finally decided I would go on in my journey. I got my passport for Italy, and, one morning, started out of Paris. I have explained to you that I did not then, and do not now, believe in premonitions, and I believe what are commonly called premonitions are partly the result of a common disposition to falsify in order to tell something strange and partly owing to a phenomenon of the mind that makes us think, after a startling fact has happened, that we had had a premonition of it, so that I will now tell what occurred as it now seems to me it did occur, with a probability that it was not really what happened.

I started out of Paris and was trying to entertain myself with the prospect of crossing the Alps on foot as the soldiers of Hannibal and Napoleon had done, and of seeing Rome, Naples, Pompeii, Vesuvius and all the wonders with which Italy is filled. I felt well and strong in body at least — and I tried to inspire myself with extra energy in thinking, in walking and in enjoyment and appreciation of this beautiful dream of my boyhood, inspired by such stories as "Sanford and Merton," that I remembered as traveling with knapsacks on their backs. But my efforts to enthuse myself were entirely unavailing, and I found that, in spite of all that I could do, my thoughts were all turning back to my home, and my steps got to be faltering, slow and heavy. Finally I stopped and sat on a stone seat on the side of the pavement in the suburb of Paris, from which went the road I was to take for Italy. I sat there for half an hour, and in order that nothing might distract my thoughts I leaned forward and put my elbows on my knees, and my face in my hands, and closed my eyes. I felt that right there was a turning point in my life, and after balancing the pros and cons, as best I could, I arose and turned my face homeward.

About that time my sister Alice, a lovely girl, aged sixteen, had died at my home. I could receive no letters from home, traveling as I was, and had heard nothing of my sister's death. She had been a great comfort to our mother, and it would now seem to me, if I were un-scientific and superstitious, that some kind of Providence, or what they now call telepathy, had impressed me that my mother, more than ordinarily, needed my presence. My story, even though I am merely touching the salient and peculiar points of my life is probably getting too long for the patience of those who may read it, and as there was nothing eventful in my journey home, which I made by rail, and in the ordinary ways of travel, I will say nothing about it. I got to Lexington, within eight miles of my home, before I heard of my sister's death. As I came down the walk to my home, my mother met me with that wonderful expression of love that a mother feels for her child. It was a blending of sadness and gladness. Though I had been reared on a large farm I knew but little about farming, but I had intended to go, at once, to work on the farm, both for the purpose of doing some good and to bury my sorrows, and the next day after getting home, I got my oldest clothes and went to work, with the Negroes, in a large corn-field. It was hard to me, because I had not been accustomed to it, but I soon became interested in it, and found in it the first mental relief that I had had for years, and I would say now to all persons, of either sex, old or young, rich or poor, that my experience is that physical labor, called a curse in the Bible story of Eden, is the greatest blessing known to humanity, and that there is hardly, if at all, any such thing as happiness without it. I found, working along side by side with the Negroes, and in talking with them as we worked, comfort of body and quiet of mind, such as I had vainly sought in the company of learned men and women.

One day a very large and tall locust tree blew down in the back yard of our home, and an old Negro man and a young one and I were all chopping it up with axes. I felt more pride in being able to strike accurately and powerfully, so as to drive that axe into that locust wood, than I had ever done from preaching a sermon, and if there was not something like a smile of pride on my face I could feel something like one in my heart. My mother came and stood and looked at us, and talked to us, and, for the first time, in a long time, I could see just the faintest suspicion of a happy smile on her face. It seemed to me that she had, for the first time, begun to realize that the fact of my being an infidel did not necessarily make me a bad man. Negroes are, in some instincts, quicker than white people. I could see from the expression on the face of the old Negro that he understood the situation and was happy in sympathy with my mother and me. In all of my experiences through life, clear up to this hour that I am in prison, the Negroes have always been my friends, and among the prisoners here they are my friends.

Our axes kept time to our talk as we chopped on that tree. The old Negro while chopping or stopping to remove some cut off limb of the tree, began telling, in the usual Negro lingo, a story to my mother which I will give, in ordinary English, and which was about as follows:

"Once there were some smart men who wanted to try an experiment by taking a little baby boy and raising him up in a nice place where he would have all kinds of comforts and good things, but they were not going to tell him anything about God, or about religion, or about the world, and they were not going to tell him anything about women. They just wanted to see what he could find out by his own thinking. So they found a beautiful valley in the mountains that was so surrounded by mountains that there was only one place where he could get out and there was always a guard there to keep him from going out. He had a beautiful house in the valley, and horses, dogs, boats and plenty of servants, but they were all men, who would be discharged if they talked to the young man, except just what had to be done to wait on him. With all of these nice things around him that child grew up to be a young man without ever having smiled and never seemed to be happy.

"People on the outside of that valley knew about the young man in there, and there were some pretty girls who heard of him and they were so anxious to see him, because they felt so sorry for him that they were determined they would see him. They had money and they bribed the guard to let them in, and bribed the servant men inside, so that nobody but them would ever know of it, and one night the girls got into the valley and hid themselves in some large flowers so that they might see the young man the next morning when he came walking in the garden. Sure enough, the young man came walking along toward where the girls were, and in their anxiety to see him well, they attracted his attention. He looked at them and was alarmed, but when he saw that they would not hurt him he stood and looked at them and seemed to enjoy doing so.

"Just then the manager of the whole place, who had been kept in ignorance of what had happened, came running, very much alarmed for fear he would be put out of his position, and caught the young man and led him away and had some of his servants to put the girls out of the valley immediately. The young man asked the manager what those things were he had seen in the flowers, and the manager being afraid to tell him they were young women, said to the man 'They are little devils.' And now, old Mistress, that's what's the matter with Marse Charlie; he just wants one of them little devils."

I saw long before the old Negro got through that he had gotten, from somewhere, a modernized version of the story of "Rasselas, Prince of Abyssinia." My mother and I both smiled, but I cannot remember what either of us said, if we said anything, but the words of that old Negro, "I want one er them little devils," went through my brain many times, but I staved it off from me and finally got rid of it by thinking of nothing but my work on the farm.

I had a brother-in-law and sister, Dr. and Mrs. Grissim, who lived in Georgetown, Ky., and they had a family of most interesting children, some of whom were just old enough to go into society. As a family the success in life of those children has been phenomenal. I went one evening, sometime in the pleasant season of the year, I cannot now remember, to Georgetown to see the family of Dr. Grissim and to spend the night there. My niece, Lida Grissim, now Mrs. S. F. Leib, of San Jose, California, was then and is now remarkably attractive personally and otherwise. She and the other members of the family told me that she and a lady friend and their two escorts were going that night to a dancing party at Mr. June Ward's, about three miles out in the country. They said they were going in a large carriage and wanted me to go with them. They said they knew I would not dance — I never could — but that there were many beautiful and elegant things there with which I could entertain myself, and that the chances were I would find numerous people there who would be glad to see me, including Mr. and Mrs. Ward; that the party was informal and that they had a right to bring any guests of theirs, and my niece and all of them most earnestly besought me to go. I had no idea in the world of going and peremptorily declined, though I had on my clerical costume that I had never discarded, and which I would have worn under any circumstances. The house of Junius Ward, who was a very wealthy and cultivated Southern planter, who spent his summers there, was the handsomest country residence that had been built in Kentucky. Mr. Ward said he paid $50,000 for the building and then went on and just quit counting. The family had traveled much and the house was filled with the most costly of furniture, books, elegant pictures, curios, and articles of [virtue] from all countries. I had heard of the beauties of the place for some years, but had never seen it. I had met the son, George, and found him a very elegant and kind gentleman. I knew the family knew about me, and knew that I would be heartily welcomed, and while I dreaded the idea of going into company, I was exceedingly anxious to see not merely the fine house, but the quaint and curious things, books and pictures that I expected to find in it, and when they came to start, while I still refused to get inside of the carriage, as they begged me to do, I compromised by getting up with the driver.

We turned off of one of the most beautiful of Kentucky's famous turnpikes into the large grounds of the Ward home. We were late and they were dancing in an immense hall when we got there. Our party was most cordially greeted by many persons, guests, host and hostess, and I was surprised and pleased to see how many people knew me and knew of me, even in instances when I neither knew, or knew of, them and on being presented to Mr. and Mrs. Ward I found them delightful people and a beautiful combination of the hospitalities of Kentucky and New Orleans. When we had talked a half hour or so, I told them plainly that I was not a society man, and felt that I was de trop, at an occasion of that kind; that I had only come through the persuasion of my friends, and that my purpose was to see their library, pictures and curios, and that I did not want them to take from their other guests any of their time to entertain me. They accepted my explanation gracefully and bade me make myself at home.

The young man who was at that time the devoted beau of my niece, and came with her in the carriage, was a fine young fellow named Jesse Webb. He and his brother Will, had gone into the Confederate army, and Will had been killed and Jesse had fought through to the end of the war. He sang beautifully and was very witty, and of infinite humor. He was a great friend to me and while I always called him Jesse, he called me "Mr. Charlie," apparently as a part of his Episcopal respect for the fact that I had been a clergyman.

I spent some time in looking at the library and then began the inspection of the pictures that were on the walls of two immense parlors that, by sliding doors, were thrown into one. When I started around the walls of one of these parlors I did not see anybody in them, but after awhile I noticed that in the other parlor, behind the part of the wall into which one of the large doors slid, there were only two persons, a lady and a gentleman, whose voices I could hear without hearing the words. Their tone was that of dignified conversation — neither serious nor frivolous, and it seemed to contrast with that of the merry talking and laughing out in the hall, among the dancers. I noticed that the voice of the young woman was exceedingly sweet, and mingled with the pictures on the canvasses, there came into my mind a kind of a picture of that woman, and I felt some curiosity to see her. I went over a good many of the pictures rather hurriedly so that I could get to the parlor in which the two were, and see the girl or woman.

In looking at the pictures my back was necessarily toward the couple, and I could only by [furtive] glances get to see the woman, at the distance of across the large parlor. These glances made me think that she was exceedingly beautiful and sweet in appearance and graceful and intelligent, and dressed in beautiful taste in half mourning — a silk of checked black and white, and she seemed to be about twenty-one years old. She was talking to a young man who was not at all handsome, but who seemed to be more than ordinarily intelligent and fluent in conversation, and it struck me as a strange thing that that couple had gone off from the rest of that gay company and were sitting there engaged in earnest and thoughtful, though apparently pleasant and entertaining conversation, when there seemed, so far as I could judge, not to be anything about love in it. When I turned another angle in the wall I could see the two better, though I did not dare to look straight at them, and while it was almost still in the parlors, I could hear a little better what they were talking about, and I became more convinced that my first impressions of the two were correct.

During all this time Jesse and others had come into the parlors occasionally and came to inquire if I was having a nice time. About this time Jesse came in and came rapidly up to me as if he had to get back for some engagement in the dance, his face beaming as if he felt a kind of inspiration in what he was going to say, and he said, "Oh, Mr. Charlie, there is a young lady here that I feel certain you ought to know. I know you would be delighted with her, and I know she would be with you. She is in second mourning for her brother and will not dance, and you and she would be delightful company for each other, and I just want you to let me, please, introduce you to her." I knew immediately that he must be alluding to the young lady at whom I had been glancing as she talked to that young man, and with the least show of resistance, some of which I felt that I had to keep up to maintain my consistency, I agreed to be presented to her. Jesse took me up and introduced me to her as Miss Lucy Peak, and he did what I think was, under the circumstances, a very elegant and appropriate thing. He said to us both that we were both his friends, and gave a little outline sketch of who she was and who I was, and said he hoped our acquaintance would culminate in a lasting friendship, as he believed it would do, and having said this with a graceful combination of seriousness and humor, and with a parting injunction to her to make me have a nice time, he bowed himself out and left us three together.

The gentleman who had been talking with her talked with both of us for a quarter of an hour, and then gallantly and gracefully gave way to me, bowed and retired to the dancing hall, leaving "Miss Lucy," as I soon asked permission to call her, and me the sole occupants of the two large parlors. Like the Queen of Sheba, I soon saw that all of my first conceptions of the young woman were more than realized in her actual presence. While her face, regarded simply as an artist would do it, was not so beautiful as that of some other women I had seen, it was exceedingly beautiful, and taken in connection with an expression in it that indicated high qualities of head and heart, it was the most beautiful face that I had ever seen or have ever seen to this day. It is strange sometimes to analyze what it is that makes a pretty woman's face beautiful. I was not prepared to say the very first minute that I saw Miss Lucy that I was in love with her, but there were dimples in the corners of her mouth either one of which I would have paid her a thousand dollars to let me kiss; and I said to myself that I was going to make it one of the aims of

143

my life to get that woman to let me kiss her on one of those dimples. She was sitting on a rosewood and silk divan that A. T. Stewart, the great merchant of New York — whose body was stolen by a friend of mine, who is now a prisoner in this penitentiary — had bought for Mr. Ward in Paris. It was just large enough for two. I sat down on it beside Miss Lucy, first in the ordinary way, and then I turned around toward her, and putting one knee up on the divan, I put my other leg over my ankle so that I could sit facing her, and she sitting with her back in the curved end of the divan faced me, and in that position we talked.

I took up the introduction to her where Jesse had left it off, and made her tell me about herself. She lived in the country, she said, about two miles from there. Her mother had died when she was young, and her father, an elderly gentleman, was a widower. She had lost her youngest brother, who was a young man to whom she was devoted, a year or so before, and she lived with her father, and she had other brothers and sisters, some of whom lived near by and some in another state. She was twenty years old, and had spent some years of her life in a boarding school and had graduated a year before. I felt that Jesse's introduction of us had bridged over the formalism ordinarily supposed to be incumbent on first acquaintance, and in apparent absence of mind, while I was talking or listening, I did not hesitate to toy with some articles of her toilet, fan, gloves, handkerchief or other things that came over my way, and I asked her to let me see her pretty watch that her dead brother had given her and she did so. She was formal sufficiently to be perfectly dignified and yet was not prudish, and she was gracefully reserved and yet not cold, and when I was perhaps just a little freer and easier in my style than the code prescribed, she did not rebuke me; and I saw plainly, from the beginning, that she was a woman with whom any attempt at undue familiarity would be fatal to any man who made it, whatever may have been his claims. We sat there and talked a good while, her face growing more beautiful to me with every new feature in it that I examined. In books she was entertaining and sensible, without being sophomoric or pedantic. There was an evident and charming absence of any purpose on her part to make what is known as the "first impression" on me, and she seemed all the time to hold something in reserve that would delight me to know of her. I felt my heart going toward her all the time. I soon got so that I felt that she could see this, and I did not care if she did — rather hoped she would. I finally suggested that we should rest some by walking; and if she was graceful in sitting, she was surpassingly so in walking. She took my arm, not in that half-hearted way that makes a man afraid that any little unexpected movement will loose the woman's hand and arm from his arm, and not with that swing onto a man's arm that some women have, that is generally pleasant to the man and a little compromising to the woman; but in that, as in all other matters, Miss Lucy had a most charming conservatism, and I felt ennobled by her companionship as I never had done before in my life. The whole world seemed to have changed again, and I was exceedingly happy.

We walked together some time and we were finally invited to go together for supper. We both enjoyed the supper, which was a splendid one, and into our table talk put a little more humor, perhaps, than we had into our former conversation. I never believed in helping a lady, on an occasion of that kind, and waiting until she had eaten, but I got us a nice assortment of good things on one plate, and we ate off the same plate. I knew it was not good policy, nor good manner, to monopolize her company, and I gave her up to her other friends, ladies and gentlemen, for awhile, and came back to her in good time to see her off home in her carriage, as she had promised me I might do.

I think it was some time in the early Fall, or late Summer, and the night was a little cool, and when she came down stairs with her wraps on, it seemed to me she was more charming than ever. Most of the time before we had been almost alone, and now we were in the midst of the merry, happy, laughing, talking company, and, while all the time very modest, she was perfectly self-possessed, and ladies and gentlemen seemed to vie with each other in complimenting her — a thing that does not often occur.

I got my hand and arm up under her wraps and took hold of her arm and led her out to her carriage. As she got in I took her hand, and in telling her goodbye held it to the very last second that I thought I could do and be within the limits of the code, and I had a kind of a feeling, when I let go her hand, that she had allowed me to hold it possibly as much as three seconds longer than was absolutely necessary in a convention-al handshaking. I felt a tremendous temptation to ask her to let me get into the carriage with her, and let me go home with her, and to tell her that I would walk back to Georgetown that night, but I was afraid and did not ask her; and when the carriage rolled off I felt like the inspiration of my whole life had gone; but, for hours, I lived in that memory as in a beautiful dream. I could hear the rustle of that silk dress, and the tick of her pretty watch and the tone of her voice, and the least bit of an occasional laugh, and I could recall just the daintiest of exquisite perfumery, and feel her hand in mine, in memory just as I had done in reality.

145

When my party was starting home and they all asked me if I had had a nice time, though it was dark and they inside, and I still outside of the carriage, I could tell from their voices that they were smiling sardonically when they asked me; and I acknowledged to having had a nice time.

You may think it strange, but after thinking it over, next day, I determined that I was going to forget all about that and I went home and went to work on the farm, and thought about nothing else for a month or more — not even about that girl, so far as I can now recall. After the expiration of about that time I went again to see my sister and her family in Georgetown, and to go, for the first time in my life, to one of the local fairs, which were, at that time, very popular. It was about two miles from Georgetown and out in the beautiful woods of Bettie Herndon's — then Mrs. Barnes — uncle. There was a temporary amphitheatre, and I went with Jesse and Lida and two others, out in a large carriage. The day, some time in the early part of October, I think, was just as beautiful as you can imagine one, and the grass and trees were all beautifully green. When we got there, there were probably five thousand people there, including many of the most beautiful of Kentucky's famously beautiful women, and the seats were so packed that many gentlemen, who had no ladies with them, were left standing. My party and I, a half dozen, and of each sex, could only get seats by climbing, by very slow stages, through the people back up to the highest seats; but when we got up there we said we had nicer seats than anybody, because we could see well, front and rear.

I was sitting there with my party, looking down at the people who still thronged below looking up for seats, when I saw what I shall never forget while my memory lasts. There was an elderly, nicely dressed gentleman, who had with him a lady who seemed to be his daughter, and the supposed daughter's face was the loveliest face and the most beautiful thing that I have ever seen. The old gentleman had an expression of perplexity on his face because he could not find a seat for his daughter, seeming to be willing to stand himself if he could only get a seat for her; and I would have given him my seat if I thought he could have gotten as far up as we were.

I was so enraptured with the appearance of the young woman, as she looked up, embarrassed and blushing, because so many people were looking at the two, that I caught Jesse by the arm and, while I pointed to the young woman, said, "Oh, Jesse, Jesse, tell me, if you know, who that young girl is, yonder!" He looked where I pointed and, without answering me, stood up and began beckoning to her and waving his handkerchief to attract her attention. The others of my party all joined

146

him in beckoning to her, and she caught their signals and recognized them with a sweet bow and smile. Then Jesse turned to some of the party and said, "Mr. Charlie asked me who that is; he is the only man in the world like him."

Then he turned to me and said, "Don't you really know who that is?" and I said, "No, I have not the least idea," and Jesse said, "Well, that is Miss Lucy Peak, the girl you had such a nice time with at Mr. Ward's," and I said, "I didn't know her because she was in party dress then, and has her bonnet and street dress on now;" but before I was half through those words I was standing and waving my handkerchief too, and beckoning, and calling, through the hum of thousands of voices for her to come up, and showing her that we could not get down. Her father glanced at our party, several of whom he recognized and I could see from the expression of his face that he was gratified to have her find such company, and when she was fairly on her way up to us he walked on. The young woman started up, several hundred people, having been attracted by the incident, and as she would manage to climb up, only one step at a time, through the densely packed people, she was so embarrassed, and she blushed so, to have attracted so much attention, and yet, with all, was so graceful and dignified, that everybody helped her by moving and crowding together, and watched in sympathy for at least ten minutes that it took for her to climb up to us. When she finally got where I could nearly reach her I stretched out my arm and hand as far as I could, and she gave me her hand, and I held to it until she got up to us, and though we thought we were crowded just as thick as we could be before, the others and I arranged for her to sit right by me, and we sat just as close together as we could sit, and I didn't feel the least bit uncomfortable from being crowded.

There was a back to our seat to keep people from falling over behind, and when I kept my arm down in its ordinary position it did really crowd her uncomfortably, but when I put my arm along the back of that seat behind her she just seemed to fit up under my arm exactly, and there was not a half inch to spare, and I was glad of it. She tried to relieve her embarrassment, while a good many people were looking at us, by talking to Jesse and Lida and my sister, Jennie, and the others, but I knew what all that meant, and I was in a position where I could get along nicely even if she didn't talk to me any. Then Jesse had to tell her that I had not known her, and she said she had no right to expect that I would know her, and I said, I thought she had a very good right to expect it, and that I would have known her but for the change in her toilet, and when we thus got to talking, and she necessarily pressed up against the

147

breast of my clerical coat, there was put into my head and brain a memory that I now have, here behind these bars, more beautiful than any conception of heaven that I have ever been able to frame, and just her voice alone was more beautiful to me than music of whole legions of angels and harps. I would rather spend eternity just as I was then, than as any angel that ever struck a harp, any seraph that ever sang hosannah, any throned and sceptered monarch that ever lived. Her tasteful "gown", they call it these days, would, by degrees, get over my knees, and when it persisted in doing so, after she had several times removed it, she finally let it stay there. Jesse and the balance of the party were so evidently inclined not to give us any more room, that we got so close together that it seemed to me she could almost feel and hear my heart beat, for it was beating pretty vigorously.

I determined then that I was going to ask that woman to become my wife and, after we had talked there for an hour or two and looked at the fine horses, she proving herself a better judge than I was, by the way the blue and red ribbons were tied on them, by the judges in the ring, I proposed to her to take a walk, and we climbed down through that crowd and went out of the amphitheater and walked on the pretty grass, and finally sat down facing each other, in a pretty place. I did not hesitate to feast my eyes by looking at her face, as we talked, and that longing to kiss her in the dimpled corner of her mouth, that I had felt at Mr. Ward's, now came back stronger than ever. She took me to dinner with her, at the elegant spread of her pretty and sweet little widowed sister, and when we came to part in the evening, I asked her if I might come to see her at her home, and she said, "Yes," and we made an appointment, only two or three days ahead, when I was to come.

She was just as lovely at her home as she had been when I had before met her, but, while just as cordial and sweet as she could be, evidently belonged to the touch-me-not variety of flowers. We had another divan just large enough for us two, but I would not have proposed to take her by the hand, except in meeting and at parting, for a thousand dollars. I first went to see her every week, but the weeks got to seem so long that I went twice a week sometimes; and when it got so cool that we had to have a fire in the parlor, we would draw up that divan in front of it, and it would seem to me that before we could get half through talking, and eating the nice things that she always brought in for both of us, it would be midnight, and sometimes after that; and sometimes, when it was quite cold, or dark, she would invite me to spend the night at her home, and her father would come in and insist that I should do so; but I do not remember that I ever did.

What did we talk about? Well, I will give you a sample, taken at random. One night we were talking about the phenomenon known as the "death watch." It is a strange ticking like a watch, the nature of which I do not believe, to this day, anybody understands. A popular superstition makes it something supernatural that presages death. The scientists — entomologists especially — say it is a noise made by a small insect, called anobium tesselatum. I do not believe the explanation of the scientists is any nearer right than the other.

One night, talking to Miss Lucy, I said about as follows: My Brother Barton died when he was nineteen years old and I about twelve. I was much devoted to him, and he to me. He died in the summer, and I went off into a remote room upstairs that we called Major Nicholson's room, and lay on a bed alone and cried until I became quiet and was lying there perfectly still. I heard a watch, as I thought, ticking on a window sill near me, though I did not see it. I was a little surprised to know that a watch was there, but, absorbed in thought about my dead brother, I lay there, still, for an hour or more. When I got up I glanced at the window sill expecting to see the watch, but though I could still hear the ticking I saw no watch. I was so surprised that I would have brought some of the family to hear it except that they then were all so distressed. I heard that same ticking there many times for a year, or years, afterward, and though it seems strange, it is a fact that I never took any body to hear it. Years after I was telling my sister, Mrs. Grissim, about it, and she told me of a strange experience they had had in the same line. They had had a pretty mantle clock covered with glass through which the pendulum could be seen. For years the clock had been out of repair and would not run, but when one of her daughters died, something in that clock began to tick, the pendulum being still, and it kept up that ticking so long and so inexplicably that they associated it with her [daughter's] death and finally had the clock taken and laid away in the garret. When I got to that point I stopped talking for a minute, and though we both had on watches we could plainly hear a watch ticking in the wall half way across the room from us. We both listened a few seconds, then got up and walked to where we both heard it, and there, in the plastered wall, we heard a watch ticking just as plainly as if one was hanging there, when there was certainly none there, and it was precisely the same kind of ticking that I had heard when my brother died. I do not remember that we ever heard it again. I have heard the same thing in several other places in my life. Of course, we thought it was a strange coincidence. Though I had never told Miss Lucy that I loved her, I thought she could see that I did, and one night at home I wrote and mailed to her a long letter in which I told her the whole story of my love, and told her that I was coming to see her, in a few days more to ask her to marry me, and that I wanted her to do her best thinking, in the meantime, and if possible, answer me the next time I saw her.

I went to see her at the time, and found her in the parlor ready to meet me. I came in and she came toward the door to meet me, extending her hand to shake hands. I took it and held it and said, "Miss Lucy, before I sit down I want you to give me an answer to the question that I have told you is weighing on my heart," and she looked at me sweetly and earnestly in the face and said, "Yes." I wanted to ask her to ratify it with a kiss but I was afraid to do so, and so I held her hand and thanked her with all my soul, and then led her by the hand to the divan and we sat down. I told her that that was happiness enough for one night and that she must think about it, and we would talk about when we would be married the next time I came to see her.

The next time I came we discussed that and she had concluded that our wedding day should be in next June, and I said it was a pretty month but it was too far off; that she was just twenty-one years old and I twenty-seven and that there was no reason that we should not be married sooner than that, and I said I thought a wedding day ought to be selected for some special reason, and I said the 14th of February, St[.] Valentine's day, was the day the birds mated, and that I wanted her for my valentine on that day, and we finally agreed on St. Valentine's day, and the next time I came to see her I brought her a diamond ring, and it had inside of it "C. C. M. to L. G. P., Feb. 14, 1867."

One night soon after that when I was saying good bye to her, to go home, I said "Miss Lucy, it will soon be Christmas, and I want you to give me a Christmas gift," and she said "Certainly I will," and I said "But I mean one particular Christmas gift," and she said "Well it depends upon what it is." Then I said, "It is what I want more than anything else and I think you might promise to give it to me." She said she would not promise anything without knowing what it was, and I argued that she ought to have enough faith in me to know that I would not ask her to give me anything it was not right she should give me, and I begged her, very earnestly, just to say, as expressing her faith in me, that she would give me anything I asked of her as a Christmas gift.

She would not make the promise but said she would like to know what I wanted. I told her I wanted her to give me a kiss for a Christmas gift and she said she would do so. Then I said "Miss Lucy, just five days before Christmas, the 20th of December, I will be twenty-seven years old; wouldn't you, just as soon give me my kiss for a birthday gift as for a Christmas gift?" and she said "Yes;" and that was only three or four days before my birthday. I then thought a great deal as to whether I would kiss her on that dimple in the corner of her mouth, or whether I should kiss her the old-fashioned way, but I finally concluded that the dimple idea was an innovation that, because it would be unexpected, might lead to an embarrassing complication, and when I went to see her, on the night of my birth-day she was waiting for me in the parlor, and when she came to meet me, as I came in the parlor door, she gave me both of her hands and looked up at me, and I loosened my left hand from her right and, putting my left arm around her, drew her close up to my heart and kissed her right in the middle of her pretty mouth — just the one single kiss that had been promised me, but that one was a good one, and I got all that was in it; presuming, of course, that the hug was only a part of the kiss as the sauce is a part of the cake.

During this time we attended some weddings and parties together and I saw her in regular evening dress, and at a church fair where we were, a beautiful smoking cap of velvet and gold lace that Miss Lucy had made was put up at auction and I bought it for nine dollars. My sister, Mrs. Brent, and I had bought a nice home in Georgetown and the room that was prepared for Miss Lucy and me was exceedingly beautiful. It was arranged that we should be married at night in the church and then have a reception at the home of myself and sister. St[.] Valentine's day came, and it was warm for the season. I went to the house of Miss Lucy, five miles in the country; I was dressed just as I had done as a clergyman, except that my clerical vest was of white silk and, of course, I wore white kid gloves and my gentleman attendants, among whom was Jesse, with Lida as his companion, were all in white vests and regulation dress suits.

When I met Miss Lucy in her bridal dress I was so overcome by the beautiful apparition that I would no more have dared to do any thing more than bow and gently take her hand for a moment than I would have dared to be familiar at a presentation at the Court of St. James. There was a charming profusion of bridal veil and orange blossoms and exquisite drapery with Miss Lucy all wrapped in it like a fairy, and I got in with her and we rode away to town, our gloved hands clasped in each other. The church was crowded full of people and as she and I walked down the aisle, she leaning on my arm, escorted by our attendants, there was in my heart an [ecstasy], such as no mere home coming conquering hero can know.

I didn't know or else forgot what the regulation was, though as a minister, I had performed the marriage service for others, so I thought if I made a mistake I would make a good one, and when we were

151

pronounced man and wife, her maids of honor raised her long veil that fell to the floor and I kissed her, only the second time that I had ever done so. It seemed strange to hear people call her Mrs. Moore, but I called her Miss Lucy and have done so to this day.

At our home we had a large and happy company, and when we had all had a nice long talk and more laugh, and Jesse, dear fellow, now dead, and dead as a bachelor, claimed that he had done it all, and was evidently happy in our happiness, we all went out to a splendid supper, and Jesse fixed a nice plate for me and Miss Lucy, and we ate off the same plate like we did at Mr. Ward's. There were quantities of beautiful bridal presents, and Miss Lucy and I looked at those. About midnight the guests began to come to bid us good-bye, and they grew fewer and fewer, and finally Miss Lucy disappeared, and I was walking the parlor floor alone, and somebody came and told me that I could go to our room. It was nicely done and was not at all embarrassing as I had feared it would be. I went up to our room in which there was no light but that of a beautiful, cheerful fire in the grate that gave a subdued but delightfully soft glow to the room. The beautiful bed had an occupant in it, and her hair was beautifully scattered around over the pillow. I walked up to the bed, put my knee on it, leaned over, and putting my hand under Miss Lucy's chin, I turned her face up and kissed her on that dimple in the corner of her mouth, and still believing in a God, though I was an infidel, I kneeled at the bedside and silently mingled my thanks and my prayers to the one unknown God. I loved a cigar very much, though I was a moderate smoker. I knew it was not good form to smoke in the presence of a lady and not good sanitation to smoke in a sleeping room, and I told Miss Lucy so and asked her if I might smoke a cigar, and she said "Yes." I lighted my cigar, threw off my coat, and in the delightfully warm room I lay down on the top of the cover, on the bed by her side, and we talked about all the things we had to make us happy. I smoked that cigar partly because I wanted to smoke and partly as a means of relieving her of the embarrassment of the ordeal through which I knew she must be going, and we talked, and I even made her laugh, and I smoked until my fine cigar was all gone, and —.

We staid at home for three days that were all occupied receiving calls from friends, and then we started on a tour through the Northern cities, stopping at Niagara just long enough to see it in its frozen glory. At Washington we went to hear Forest, McCullough and Edwin Booth in "Othello." When the jealous Moor smothered "Desdemona" with the pillow I was thinking of my darling that night I smoked the cigar, and the tears came gushing to my eyes, but Miss Lucy laughed and said it was better than the usual farce, because it was not so intended. In New York we saw "The Black Crook" at Niblo's Garden, till then, and probably until "America" at the Chicago World's Fair — the most gorgeous scenic effect that had been seen on the American stage. We came back to our home, in Georgetown, and I believe I have told you, somehow in advance, about my being engaged in a bank there, and how while there I suggested the building of the Queen & Crescent Railway, now one of the most beautiful in the world, and I believe I told you about my fire company, and how by a catfish getting fastened in the nozzle of a fire-hose, the whole of the old part of the town was burned, and subsequently most beautifully built, much of it out of the money of a fire company for which I was agent, in connection with my banking business, and my claim that, to this day, Georgetown owes me a monument with a bronze heroic statue of me on it, with a fireman's helmet on my head, a fireman's trumpet in one hand and an insurance policy in the other, and on the pedestal under my fireman's boot, "Omnia ex igne."

When we had been married a year and a half, our first child, a beautiful little girl, was born, and some time after that we went to live on my farm in the country, and in connection with banking and railroad building, I am going to tell you of an incident of my life to the truth of some of which Col. R. H. Fitzhugh, of the staff of Confederate General Lee — the Colonel now residing in Lexington — can certify, as he was engaged as an engineer for the same railway syndicate that engaged me as a secretary. I will call the leading character in this story Major Brown, because that was neither his name nor his military title. He spent most of his time in New York City, and a considerable part of it in Washington, and then he came and spent a considerable part of his time in Lexington, his most intimate friends there being Mr. Joseph S. Woolfolk, then and now a prominent citizen of Lexington, and Regent John B. Bowman, of Kentucky University, who then lived at "Ashland," the home of Henry Clay. Major Brown and I met, and he seemed to take quite a fancy to me. I thought he did this partly because he liked me personally, and partly because he believed I had almost unlimited influence with one of the most beautiful and brilliant young women I ever knew, whom the Major wanted to marry. Brown was homely, personally, but otherwise he was one of the most intellectual and engaging men I ever saw. He had seen much of the world, and of the finest of society, especially at Washington. He appeared to be an accomplished gentleman and a splendid talker. He was a devout Episcopalian; would "ask the blessing" at the table, and every night in his room would kneel at his bedside and

153

say his prayers; but there was nothing about him that appeared sanctimonious and I knew of some exceedingly good things that he did.

He came to see me a number of times. He was apparently engaged in organizing rich New York syndicates for railroad building, and had an immense fund of railway information. One pleasant day at my house on the farm after I was out of the banking business, he asked me to walk out and sit under the trees to have a business talk with him. He told me that he was an organizer of railroad syndicates, and that he wanted me for his secretary, and said he would pay me $300 a month and all my traveling expenses, and yet that I would have time to attend to my farming affairs. I accepted the situation, and soon after he gave me $10,000 and told me to buy him a pretty home with it somewhere in the country, near Lexington, but not to be in any hurry about it, but simply avail myself of any opportunity that offered. He would take no receipt for the money, and I deposited it to my credit in the banking house of Grinstead & Bradley, in Lexington. Another day he made me a present of $25,000, in the beautifully engraved stock certificates of a road that was soon afterward built. It seemed very strange to me that he would do this, but he seemed to be a very rich man with no relations, really with no home, and while he was well received every where he went, he always said that the life of a man of the world was not congenial to him, and he seemed to regard my own family and those of my sisters as the only people in the world with whom he really felt happy.

We went to New York City together and stayed at the finest hotels, he paying all expenses. He seemed to want me to talk with him, and advise with him about his plans, and he seemed to want me as a man in whom he could confide anything. On Wall Street, in New York, he and I would go into almost any bank we came to, and we would be taken back into the private offices of their managers, and he talked to them just as familiarly as he did to me. Gen. John C. Fremont and Gen. N. P. Banks were associated with him. Gen. Fremont had an engagement by telegraph to take breakfast with us one morning at Delmonico's, but he failed to come, and I never met him. Gen. Banks and I were riding together one day in a very handsome carriage on Broadway, when we passed the handsome office of the Howe Sewing Machine Company. I noticed it and started to tell Gen. Banks about Howe, as I had gotten the information from an interesting sketch of his life that I had read, he being the inventor of the sewing machine. Gen. Banks said, "You can't tell me anything about Howe; I worked at the same bench with him," and he told me about Howe.

At the finest hotels the Major knew the waiters by name, and they knew him and were glad to show him every courtesy. The Major said he would pay me my salary at the end of each month, and he was ready to do so to the day, but I had so much of his money in my hands that I told him to wait until we went back to Kentucky. But all the time, though I could see nothing wrong in the man, and though he seemed to be devoted to me, I could but feel that, back of all this, there was some scheme that I did not see, because it seemed to me that I was getting too much for the value of what I was doing, and I watched the Major closely. I never discovered that he had any designs against me, but when I had been with him two months I found that he was using me in a deep laid plot of villainy against another. It was a scheme so ingenious that it was hard for me to realize that I had detected him, but when I had done so I told him plainly about it, returned to him every cent of money that I had ever gotten from him, including my traveling expenses, and even refused to have a single cent of my salary, and I exposed him, and he soon disappeared from about Lexington, and I have never since heard of him.

About the close of the war my old family home was burned, and a smaller house was built upon a part of the old foundation. I had, on my part of the old farm, a very old stone house that from my admiration of Dickens and from its appositeness I called "Bleak House," and I even had the "Growlery" upstairs. It was on a hill and had no trees near it, but the thick stone walls made it warm in winter and cool in summer. Its desolate appearance was proverbial. When I had lost my position in the Deposit Bank, in Georgetown, because I was an infidel, and before I had gotten a position in the bank in Lexington — during which latter I conducted the farm also — I went with my wife and baby to live at "Bleak House," and conduct the farm. The baby was just old enough to begin to walk a few steps, and her name was Eliza Campbell, the Campbell being for the family of our distinguished kinsman, the Duke of Argyle.

My wife soon demonstrated what good taste can do, in beautifying even under disadvantages. We had pretty furniture and books and other pretty things that had been in our house in Georgetown, and while "Bleak House" externally was but little changed, my wife made it so sweet a home internally that it was a surprise to all, and our beautiful dining table and its pretty accompaniments held an abundance of good things, prepared most scientifically with reference to pleasure and health by cooks descended from our old home cook, and trained in the advanced ideas of the culinary art by my wife. We were building a new kitchen to our old house, and though it was about completed we had not put in the windows and doors, because the weather was so warm. There were shavings lying around the building. We had been told by the Negro servants for some time past that there was an insane Negro woman in the neighborhood, and it was thought that she would come in our open kitchen at night to get something to eat. So far from trying to detect her we were rather glad she did so, and saw no harm that she was doing. One night my wife aroused me, and asked "What is that roaring?" I knew the house was on fire, and though I had been an insurance agent myself, I had no insurance on it. It appeared that the insane Negro woman had accidentally set it afire.

Though I had quite a number of Negro men employed whose quarters were in full view of the fire, we were all so sound asleep that my wife was the first to awake, and the fire was so nearly upon us that by the time I could get my wife and baby downstairs and a safe distance from the house in which there was a large can of powder that I had placed near the roof so that its danger would be comparatively small in case of fire, and then go again back to our bed room the flames were so rolling through the windows that I could not even get to our pretty watches that were lying on the dressing stand, and they were burned. The Negro hands, men and women, were working faithfully. We carried out my wife's elegant, heavy piano, I lifting my share. All the time I was watching when the flames would get to that can of powder, and calculated closely how long before it would explode, then told the hands and we all ran until it exploded, and during the time we were waiting for that explosion there were being burned things the loss of which we feel to this day. My wife was sitting on a stile crying like her heart would break, and little Lida Campbell, whose death when she was eleven years old, put the first gray hairs in my head, was laughing and clapping her chubby little hands in glee as she enjoyed looking at the bright fire. I was strong and well and felt that life was before us, and I was not much distressed. But a few days after that I found that I had lost $3,000 by a security debt, and soon after that I lost $200 by going security for a preacher, and soon after that a smaller amount as security for another man.

Fifteen years afterward the $3,000 was paid back to me. After I lost my position in the bank in Lexington because I had talked against [horse] racing, the bank being specially patronized by race horse men, I furnished the money to build a flour mill in Lexington, in which I was an equal partner. I lost about $1,500 the first year and sold my interest to my partner. I began to think I was not a successful business man, and I paid every cent in the world that I owed, then deeded all my property to my wife and children, and published in Lexington newspapers what I had done so that nobody might credit me ignorantly. It made no difference in my financial standing, and I have always had in any bank or other business house in Lexington more credit than I wanted to use, and have to this day. My wife and I had been engaged to be married four months, and it was within two months of our wedding before I ever had any idea whatever regarding her fortune. I did not know that she was worth a dollar in the world, and never would have known until after we were married had not a friend of ours volunteered to tell me that she was worth just about as much as I was, which proved to be true. I gave my property to my wife and children, though my wife begged me not to do so, but I have always been proud that I did so, and think that the majority of men of means would be happier, if, in all cases where they can, they would put their families above want, even if it restricts the men financially in business operations and in the indulgence of themselves. There is nothing of which I am prouder than the fact that the proper court records, and facts known to my neighbors, combine to show that purely for the love of my wife and children, and not to avoid the payment of any debt, and when my wife did not want me to do so, I gave every-thing that I had to my wife and children and so arranged that they could not dispose of the principal until the youngest child was of age. I may be a convict charged with having advocated "free love" in my news-paper, but the court records will always show that I made it one of the first purposes of my married life to provide for my wife and children, and when we are both now gray-headed, and she writes me in prison and says, "Under the circumstances I am proud to be a convict's wife," and that utterance of hers is applauded by good men and good women all over America, and even across the ocean, I am simply certain that I have been honored, and my enemies dishonored by my being put in this prison.

I do not mean it as an invidious comparison, but simply as a truth, the benefit of which I want other young people to have. Certainly, I have said enough of the attractions of Dessie Campbell to arouse, to this day, the jealousy of my dear wife were she not a superior woman, but I can see now that the difference between the two women is the difference between "Dora" and "Agnes," in David Copperfield. Had I married Dessie Campbell my only distinction would have been that I was Alexander Campbell's son-in-law. As it is now, I would not give my own distinction, as I see it realized even now, for that of all the priests and preachers that ever lived, and while I have the kindest recollections of Alexander Campbell and of all his family, I would rather be a dog and drag a clog all my life, than to be chained for life to the clog of super-stition that gave Alexander Campbell all of his fame. Take my mere bodily liberty if you will, and give me handcuffs and prison bars, but give me the mental liberty that makes me proud that I am of sufficient importance to have been honored with the anathemas of the church, while every heart beat of my Lucy is in sympathy with mine.

> "John Anderson, my Jo John,
> We've climbed the hills togither
> And many are the cantie days
> We've spent with one anither.
> Now we maun totter down, John;
> But hand in hand we'll go,
> And sleep togither in the grave,
> John Anderson, my Jo."

We built a pretty home in Lexington, and a plain, but sweet one, in the country, on the farm, now all embowered in trees, the latter being our home at the time I was sent here, and during the last twenty-five of the thirty-one years that we have been married we have lived a part of the time in Lexington, and most of the time in the country, and I have been engaged in farming all the time and in journalism nearly all that time. Like "Helen's Babies," I wanted to "see the wheels go 'round," and for about two years owned another flour mill and came out about even in conducting it. My wife and children once went to California and lived there for six months, our purpose being to go there and live, if we liked it more than Kentucky; but they came back preferring Kentucky, and they would all rather live in the country than in the city. Byron speaks of the common ambition to see our names in print, and it is a proverb among printers that a man who once gets printer's ink on his fingers never gets it off.

When I was educated the common sentiment about education was that it was simply an accomplishment essential to the highest society. Now, education is nearly always with regard to its business value. The latter is more sensible. Having no special calling in view — though I subsequently went into the ministry — my education was general, rather than special, and seemed better adapted to journalism than anything else. My only other literary labor has been a theological book, "The Rational View," written in defence of the modern rationalistic view of Christianity. My literary life seemed to come to me accidentally. One day, before I had finished my college course, I was walking through a large and beautiful woodland at my old home, and saw many young crows in the trees that were just getting old enough to fly. I believed that our crows were so nearly identical with the English rooks that the young ones would be good to eat, and I wrote an article for the Lexington "Observer & Reporter" — then the most important paper in the Bluegrass Region, and when the metropolitan dailies were scarcely known among the country people — headed "The Edibility of Crows." I meant it, in hard earnest, as a means of getting rid of crows. It was given prominence in that paper, and that was the first writing I ever did for print. Some parties acted upon my suggestion and tried eating young crows. They subsequently spoke of me in bitter terms. "Eating crow" was then, as now, a political slang, and some persons discovered a deep-laid political significance in what I had said, and I think that was the view of it taken by Editor Wickliffe, of the O. & R. Dean Swift wrote "Gulliver's Travels" simply as an amusing story, and when many political wiseacres announced the deep-laid political significance of the story, Swift simply "sawed wood and said nothing." My article proving utterly abortive in the line for which it was intended, I left its political interpretation to those who saw more in the piece than I had ever done. It gave me some political prestige, and I was sent as a delegate to the Presidential ratification convention, at Louisville, of Bell and Everett, and in the theater room in which the convention was held, I was in an opera box with Gen. Wm. Preston, also a delegate, afterward American minister to Spain, and then a distinguished general in the Confederate army. I did not know anything about politics and cared less. Edward Everett I knew to be one of the most scholarly men in America, but I have never known who Bell was to this day. I believed it was a case where the tail could wag the dog. A cartoon that I think was one of Nast's earliest, represented a race track in which my man was running with a big dinner bell on his head, and so far behind that it was evident the distance flag would drop on him, while Lincoln was away ahead of all the entries. If I had managed fairly well the political boost that my crow piece gave me, I would have gone to Congress instead of to the penitentiary.

The next piece that I ever wrote for any newspaper was two or three columns for the Wheeling (Va., now W. Va.) Intelligencer. It was written when I was at college, and was a report of a somewhat dramatic episode in which I had participated as a member of a Sheriff's posse, in Pittsburgh, Pa. The next piece that I can remember ever to have written was a pretty long article in the Lexington Daily Press, headed "A Lay Sermon to Preachers." The first intimation I ever got as to how it had

159

been received was from Billy Breckinridge, then just beginning his brilliant career as one of the most famous of American orators. We met on the street in Lexington early in the morning of the day the piece appeared, and Billy, in shaking hands with me, quoted to me, from Byron, those lines about having awaked that morning to find myself famous. I did not know to what he alluded until he explained to me, that early as it was he had read my article in the Daily Press. It was a seven days wonder, and some parties carried copies of it with them for weeks afterward and read it to groups of people. And yet had it been written at this day, by me or by anybody else, it probably would not have created much if any, interest. It was not an attack upon religion, but was a covert attack upon the church, based upon a real experience that I had had at the Episcopal church. Captain Jesse Woodruff, a soldier of the Mexican war, still living in Lexington, was, at that time, employed as managing editor of the Press. He was regarded as the most competent political editor in Lexington, but for allowing my article to appear in the Press, he was put out of his position on the paper, and has never had anything to do with journalism since. He was for many years my personal friend and literary admirer, but finally turned against me and so remains.

Though Henry T. Duncan, editor and proprietor of the Press, discharged Capt. Woodruff, as I have said, such was the reputation as a writer that "The Lay Sermon" gave me that Col. Duncan put me on the staff of his paper at a salary of $75 a month, and I held that position until he had to appease the religious public by discharging me for an article that was not more than three "sticks" long that I wrote against Talmage. I then took a position on the Daily Transcript, and as a combination of editor and reporter I spent four or five years on those two papers. Both of them were continually afraid of the explosive things that I was, at any time, liable to say — as they said; though they all read alike to me; some of them looking more startling in type than they did in my lead pencil copy. But because I carried a certain clientele with me, when I was put off of one paper and went to the other, neither of the rival editors was willing that the other should have me.

The same people were alternately my friends and my enemies. Mrs. Maria Dudley, one of the most prominent ladies in Lexington, cut from the columns of one of those papers, and pasted in her scrap book of humorous literature, and read to many, an article that I had written called "The Lightning Rod Man." Like everything I wrote it was simply a recitation of facts in my own experience. And yet the last time I was put off the staff of the Transcript was because Mrs. Dudley wrote its editor a note telling him to discontinue the paper to her if I was to remain on its staff. The chief feature in my writing was its realism and it was realistic, because, then as now, I could write only what really occurred. I once wrote a piece called "Looking for the Pantry Key." Its republication was repeatedly requested by ladies, and I was given the credit of having drawn on my imagination for an interesting combination of fun, pathos and marital devotion, and yet it was an incident all the main facts of which had occurred only the day before in my own family — barring only a little that was evidently intended to be understood as extravaganza and hyperbole.

One day after I had been engaged in journalism until I was forty years old, and was engaged as editor of the Transcript, I was sitting behind the counter, in the office of that paper when a man came in and walked up to the counter and presented his card, showing that his name was Strahan, and that he represented the roasted coffee house of E. Levering & Co., at Baltimore. I have since voted for Joshua Levering, of that firm, for President of the United States, on the Prohibition ticket. Strahan was a gentlemanly fellow and wanted some advertising done in the Transcript. I handed him over to the man who had charge of the advertising department, but never having heard of such a business as roasting coffee on so big a scale, and knowing nothing about it except as done by cooks in private houses, I asked him about it, and when he had arranged about his advertising, he and I got into conversation.

It seemed that he was being paid $100.00 a month, and all expenses paid, for traveling anywhere in the United States that he wanted to go, and only had to carry in his pocket a little miniature sample package of the roasted coffee that his house had to sell. I told him that I thought he had one of the nicest jobs of any man I had ever seen — that he had nothing to do but travel on railroads and steamboats and live at the best hotels, and talk and act like a gentleman, and have all expenses paid, and a fine salary beside. He said to me, "Would you like to have a job like it?" I said, "Yes; I have been in the newspaper business until I would like to have a change, but I don't like coffee, and don't know one kind from another." He said I could soon learn that and that they would give me a job, paying all my traveling expenses and beginning on $35 a month, and pay me more according to my success. I took the job and they soon raised my salary to $50 a month and then to $75 a month and all expenses paid, and I had never gotten but $75 a month as a journalist.

I could go wherever I wanted to and draw on my house for money from any place, and did so. I soon quit making out my expense accounts for they were about the same all the time, and I could be selling coffee while I was doing that. I was ashamed to commence drumming — I called myself a "commercial evangelist" — in my own town, Lexington, so I got aboard a Q. & C. train and stopped at Nicholasville, twelve miles from Lexington, to try my luck as a salesman. I went to every grocery in the town and did not sell a single pound. I found that there was a great firm of coffee roasters named Arbuckle, and they seemed to have a monopoly of the business, because they were the pioneers in that department and had lots of money, and that [while] their coffee was well known and sold itself, the other coffee firms had to have their agents. I argued the question as best I could — which was bad enough — with the Nicholasville grocers, but they all said that they were supplied with Arbuckle's roasted coffee, and that everybody knew about that, and when they wanted to sell any other brand they had to stop and explain about it, and they did not like to do that; and it seemed to me that their argument was good and that there was not anything I could say to answer it.

I left Nicholasville feeling greatly discouraged, and with a sort of impression that I had compromised my dignity, and that I was wasting the money of the Leverings and doing no good. I looked at my railway map and said I was going clear out of Kentucky before I tried selling any more coffee. I saw on the map a place named Greenwood, soon after the Q. & C. got into Tennessee, and I determined to stop there, principally because the place had a pretty name. If the place had been named Smithtown or Jonesburg I never would have stopped there, but I thought that nobody who would name their town Greenwood would not be green — would have a nice town and I bought my ticket for that place. When I got there I found the town consisted of one house and one inhabitant. The house was a combination of grocery, post office and railway station. But I noticed that it was a pretty big house and had a large supply of groceries in it, and he explained to me that the house belonged to a large coal company and that he bought supplies for them. I never collected any money, simply sent the orders to the Baltimore house, and though I afterward sold to almost anybody that wanted to buy my coffee, I made so few bad debts that it surprised the house and me, too.

I saw that I would have to wait at Greenwood several hours before I could get another train going south, so I concluded to try a new policy on that man. I saw he was there alone and that he wanted to talk, and it was a pleasant place, and we got some chairs and sat out in the shade and talked. About a quarter of an hour before train time I looked at my watch and said I must be fixing to go, and remarked, in a kind of an off-hand manner, that I was selling Levering's roasted coffee — by the way, the Leverings ought to give me a hundred dollars for this advertisement — and I asked him if he wanted anything in that line, with the air of a man who was tired of selling millions of cases of coffee and who didn't ordinarily bother with a small place like that. The man said, "Yes; you may send me seven cases." There were a hundred pounds in each case, and I stuck down in my order book my first order for coffee — 700 pounds — taking pains not to let him see that it was my first order, and I talked on as I wrote it, as if I had taken so many coffee orders that I did not want to be bothered with them while I was talking. But I got aboard that train happier than Dewey was when he gave the devil his Dewey at Manila, and knocked l out of what used to be spelled Manilla.

I found out that the way to sell coffee, and to do a good many other things, is not to let the other fellow know that you want to do it very much. It is the best way to sell newspapers and books, also. I started out to travel all over the United States from ocean to ocean, but I found that this was quite a large country, and I never traveled further than Kentucky, West Virginia, Ohio, Indiana, Illinois, Tennessee, Alabama and Georgia, and then I was tired of making new acquaintances.

One day I went to Henderson, Ky. The weather was so hot that hardly anybody was to be seen on the streets. I had never been there before, and I knew nobody in the town, and nobody knew me, so far as I knew. I started out to sell coffee. I came to a large, fine looking grocery, and had put one foot on the door sill to go in when I saw a man in the extreme back part of the house, throw up his hands in a frantic manner. He had pulled off his coat, vest, cravat and collar, and unbuttoned his shirt bosom, and leaning in his chair back against an open window was using a large palm leaf fan with great vigor. There was nobody else in the house. If there was anything about me to indicate that I was a drummer I did not know it. But that man with his hand raised as if to surrender, and in a tone of appeal, called to me and said, "For god's sake, mister, don't come in! Just send me some of it, but don't come in!!" He could not have known what I had to sell, but he was willing to buy it at random, and without knowing the price, rather than to have to tackle a drummer on that hot day. I never said a word to him. His house seemed to be full of goods except a corner near the front door that I estimated would hold about thirty cases of coffee — 3,000 pounds. I stepped back out of the door and looked up at the sign to see what the firm name was, and I sent that man enough roasted coffee to fill that corner; as large an order as I ever sold to the retail trade.

A few months afterward I came through that town again and went into that house, and asked the man if he wanted any of Levering's coffee. He looked at the few cases he had left and gave me another order, and neither of us alluded to the peculiar circumstances of the first sale. A few days after that I stopped at a small town in Tennessee. The weather was still hot. The station was a quarter of a mile from the town, and there was nobody at the station when I got there but the telegraph operator, and I was the only passenger who got off there. Nobody in the town knew me. The operator was listening to the tick of his instrument and turned to me and said, "Garfield is assassinated." He knew no other particulars. I saw that I was the only man to whom he had told the awful news. I walked alone down to the town expecting to tell the startling news. There were no telephones then. As soon as I got to the town, and before I had spoken to any one, I heard a man say, "Charley Moore says Garfield is killed." I was surprised, and then heard several others tell the sad news as having been brought by "Charley Moore." I walked up to one of these men and said I had been the first man to hear the news at the station, but that I had said nothing about it to anybody and was curious to know how they knew my name, and how they knew about my having heard the news. The man could not understand my perplexity until I told him all the facts, and he said that another man named Charley Moore had just come to town on horseback, and brought the news of the Garfield killing from a station on another railroad.

I traveled for the Leverings a year and a half, and then gave it up because I could not stand the separation from my family. During all the time that I was traveling for them I amused myself writing for the newspapers, and the point of my writings was to get in my advertisement of Levering's coffee, the papers printing the advertisements for the benefit of the other features of my communications. They were written in prose and in poetry, and, in allusion to my peripatetic life, my nom de plume was "Perry P. Tetik." My wife has saved clippings from my newspaper articles ever since we were married, and I want her to finish this chapter by furnishing to the printers of this book three or four specimens of my Levering coffee poetry. Mr. Strahan took the newspaper extract which he thought was the best of all my coffee poetry to Chicago, and had it printed in large quantities for advertising purposes, and I know that my wife has no copy of that. I will give you here the facts about one newspaper article that I wrote as a part of my experience as a coffee drummer.

In traveling I did what was common among drummers — arranged my business so that I would lay over Sunday at some point of interest, and at the time of which I speak I had arranged to stay over Sunday at Crab Orchard Springs, in Kentucky, and, with this intention, I got to Standford, Kentucky, the Saturday evening before, to put in a part of the evening there selling coffee, and then go out to see the "pink cottage," two miles in the country from Standford, and report it for the newspapers and then go on to Crab Orchard Springs that night. Rev. George O. Barnes was one of the most remarkable preachers that ever appeared in America. He was then — which was about twenty years ago — about fifty years old. He was a graduate of Center College, at Danville, Kentucky, and was ordained to the Presbyterian ministry. He was exceedingly gentle and affable in his manners, and had the art of pulpit oratory to a degree that I have rarely seen excelled, and his influence upon his audiences, that embraced the finest people of Kentucky, by thousand and thousands, was far more remarkable than that of any other man I have ever seen and heard in the pulpit, or on the stand, for the larger part of his preaching was done in court houses and opera houses and theaters. Though he never knew me until I was an infidel, and he was a most radical believer in Christianity, he and I were always friends, always talked freely when we met and he was always just as kind to me as he could be, though I rasped him pretty roughly through the newspapers for things that he said and did that I thought were glaringly irrational, if not worse; but I always, at the same time, had kind things to say for him, as I do now. He is still living and preaching, but fame and influence have so waned in his old age that he is left almost destitute, and I hope that what I am here saying may cause somebody to help him in his old days.

That his errors are great is certain, but I have always hoped that they were of the head rather than of the heart. While it is true that in his palmy days he lived in luxury, and was feted and praised as is true of all very popular preachers, I never heard an intimation of any kind of immorality against him. He had spent the first years of his life as a missionary in India. All through his remarkable career in Kentucky his daughter, Miss Marie, traveled with him, their only church music being her voice and a little organ that they carried with them all the time. The music was beautiful and so new and catchy that the people learned it as they do the most popular secular songs. Miss Marie was quite pretty, and her manners sweet all the time, to the last time that I ever saw her. "Bro. Barnes," as everybody called him, was a name that was daily, for years, upon thousands of Kentucky lips. He left the Presbyterian church, or was excommunicated, for heresy to Presbyterianism, and preached independently, and was heard without regard to any church connection.

He believed that he could heal the sick, blind and maimed by anointing them with oil and praying over them.

Once at Lexington, I led a poor blind Negro man, who believed in Bro. Barnes, up on a large stage and demanded that Bro. Barnes should heal him. My purpose was to expose Bro. Barnes, and he knew that, and it seemed to me that the exposure was plain enough to have effected its purpose, but it made friends for Bro. Barnes and enemies for me. At Louisville I saw him preaching to audiences that packed, until there was no longer "standing room," the largest theater building in the city, and I saw him [anoint] blind people and sick people and crippled people and pronounce them healed, there and then, and I saw many men and women whose appearance indicated that they were as fine people as lived in Louisville, rise from all over that vast throng of people and announce their faith in the Christian religion, based upon the miracles (?) that had just then and there been performed before their eyes. The Courier-Journal daily printed columns about the marvelous cures performed at these meetings of Bro. Barnes, and never printed a line indicating that there was any doubt about the genuineness of the miracles alleged to be occurring there, every day, for weeks at a time, that these meetings were being conducted. Such was the popularity of Rev. Barnes that there was rivalry among the wealthiest and most intelligent citizens of that city to entertain him and the members of his family, and sometimes others who traveled with him; any hotel in the city was glad to have him without any charge. I was the only being in Kentucky who dared, in print, to talk about him, just as I am now doing and to ridicule the alleged miracles.

Bro. Barnes had lived at the "Pink Cottage" near Standford, and when he left there it was used as a place where people were cured by prayer. The Interior Journal, published at Standford, teemed with accounts of the miraculous healings that were constantly occurring at the "Pink Cottage," and that paper was the organ of Rev. Barnes, and printed long letters from him through which, as in all his sermons, there was constantly repeated the catch, "Praise the Lord," and which, some years afterward, was changed to "God is love and nothing else," which Rev. Barnes wanted everybody to remember all the time, saying the initials of the words spelled "Gilane." When I got to Standford I saw in the people a disposition to make money out of the fame of the "Pink Cottage," like that at Lourdes and Oberamergau. I soon found that in Standford it was an easy thing to get a fight on my hands by ridiculing the miracles of the "Pink Cottage." I hired a saddle horse and rode out there about 3 o'clock in a summer evening.

The cottage had pretty grounds around it, and the cottage, which was pink, of course, was a one-story building, of five rooms, with a porch in front and one in the rear. I hitched my horse, and, ringing the doorbell, was shown in by an ordinary looking country woman, who, as soon as I was seated in the parlor, without any preliminaries, sat down by me and asked me of what disease I had come to be healed. I told her that I was not sick or diseased, in any way, but that I was a newspaper man and had come to get items for a newspaper article about the cottage. She seemed to disregard the newspaper feature of my visit entirely, and said, rather disdainfully, that she knew I was sick in some way, because she had never seen anybody who was not. I said that I supposed there was nobody in the world who was perfectly healthy, any more than perfectly anything else; that really there was nothing that was absolute — all relative — but that so far as I knew there was nothing about me of which I could wish to be healed. She said that she did not mean that I had to be sick in body, but might be in heart or in soul. I said that so far as I could judge my mind was all right, and that morally I was as "sound as a Spanish milled dollar." She still insisted that she knew there was something wrong about me, and I said, "If there is anything wrong about me it is in my morals, and it is the fact that I use tobacco." She said, "I knew all the time that there was something the matter with you; one of the greatest proofs I have that God heals people in answer to prayer is that he cured me of dipping snuff in answer to prayer. Come on out here in the back porch and we will pray to the Lord for you."

She started on out and I followed her. In that porch I found about a dozen lazy and ignorant looking people, about equally of the two sexes, and the woman who led me out said, "This man has come to get us to pray that he may quit using tobacco." They set a chair for me about the middle of the porch, and in less than a minute, they were all kneeling around me, and the woman was praying for me. She said to the Lord that I used tobacco, and that I had come there to get them to cure me, and that he had promised, in the Bible, to cure people in answer to prayer, and that now she wanted him to be as good as his word and cure me. I sat there taking notes in shorthand while they were praying, and they finished the prayer in five or ten minutes, and all got up, and said nothing more about tobacco or prayer, and soon got to talking about Bro. Barnes and the "Pink Cottage" generally.

I went on to Crab Orchard Springs that night. Next morning, Sunday, I had eaten my breakfast and started out to walk about the grounds. The buildings of the place are houses around three sides of a square containing several acres in pretty trees and grass. These houses are two-story, and there is a continuous two-story porch that runs in front of them looking out upon the square. I was sauntering along on the upper story of this porch when I came to a man who had brought his chair out upon the porch and was sitting by the railing and was filling a fine meerschaum pipe out of a package of fine tobacco from which he had just taken the first pipeful. There was nobody near the man. I had never seen him or heard of him before, and knew nothing about him. I walked up to him and said, "I never saw you before, and I am not a physician, but I want to tell you something. You have come to this watering place to regain your health, and you are ruining your health using tobacco." I said it slowly and deliberately. The man looked at me earnestly, but said nothing, but as I started off I saw him invert the bowl of his fine pipe and strike it on the railing so that the tobacco all fell out. I walked on around the porch, and, in about an hour afterward, came to the office and was standing by the counter talking to the clerk. A little boy came in and laid upon the counter a package of smoking tobacco that seemed to have had about one pipeful taken out of it. I thought I recognized it as the same bag that the man with the meerschaum pipe had had, and I believe he had thrown it away and that the boy had found it, and I told the clerk what had happened between me and the man with the meerschaum pipe, and I told the clerk that I would go and see. I started sauntering along that porch just as I had done before, and found the man sitting there alone and in the same place. He was not smoking. I told him about having seen the boy bring in a freshly opened package of tobacco, that looked like the one I had seen him have and I said to him, "Did you throw it away?" He said "Yes," and did not seem inclined to talk. I said to him, "Did you throw it away because you are going to quit smoking?" and he said "Yes."

I had begun to smoke when I was in my senior year at college, when I was nearly twenty years old, and I used tobacco twenty-one years. I was not an "excessive" tobacco user, if we can conceive that such a thing can be used in moderation, but I had smoked a meerschaum, or old Sister Lynx's cob pipe, or a fine, strong, dark cigar, and then I began chewing tobacco. I chewed only the finest of fine-cut tobacco. I loved it very much, and tobacco chewing, as I have told you, had been the only bad habit of my father. I used it so moderately that a nickel's worth would last me a week, except when, sometimes a fellow would ask me for a chew and put into his mouth, at one time, as much as I would use in a day or two. I kept my fine-cut in a pretty, bright tobacco box, in my hip pocket, and while I was talking to that man my box was nearly full of splendid tobacco. I pulled out my pretty tobacco box, and said to that man, "Do you see that box?" He said "Yes." I drew back my arm and threw that box as [far] as I could sail it out into the same square where the man had thrown his package of tobacco. My box went glittering through the sunshine, and fell far out in the deep blue grass. I was just starting to walk off, when a gentleman called me and said, "Wait a minute," and came walking up toward me and the other man and said, "I was sitting at my room door, yonder, and saw and heard what transpired between you two;" and putting his hand in his hip pocket he pulled out a plug of chewing tobacco. He said to me, "Do you see this?" and I said, "Yes." Then he stepped back and threw his plug of tobacco just as far as he could send it in the same direction I had thrown mine.

I said to the two, "This is an interesting incident; I want to make a suggestion to you. We will not say we will never use any more tobacco, but let us here take each others' addresses and pledge each other that we will never use any more tobacco until we have first written a letter to each of the other two saying that we are going to use tobacco again. We all agreed to it, and each of us was writing down the addresses of the others when a fourth man came up and said, "I quit using tobacco six weeks ago, and I want to go into this arrangement with you;" and all took down each other's addresses. About a year after that I was changing cars at a place where two railroads crossed each other, and there was quite a number of people changing and all were in a hurry. In the midst of it a man caught my hand and shook it cordially, and called my name. I said to him, "You have the advantage of me; I do not know you." He said, "I am one of the men you cured of using tobacco at Crab Orchard Springs." I said, "Have you never used it since?" and he said, "No." I asked him if he had ever heard from the man who had the meerschaum pipe, and he said, "I saw him not a great while since; he has never tasted tobacco since; he is a dry goods merchant in Tennessee, and is a very determined man, and will never taste tobacco again;" and then we had to jump aboard our trains. I have lost the three addresses of all the parties, and though it has now been about twenty years I have never, even by an accident, had a crumb of tobacco in my mouth, in any shape, since that Sunday at Crab Orchard Springs. I have printed the story in the Courier-Journal, and said I was the only man who ever was cured at George O. Barnes' "Pink Cottage," by prayer.

In the penitentiary here the State and the United States furnish prisoners with chewing tobacco. They paste labels on the doors of such as use tobacco, on which is printed simply the word "Tobacco," so that the man who goes around to the cells with the tobacco may know where to leave it. Before I knew it they had pasted a tobacco label on my door.

I told the man I did not use it and didn't want the label on my cell door. He said, "You can just keep the tobacco and swap it off for something else." I said, "No, I don't want any body to think I use tobacco even if I am in the penitentiary." Next day I found that the label had been soaked off.

I have alluded to my writing shorthand. I found I would have much spare time at the hotels and on trains and steamboats and I concluded to learn shorthand. I got Graham's textbook on shorthand. It is nearly the same as Pittman's with a few little improvements on Pittman. I soon found it a wonderfully interesting study, and one of the most ingenious of discoveries, and exceedingly difficult of perfect understanding and accomplishment. I studied it as I traveled and had no assistance except my text book, and, from the fact that I had to overcome all the difficulties in it, just by my personal application, I learned it very thoroughly. In order to familiarize myself with it I encouraged the habit of thinking in shorthand and afterward, whether purposely or unconsciously I know not, I got to moving my right forefinger and thumb, in sympathy with my thoughts, writing shorthand in my imagination. The disposition to write with my forefinger and thumb in sympathy with my thinking began to be an annoyance to me, and I tried hard to stop it. I succeeded in stopping the disposition in my forefinger, but it seemed to only increase that in my thumb. I wrote shorthand in my mind and with my thumb until it seemed to me liable to derange my mind, and I went to our family physician, Dr. W. N. Atkins, to advise with him about it. He readily recognized that there might be such a difficulty, and advised me kindly and I suppose scientifically; but it did me no good. I reasoned that there was in my composition a certain amount of intellectual and physical energy that had to be expended in writing, just as our appetite for food demands gratification. I noticed that while writing the ordinary long hand, in any kind of composition, my mind and thumb were relieved from the shorthand writing, and I felt that I was simply bound, in self defense, to keep myself either constantly writing longhand or thinking about what I was to write in longhand, and I am, to this day, in prison, forced to keep writing or thinking about writing in longhand.

When I now get despondent, which is common with me, or get into any kind of trouble more than ordinary, I cannot control my thumb and write shorthand until I am almost distracted. I have tried to stop it by fastening my thumb and forefinger together with a gum band; but it did no good. It was, indeed, exceedingly fortunate for me that Warden Coffin, of this prison, made me assistant superintendent of the printing department of this prison, and put me to doing the principal writing on

170

the prison paper; and so between my daily literary duties and the writing of this book at spare times, which will occupy about a month, I am nearly entirely free from the annoyance of mentally writing shorthand all the time. But for years I have been compelled to write longhand to relieve myself from writing shorthand, and I expect, to be compelled to do it the balance of my life for the same reason, and, whether financially successful or not, I expect on this account, if for no other, to remain a writer for print so long as I can write. The things that I write in shorthand in these cases of mental trouble are just any random words that may be the last I have heard somebody speak, or that I saw in print, or that just accidentally occurred to me, and, in spite of my efforts to the contrary, I will write the words over and over again. I have even tried to forget shorthand and have tried to change my habit by writing with some of my fingers rather than my right thumb, but I cannot do it; cannot even change it into the habit of writing with the forefinger of my right hand.

I rarely use shorthand practically except to make memorandums, and in cases where I want to put down much in a little space and rapidly, and, sometimes in writing for print, when my mind goes ahead of what I can write in longhand, I put down shorthand memorandums on the margin of my paper, knowing that they cannot confuse the printers. Once a young lady came to me in Lexington and said she knew I wrote shorthand and that she wanted to learn it. I told her what text books to get and, with other instruction I gave her, told her to get in a habit of thinking in shorthand. About two years afterward I met her on the street and she said to me, "Mr. Moore, you remember that when you told me about learning shorthand, you told me to learn to think in shorthand. I did so, and now I have gotten so that I write shorthand all the time with my right forefinger, and can't stop it." And with an expression of pain on her face she showed me, all the time we were talking, how her right forefinger wrote shorthand on the black silk apron that she had on. I had never mentioned to her the trouble of the same kind that I had, and I do not know that I had made it known to any one. My son, who lives in Washington City, has told me of a man that he knows who is troubled with shorthand writing just as I am.

Years before I learned to write shorthand I wrote in longhand, with the big toe of my right foot, "Robt. J. Breckinridge." I have written that name, in that way, thousands and thousands of times. In writing, the connection was only between my mind and my big toe; but, of course, my whole foot moved with my toe. I never wrote out the full name, Robert, but simply the contraction, Robt. I always wrote the whole name without raising my pen, so to speak. I do not believe that the power of thought is in the brain any more than in any other part of the body — certainly no more than in the medulla oblongata, or spinalis, and I think what I have given is some evidence of my view. My right thumb has a mind of its own, that not only operates independently of my volition, but in opposition to my volition. And yet I know, apparently in contravention of my own theory, that a man who has his right leg amputated at the hip will suffer with cold in his right foot, and I believe that if my right leg had been amputated before I learned shorthand, I would still have written "Robt. J. Breckinridge" with my right toe, and that if my right arm were now amputated I would still, in my mental depression, write shorthand with my right thumb.

Insanity of body or mind is the inevitable result of a vis a tergo, for which heredity and environment — not ourselves — are responsible. An absolute instance of "mens sana in sano corpore" does not exist in the universe. There is nothing absolute except mathematics. The multiplication table is absolutely accurate; the three angles of every triangle are absolutely equal to two right angles. All else is relative, and mental sanity depends upon who is to umpire the case. Some of the most prominent of the clergy of Lexington have said, in public print, that they thought me insane, while, to my mind, there can be no higher evidence of a man's insanity than the fact that he believes any religion, and especially the Jewish or Christian, to be true. Upon this issue there is now an "irrepressible conflict," to the bitterness of which my imprisonment will add.

I am going to ask that here my wife may give to my printers three or four Levering Coffee poems that I wrote, and to put them in a separate chapter to themselves, printing them with the same heads that they had in the newspapers. I will here begin

Chapter IX
Jones
An Epic — by Perry P. Tetik

Jones was a gentleman, born in Kentucky;
Was bright, young, handsome and withal so lucky
As to have inherited houses and land,
And a cool hundred thousand of cash in hand.

In science and ethics Jones was a scholar;
Sound in the faith as a Spanish milled dollar;
Thought Ingersoll crazy and Darwin a fool:
Had a pew in a church of the orthodox school.

And Jones had traveled and feasted his eyes,
And stomach on foreign menus and skies.
"Coelum non animum mutant" — you know it,
Jones found to be true in the heathen poet.

For Jones had sauntered all through the Tuilleries,
Parisian, Venitian and Florentine galleries;
Had done great Rome on the Tiber Fluvius;
Smothered a dog, boiled eggs, at Vesuvius.

Jones knew, like a book, the land of Pharaoh,
Had ridden a camel from Joppa to Cairo,
Had bought everything that bucksheesh could buy
To tickle the palate or dazzle the eye.

As for Golden Horn and Constantinople,
Not only did Jones know all the people,
But every dog knew just as soon as he'd sight him,
And every flea flew just delighted to bite him.

All Sardis, Micale, Arbela he knew,
And Leuctra and Cannae and Salamis too;
Platea, Pharsalia and Marathon, he
Just knew them by heart, and Thermopylae.

(Which last is the place where Leonidas bold,
Told the whoppingest yarn that ever was told,
'Bout arrows so thick that they thought it was night,
And lighted the gas to see how to fight).

Baalbec, Persepolis, Thebes, Palmyra.
Babylon, Carthage, Miletus and Tyra,
Tenedos, Tarentum, Pactolus and Paphos,
He knew like a book. (He summered at Samos).

He'd been where was born, and where now reposes,
Each one of those coons but Homer and Moses;
Hipparchus, Hesiod and Alcibiades,
Epaminondas, Zeno, Miltiades;

Herodotus, Solon and Hippocrates,
Scipio, Sallust, Sesostris, Socrates,
Pittacus, Pisistratus, Pythagoras,
Epictetus, Xerxes, Anaxagoras,

Sophocles, Sennacherib, Shalmanezer,
Pompey and Crassus and Julius Caesar;
Names like Sardinapalus and Xenophon,
Which to get into meter is not any fun.

Jones knew, beside, each one of the ologies,
Treated in books or taught in the colleges;
Anatomy, Botany and Geology,
Psychology, Philology, Phrenology;

Then Ichthiology and Stenography,

174

And Ornithology and Geography,
Also Astronomy and Astrology,
Paleontology and Theology.

And Jones played the fiddle, flute and piano,
Sang tenor and bass, alto and soprano;
In German and racquet, in waltz or Lancers,
Tip'd the light fantastic among the dancers.

But here's the surprising part of my story.
Jones wasn't happy either since or before he
Got married; for he'd a beautiful wife,
And as sweet as you ever saw in your life.

They went to theater, concert, opera,
Lecture, skating rink, beer garden, hop or a
Church (to alleviate worldly distresses
By saying their prayers and looking at dresses.)

And Jones kept a table with viands and mets,
In Haviland's hand-painted, French china sets,
And all the new dishes that ever were seen,
Gotten up in the style of the French cuisine.

His wines were Catawba, Sauterne, Pommery,
Claret, Souv'raine, Piper, Mumm's Extra dry,
Hockheimer, Topaz, Kelly Island, Chateau,
Rhine, Port, Sherry, St. Emilien, Bordeaux.

Yet Jones was not happy; some great aching void,
Some horrid hiatus his pleasure alloyed;
Some desideratum he never could find;
Some sine qua non for a satisfied mind.

Jones met by rare chance one day, do you know, sir,
A cultured, pious, intelligent grocer.
And, under the guise of inspecting his wares,
Just walked in to talk and unbosom his cares.

"What's that brown package?" said Jones, "may I know, sir?"
"That's Levering's coffee," responded the grocer.

"Is it good?" said Jones, his eyes opened wide;
"The best in the world," the good grocer replied.

Then Jones, like a Christian, gentleman, scholar,
Put his hand in his pocket and pulled out a dollar,
Which bought him five pounds, (that's the lowest figger),
And had it sent 'round to his house by a nigger.

* * * * *

Some months have passed by, Mr. Jones and his wife
Are the happiest folks you've seen in your life;
And that pious grocer, from whom Jones did buy
Lives in a brown stone front, four stories high.

A Dream of Ham and Coffee
by Perry P. Tetik

Ham for supper! Old Moses was level,
When he said that a hog wasn't fit for the devil;
And only some heathenish son of a gun
Would ever have thought of eating one.
I may be at fault; decidedly am
Inclined to believe that the curse upon Ham,
That old Noah uttered when once on a tight,
Referred to the eating of bacon at night.

Supper was late, and, hungry as thunder,
I committed a terrible hygienic blunder; —
First, under my vest I proceeded to cram
Half of a sugar-cured Magnolia Ham,
Then smoked a cigar and rolled into bed;
But dreams that floated around in my head
No artist can limn, nor poet scan,
Of the Levering's Roasted Coffee man.

I stood again where the Magnolia blooms,
And its fragrance on Southern zepher comes;
And I drew in the breeze of the Magnolia dell;
But nothing but Levering's Coffee could smell.
Then, where the waves of the fruitful St. John
Through Florida, and to the sea, roll on,

I plucked the ripe golden orange and bit;
And nothing but coffee could taste in it.

Again, where the Father of Waters pours
Into the sea, and where the sea roars,
I stood and watched the dusky waves
That rushed and roared into ocean caves;
But as far as the eye could stretch and behold,
Nothing but billows of coffee rolled;
And the jetty of Mr. Eades but surrounds
Thousands of acres of "coffee grounds."

And sea serpents, mermaids, dolphins and whales,
Rose out of the sea and stood on their tails,
And of Coffee A sugar rolled up a whole mountain
Right into the mouth of that terrible fountain,
And while Yosemite poured in a stream
Of the richest and best of Alderney cream,
They drank out of shells selected at will,
From the size of a coffee-cup up to a still.

And then, where the Geysers of Iceland spout,
And where the hot springs of Arkansas run out,
And the fountains leap up at Fontainbleau,
Where the great Croton pipes do rush and flow;
There hottest of coffee leaps and dashes —
Levering's best coffee spouts and splashes —
And Vesuvius e'en her wrath forgot
And steamed like a jolly old coffee pot.

Then, again, at Niagara I wondered,
While coffee adown its fathoms thundered,
And great ships a coffee ocean sailed o'er,
From Java and Rio to Baltimore;
While over my head did great black clouds rise,
And rain down coffee from thundering skies;
And yet more astonishing still to tell —
But I woke — Yes, that is the breakfast bell.

A Song of Coffee
by Perry P. Tetik
[Air — From Greenland's Icy Mountain.]

From Vermont's icy mountains,
From Indiana's land,
Where California's fountains
Roll down their golden sand,
From land and lake and river,
And every other place,
The call is to deliver
This coffee by the case.

What though sweet coffee breezes
Blow soft o'er Java's isle.
What wife her husband pleases
Who makes his coffee vile?
And how unpaid the kindness
Of Levering to our land,
If people in their blindness
Use any other brand.

Shall we whose heads are level,
And use the E.L.C.,
Let men go to the devil,
As fast as fast can be
From drinking low grade coffees,
And never once proclaim
The sweet content that offers
In Levering's matchless name.

Quaff, quaff this drink, fair women,
From gloom dispelling bowl,
Till like politics with the men
It spreads from poll to poll
Till o'er our handsome nation
The Levering's coffee fame
Will make the whole creation
Rise up and bless his name.

178

Johnny and His Sled
A Pome — by Perry P. Tetik

Little Johnny for a ride
Concluded he would go and slide,
For Johnny thought the best of riding
Was getting on a slide and sliding.
And so he started up the road
And then he took his slide and slode,
And down the hill he fairly flew,
So slickly on his sled he slew,
And not sufficiently had ridden
Until he four miles had slidden.
While doing as his mother bid
Upon his slide he safely slid
But, alas! too long he stayed
Upon his sleigh too long he sleighed
And he was ordered to his bed
For sliding so long on his sled,
And told that he was very bad
Because upon his slide he slad,
And got bedabbled in the mud
In consequence of having slud,
And any boy should feel the rod
Who disobediently had slod,
But if he'd take his slide so slick
Up to the grocery right quick
And a load of Levering's coffee bring
She would forgive the naughty thing.
And Johnny did as he was bid
And to the grocery quickly slid,
And as soon as he got his load
Right straight back home he slickly slode.

Chapter X

When I had spent a year and a half traveling for Levering's Roasted Coffee firm, though the relations between us had all the time been as pleasant as could be, and I thought I might get a salary of $100 a month and my expenses, I became so tired of traveling and so home sick, and so tired of talking about coffee that I wrote the Leverings that I did not think I could do them justice, and I gave up my position. That was about 1882. I came back to Lexington and went into journalism, again employed by the most prominent daily in the town. I wanted to say things all the time that the editor and proprietor would not let me say, and several times I was discharged because I would say things that he did not want me to say. I was very much disgusted at seeing how the press pandered to the church and to the liquor traffic. It disgusted me to see how priests and preachers would manage to get "puffs" of themselves into the papers, and that the most common-place pulpit platitudes from the most ordinary men were always spoken of as "eloquent," and nothing religious was ever fairly criticized[.] It disgusted me to see how crimes committed in saloons were kept out of the papers and that the editors were brought to do this by the advertisements of saloon keepers. I saw horrible crimes committed in saloons, and when I reported them fairly, I found, in several instances, that my reports of them had not appeared in the paper. I thought it possible that there was some good reason for it and said but little, if anything about it. Finally I wrote a fair report of a saloon crime and it was not published. I felt that I was in a position where my paper would report anything good for the church and for the saloons, but nothing bad, and I knew I was the principal writer for the paper, and I felt that I was being used as a tool to give a one-sided view of those two very important things, and I was not willing to do it. My habit was to spend my time in Lexington until midnight every Saturday, and then start afoot to my home eight miles in the country and stay until Monday morning. One night in 1884, as I was walking home from Lexington, and was about two miles from the city, and was feeling disgusted with the way newspapers pandered to the pulpit and the saloon, it occurred to me that I ought to start a paper of my own. In five minutes the suggestion matured into a determination, and I began to think of a name for the paper, and, in less than a minute, the name BLUE GRASS BLADE occurred to me; my purpose being to have the name a play on a blade of bluegrass and a sort of metaphoric Damascus blade. The name seemed to suit my purpose exactly, but I could not realize that the very best name for my paper would occur to me in only a minute's thought, and I thought of several other names for it, but each time my judgment would turn to the first name suggested to me, and I determined that the paper should be named THE BLUE GRASS BLADE.

It soon became known that I was going to start my own paper, and there was considerable curiosity to see it. My expectation was to make it merely a local paper, to extend no further than the boundaries of the "Blue Grass Region" of Kentucky. I arranged at once for its publication and its first issue was caught up with great avidity. I said, in my first editorial, "I am not a prohibitionist." I wrote everything in it first-personally, using the pronoun "I" instead of the customary editorial "we." I was much in earnest in all I said and while it was not my purpose to make it a "funny paper," I had an acute sense of the ridiculous, and when things naturally suggested themselves to me in that light I treated them in that manner, and as contrasted with the very dry style of Lexington journalism up to that time, it amused people generally, and many people, while they laughed, read my pretty severe strictures upon religion, and upon the liquor traffic, when they would not have read them in the ordinary way of opposing those two institutions.

When I had run the paper three months and it was all the time a success, there came into my head the idea, "Quit while your credit's good." It was started by the suggestion of my wife, whose criticism has always been more to me than all the balance of the world, that I could not expect to keep my paper up to the interest it was then creating; and for no other reason than that, I stopped my paper and sent back to all subscribers the pro rata of their subscriptions. I stopped it for three months and started it again and ran it for another three months and stopped it for the second time, refunding the subscription money as before, because very bitter things were beginning to be said and written against me. I had been conservative and kept back many things that I wanted to say; out of a 1,000 people who will help a man to gain distinction 900 will turn against him and help to drag him down when he has attained it; and this was my experience. I then started the Blade the third time, determined to say just what I thought ought to be said about anybody and anything. The sensation produced was such as was never caused by any newspaper printed in America except those that were printed against slavery, including the one printed in Lexington by Cassius M. Clay, resulting in his office being torn down by the leading people of Lexington and thrown into the streets, and in his being attacked by men, one of whom he killed with a bowie-knife, and the other of whom he cut so badly that he barely survived it.

My paper was printed the third time I began it by Mr. J. M. Byrnes, who then had the same fine printing house, in Lexington, that he now has. After the first issue of my paper it got so that a considerable time before the hour came for its appearance a crowd would so gather around the door that Mr. Byrnes would not only have to lock the street door, but stand outside to guard his doors and windows. Beside my regular edition, that went to nearly all the leading people in the city, I have sold as high as 750 papers on the streets of Lexington. When the issue would seem likely to run short the newsboys would sell them for 25 and 50 cents each, and I have had a dollar offered me for a single copy in the office.

A meeting of the citizens of Lexington, at the court house, was called to oppose the influence of the Blade. It was presided over by a prominent Christian Circuit Judge, and the leading speakers against me were the most prominent preacher in the town, and the most prominent saloon keeper in the town, who had been indicted for selling liquor to minors and allowing gambling in his house. I was insulted and threatened on the streets until it was daily expected by the public that I would be killed, and it seemed to me highly probable that I would be. I was first assaulted by a small man, who was then and is now, a prominent citizen of Lexington. I did not strike him, but simply caught him and held him. I was next assaulted by a very powerful and athletic young man, occupying a most prominent position in society. He drew a pistol on me, but did not shoot when he saw I had none. The first intimation of his presence was a terrible blow in my face that cut my face and came near putting out one eye with the broken glass of my spectacles, leaving me almost blind. The blow came near knocking me down. I had by practice and precept done all I could to oppose the violence for which Kentucky is famous, and had preferred to be thought a coward rather than to resort to brute force, and such is my position to-day. But when I thought that I saw that the man would kill me, or seriously wound me, if I did not defend myself, I fought him and he retreated leaving me where he had made the assault. He came back at me a second time, and after the second round he retreated again. We were both arrested and I was put in the city jail, because I refused to give any bond, when the best people in Lexington begged me to let them go on my bond, and when the trial came he was fined and I was acquitted, the people applauding the verdict until the judge threatened to punish them for disorder, and every member of the jury congratulating me by shaking hands with me.

Insults and threats to kill me, made by Christian people, became common. I do not care to give the names and the details of the cases, because I do not wish unnecessarily to subject my family, or myself to further danger. Though, as I have told you, my only active part in the war was a short experience in two Confederate hospitals, a Major in the Federal army and his wife drove to my house, eight miles in the country, to tell me of a plot, to assassinate me, and, for weeks, my wife kept our windows darkened at night, for fear I would be assassinated by being shot, through the windows. The parties who it was thought would assassinate me were and are Christians, who had been reared by parents of extraordinary zeal in religion. There were four men who were especially formidable to me as enemies. They were all Christians. All of them were Confederate soldiers. Three of them were judges, and from two of those judges I had threats of bodily harm, one threatening to kill me in plain words. Of these two one has done more by his speeches and writings to uphold the Christian religion than any man who has lived in Kentucky in my day. He and the other Judge who threatened to kill me, and who for so doing was applauded by all the newspapers in Lexington have come to me and said they were sorry for what they did, and we are friends to this day, and one of them has written, in most beautiful and complimentary style, about me, in different publications since my imprisonment here.

The Judge who never threatened any violence to me, and who has never expressed any regret for his opposition to me, has been succeeded by a Judge known to be an infidel, who has, all the time, been my friend, and who, when I was tried for blasphemy against the Holy Ghost, at the instigation of a Methodist preacher in Lexington, made the decision in my favor that will probably be the last ever rendered in this government for blasphemy against the Holy Ghost, or any other ghost, or for blasphemy against anything else. The fourth of the Confederate soldiers who assaulted me was the most prominent of the four men, all of whom were unknown to me, and who lay in wait for me, and ran up behind me and dragged me back as I was getting on a train, just moving off, when I was returning to my home from a call to see a sick Campbellite or Christian preacher, R. B. Neal. Those four men were spoken of by the New York World as "four deacons" of a church that the paper named, and their object was to get the name of a member of their own church who had furnished me the information that I printed, their purpose being to do personal violence to the man who informed me. They never got what they wanted and never will, though all that I printed was evidently written by just such a party as I represented, and the Commonwealth's attorney who prosecuted me said to the grand jury, in my presence, that the fact that all I said was true, made the offense all the greater.

That Confederate soldier was afterward killed in a saloon by a policeman while resisting arrest. He said before he died that he was ashamed of what he had done to me, and I printed in the Blade what he had said and asked that my friends lay some flowers on his grave. To guard my publishers and because I do not care again to agitate questions that have been decided in my favor by all good and fair people who know of them, and because my paper has, largely in consequence of the injustice that has been done me, developed into a national paper that is not intended to discuss mere local and personal things, I will now avoid identification of persons and places. In no case will I give the specific words, that I printed for which I have three times been imprisoned, twice in jail and once in the penitentiary, because such might lay my publishers and my family liable to prosecution and persecution by my Christian enemies; though there is nothing that I would rather put in this book than the exact words, from my paper, for which I have been imprisoned three times by public prosecutions, because nothing could so plainly tell the injustice that has been done me as for me to print, here, from my paper the exact words that I have written and for which I have been imprisoned.

The first time I was imprisoned was by a church, for which I had once preached, in a Kentucky town that is not Lexington. I made no defense. I believed it would be better for me, and for my views, about religion and liquor to be imprisoned. The witnesses against me were preachers and distillers, the leader, in whose name the prosecution was conducted, being an elder and leader in the most prominent church in the town, he also being a wholesale whisky dealer. I was fined $100 and sent to jail for two months. One Methodist preacher who was a Prohibitionist gave me $75, and others gave me more than the $100 that I had been fined. I spent the two months in jail only nominally. The jailer's unmarried daughter, a young lady, gave up her own beautiful room to me, and the jailer and all his family invited my wife and all my family to come and be their guests as long as I was there, and my wife spent a part of every week with me. The parlor of the private residence of the jailer's family was put at the disposal of myself and my friends, and I had so many callers, including preachers and saloon keepers, and the finest gentlemen and ladies of the whole country, that it was such a tax to me to see and talk to them all that I sometimes had to excuse myself. The jailer kept a splendid family table at which I ate, and frequently my friends with me, and books, papers, flowers, fruits and delicacies to eat were sent me in great abundance, from people in different stations in life, with their compliments and expressions of sympathy and admiration. I had a cell in the jail that was all nicely fitted up for me, in which, or in the private rooms of the jailer, I could stay at any time, and at night, during the delightful weather, the jailer's son and I would take long walks into the country. My imprisonment there was a continued ovation to me, as seems likely to be the case here from my experience so far, which is less than a month to the time that I am now writing.

Before the time came for me to go home from that jail a livery man had asked the privilege of sending me to the railway station at his expense and I had accepted his kind offer, and when the last hour of my imprisonment came there was his nice carriage for me, and my friends to bid me goodbye, and other friends to go with me to the station. Since that time a great disgrace has befallen the family of the preacher who was the leader in my prosecution. At the same time that I was put in jail there, there was for a short time imprisoned with me a gentleman named W. T. Ficklen of Paris, Ky., who is still living. He was, and is, a Prohibitionist. He was at the time of his imprisonment nearly 70 years old, and for fifty years had been a member of the church that imprisoned him and me, and all the time he has been a most exemplary citizen. He has been ever since then an agent for my paper and for my book, "The Rational View," and will be an agent for this book.

I was afterward put in jail in Lexington, charged with blasphemy against the Holy Ghost. I could have avoided going to jail at all by simply giving bond for my appearance at the next term of the court. I refused to give the bond, though I had friends who begged me to do so, and I could have given bond, in one hour, for a million dollars, but to show that Christians would, to this day, send a man to prison for blasphemy against the Holy Ghost, the leader of them being a Methodist preacher, I went to jail to stay there for three months, until the next term of the court, I having been held over because the Commonwealth was not ready. The jailer gave me a large room that had been intended for invalids, in a splendid new jail that had just cost $80,000, and Mrs. E. B. Wrenn, then and now living in Lexington, she and her husband then and now loved by as many people as any two people living in Lexington, sent me by their servant, on an exquisite table service, meals that were as fine as could be made, and two or three times as much as I wanted, and when I had stayed in jail just long enough to show plainly to the world that the church will imprison a man for his religious opinions to-day, if it had the power, just as it once did when it had unrestricted power. I gave the bond and came out of jail, and defended myself through attorneys, and was acquitted. I only came out of jail because I was over-persuaded by my friends, and afterward rather regretted that I did not let the Christians imprison me, because I thought the effect of it would be good as showing the persecuting spirit of Christians. So that when I came to be tried for the penitentiary I resisted all the requests of my friends to employ counsel to defend me, because I believed that it would be for the greatest good to have the Christians send me to the penitentiary, and I still believe, now that I am a prisoner, that I did the right thing, and am glad I did just as I did. I believed then, as I believe now, that had I kept myself from conviction, the Christians would have claimed that they did not intend actually to send me to the penitentiary, but it is seen now they did intend to do that, and from a publication of an interview with all the prominent priests and preachers in Lexington, that while none of them regretted my imprisonment many of them were evidently delighted that I had been imprisoned. Regarding my trial I shall, personally, have but little to say.

Rev. J. W. McGarvey, president of the theological department of the University of Kentucky, as reported by the newspapers of Lexington, once did and said as follows: He walked into the pulpit of the Broadway Christian — or Campbellite — Church, one Sunday, in Lexington, to preach a sermon which it had been announced from that pulpit and by the papers, would be "to men only." There were 2,000 men present. Rev. McGarvey took into the pulpit with him a copy of my paper, the Blue Grass Blade, and reading from it based his sermon upon what I had said in that issue of my paper. During his sermon he said, "Charley Moore has said some hard things, but I have never caught him in a lie." When he said that he was applauded. It was the only time that I ever heard of any sermon being applauded in Lexington.

When I was sent to jail, soon afterward, the Commonwealth's attorney who prosecuted me, actually made the point that my statements were all the more libelous because they were true, and I have been told many times that the utterances of my paper were specially dreaded because of my reputation for telling only the truth. I have been four times prosecuted for what I have said in my paper. I have been a juror on every variety of jury from grand jury down to coroner's, and have nearly always acted as foreman of the juries upon which I was, either by appointment of the presiding judge or by election by the jurymen. Beside this I have, as a reporter for newspapers, been present at the trials of all sorts of criminals known to our courts, and I have never seen any man arraigned before any court that was treated with the injustice and discourtesy that was shown me at Cincinnati when I was convicted and sent to this prison. It is but right and fair in those who here read this statement to remember that in this case I am an interested witness, and to make what they believe to be a proper allowance for my possible, or probable, prejudice in my own favor. I will leave a report of the case to Dr. J. B. Wilson, of Cincinnati, who was present at the trial, and who wrote this report in the Blade of February 26, E.M. 299, when I was in the penitentiary. I will say about him that he is in no way in the world related to me, or identified with me in any business interest; that he only became acquainted with me through my paper, and that in my best judgment he is more liable to be damaged financially than benefited by any friendship shown me. In Dr. Wilson's article that came to me here in prison here in my paper, it is so evident that he is not prejudiced in my favor that it seems to me he says things that are unnecessarily hard on me, and almost unjust to me. His report of the trial, headlines and all, is as follows:

CHAS. C. MOORE
SENTENCED TO OHIO STATE PRISON FOR TWO YEARS. — REPORT OF THE TRIAL

It was a scene which few men have opportunity to observe in a lifetime. A white-haired man, whose years are few at best, sitting in the seat of Justice sentencing another man, likewise gray with age, to imprisonment for two years, for a few trivial words sent through the mails. Words, which to the students of sociology or to any liberally-minded man, cannot be so twisted into any shape as to render them indecently offensive — words which some of the best lawyers and judges in this city have declared, contain no particle of obscenity. The naked truth, like a nude statue morally [impresses] men differently. It shocks and shames some, and to others it is pure and beautiful.

Men differently see justice. One political party sees [little] to commend in the judgments of another. The various religious factions hate each other. The various constructions they place [upon] meaningless dogmas have led them to massacre, and torture, each other. There is in reality no such thing as party or religious justice. Only where judgment rises above party, religion, friendship, and kindred even, can mankind look for justice? It is for this reason that justice is represented as blind.

William Bunday the District Attorney and Judge Thompson who prosecuted and sentenced Mr. Moore may honestly believe that they have performed their duty and rendered a just sentence, in depriving Mr. Moore of his liberty, taking him from his family, and confining him in the penitentiary for two long years. As I said before different people will place different constructions upon a statute or a dogma, and do so both naturally and honestly. The weight of a single word has thrown nations into violent disputes, both sides fighting to the death in support of their ideas of justice.

Religious men have condemned a dissenter to the stake honestly believing that justice (?) demands that there shall be no difference of opinion on ghostly subjects. The Puritans honestly believed that justice (?) was meted out to the man, who was sent to the pillory for kissing his wife on a Sunday. Elizabeth may have honestly believed that her sentence of death to the Queen of Scots was a just deed; but it is recorded of her that she never slept well thereafter.

There are no questions which involve so much discussion as the sociological questions of to-day. These questions are only in a state of development. What seems justice to one seems persecution to another. Take the divorce question for instance. Some of our religious creeds say there is no justice in granting a divorce; for what God, the priest, hath joined together, let no Judge, the mortal presume to put asunder.

It is altogether in the way different factions are taught to view these things. The Catholic teaches that it is immoral, lustful and lascivious for a divorced person to re-marry. The Protestant teaches that it is both moral and virtuous. Both may honestly entertain these different ideas of justice, and both may be honestly right in some cases and both again be honestly wrong. It is a question which involves human affections, and never was the man born so wise as to be able to comprehend the nature, the wants and happiness of the heart of another, or decide the laws which shall govern it.

The growing evil of divorce, the marital jealousy and unfaithfulness which lead to murder, suicide, the yearly prostitution of hundreds of thousands of somebody's daughters, the secret abuses of youth, the venereal and other diseases that propagate consumption and insanity, the dense ignorance of procreative law, which incapacitates three-fourths of mankind from making proper marital selection, and the rapidly spreading secret vices which cannot be thought of without a feeling of shame, surely make the proper knowledge of sex, the greatest moral issue — the most vital issue in this country to-day. Every political and military question before this country today is a trifling insignificance beside it. The holy hush which is put upon the sex question only tends to vulgarize it. It is better to have a free and open discussion of these questions, that youth may be enlightened, and directed wisely, than go headlong on to abandon as this nation is surely progressing. People will have different ideas as to what is just in this direction, and as to what are the best methods of attacking and solving social evils. Some think the present matrimonial arrangement has solved it as nearly as it can be solved; others look abroad over the field of marital infidelity, and the byways of divorce, prostitution and vice and think it has not solved it. One thing is sure, if it is never publicly discussed, it will never be any better, and if never any better, it is bound to grow worse, especially as this nation grows in wealth; for it is the history of all nations that as they develop great wealth, they progress toward abandon, degeneracy and racial extinction.

Mr. Moore, as is well known to everybody who has read the Blue Grass Blade for these many years, and from the very start of its publication, published it as an Infidel-Prohibition journal — its most distinctive feature being that of Prohibition. With all his might and power he has fought to protect the American home and the American youth from the far-reaching evils consequent upon the use of liquor, and this, too, in a community where more liquor is manufactured than any other place in the world. He has dared to do for the right that which no other man in his community would openly do, expose the hypocrites, religious and political, who occupied high places, by grace and permission of the manufacturer and retailer of whisky. That he has done this, many times at the risk of his life, is equally well known. He has been mobbed and imprisoned for his defense of "the [American] home." He has again been prosecuted and imprisoned and published as an editor of a Free Love paper, and an enemy of the American home. There are a million or more people in this country who know that the Blue Grass Blade was never anything else but an Infidel-Prohibition paper, and that Mr. Moore is not a Free Lover, and never was an advocate of Free Love, and more than any other man has scathingly denounced it. Having always bitterly opposed Free Love, I do not know how he happened to insert the two articles upon which he was indicted, and make the comments he did upon them. It can only be accounted for in this way: Mr. Moore believes in the open discussion of all sociological questions, especially those which affect the morals of the community. He opened his columns to the free discussion of every subject which seemed to him a moral or vital issue. Why should any paper subsidize a question involving a moral issue?

Mr. Moore is a man who believes that truth can stand any test, and that the best compliment we can pay to truth is to show our confidence in it. He is not a practical man in any sense. He applies policy to nothing he does. He is so frank and open in his manners and character that he is a mere child in some of the practical things of life. Carlyle says that "Caution is the lower story of prudence." Mr. Moore is seemingly devoid of that faculty, and for lack of it often says hasty, thoughtless and imprudent things. He has not even that caution essential to self-protection. Then he knew the law and should have been cautious enough not to have approached its limits. He knew that an infidel is liable to arrest if he steps out of Christian latitude; that superstition must have a victim occasionally; and the better the man, the more he is wanted; but no one who knows Mr. Moore will believe he would intentionally abuse the privilege of speech or instigate an immoral thought. His whole life belies such an action. It was the religious guerrilla's opportunity and he took advantage of it. When a man has to fight enemies of that kind, he should adopt like tactics, and not recklessly expose himself in the open.

Right here J. J. Rucker, a professed friend, a subscriber for years of the Blade, a co-worker with Mr. Moore along the line of Prohibition, comes upon the scene. Mr. Moore has requested that I should report the prosecution just as I witnessed it, and made no particular suggestion of what should be said whatever, further than to give the full details leading up to it. "For the rest," he said, "I am not the proper one to report my own grievances. It would not be received with the same spirit as if told by some one else, and I leave you untrammeled to present it as you choose." The readers of the Blade are acquainted with the circumstances which have led to the prosecution and imprisonment of Mr. Moore; but for those who are not I will enter into the full details, at the risk of being tedious. I will endeavor to report accurately and impartially, and while my sympathies are with Mr. Moore, they will not bias my judgment wherein I think he should not be spared.

Prof. Rucker, a Christian Prohibitionist, of Georgetown, Kentucky, and Mr. Moore were friends of long standing and co-workers in the Prohibition cause. Rucker patronized the Blade for years, and Moore sent his sons to the college presided over by Rucker, to be educated. Prohibition was the tie that bound. This friendship continued for some years. As it has been stated often in the Blade, Rucker started a rival prohibition sheet called "The Temperance Star." It is supposed by Moore and a great many others that Rucker thought that the Prohibition cause was not presented in its best light associated with Infidelity; and if Moore could successfully conduct a paper on the Infidel-Prohibition plan, he (Rucker) would startle Kentucky, as well as make a lot of money, by editing one on the Christian-Prohibition plan. He failed. His paper cut so little figure that people living within ten miles of Georgetown never heard of its existence. At some time within this period, Atherton, the Kentucky distiller, presented $7,000 in all to a church in which Rucker was an official, and to the college over which Rucker presided. These institutions accepted the money without protest. Moore finding this out, exposed Rucker's hypocrisy. Time and again he held this act of Rucker's up as an illustration of Christian pretension and inconsistency. This is Moore's side of the story. If it is not true Mr. Rucker has had a long time in which to obtain legal redress. It is to this exposition of Prof. Rucker's professed Prohibition and to religious hate that Mr. Moore attributes the revenge sought by reporting the Blade to the Postal inspectors about one year ago.

The postal authorities at Washington referred the matter to the District Attorney Harlan Cleveland, of Cincinnati, in which city the Blade was published. Cleveland drew up the indictment, and in the meantime was superceded as District Attorney by William Bundy, who prosecuted Moore and Hughes. Mr. Bundy is a nephew of Senator Foraker, through whose influence he secured the position of District Attorney. He is a young man, a successful lawyer, and stands high in the community. Judge Thompson comes from Portsmouth, Ohio, in which little city he has been a successful politician, having represented that district in Congress once or twice, and held minor political appointments. Mr. Moore and Mr. Hughes stood charged in the indictment with having mailed or caused to be mailed "certain lewd, lascivious and indecent matter." The statute under which they were indicted reads as follows:

"Section 333. Obscene matter. — "Every obscene, lewd or

lascivious book, pamphlet, picture, paper, letter, writing, print, or other publication of an indecent character, whether sealed as first-class matter or not, is hereby declared as non-mailable matter, and shall not be conveyed in the mails, nor delivered from any post-office, nor by any letter carrier; and any person who shall knowingly deposit or cause to be deposited for mailing or delivery anything declared by this section to be non-mailable matter, and any person who shall knowingly take the same or cause the same to be taken from the mails for the purpose of circulating, or disposing of, or aiding in the circulation or disposition of the same, shall for each and every offense be fined upon conviction thereof, not more than $5,000 or imprisoned at hard labor not more than five years, or both, at the discretion of the Court."

The trial began with the reading of the indictment, and the statute covering the case. Judge Feland, of Lawrenceburg, Ky., asked the court for a separate trial, stating that he had been engaged as counsel for Mr. Hughes, but not for Mr. Moore. This situation of the case had the effect of obtaining a separate trial, which was protested by the District Attorney, but reluctantly granted by the court. Otherwise Mr. Hughes would most probably have received the same sentence as Mr. Moore. The court summoned the jury and the trial of Mr. Moore commenced. Very unwisely, Mr. Moore assumed charge of his case, and doing so verified the old adage of the man who acts in the capacity of his own legal adviser.

The first witness in behalf of the government was a man, the daily practice of whose life has been to do good to those who hate him; to do as he would be done by; to return good for evil; to turn the other cheek when smitten; in fact a man who is the most perfect illustration of the Christian (?) gentleman that Kentucky can produce; Prof. J. J. Rucker, of Georgetown, the shining Prohibition light, the man of strange bed-fellows, Atherton, Moore, &c..

Rucker is both an anatomical and facial study — cavernous-faced, tall, gaunt, hollow-chested, narrow, as perfect a case of splenetic and debilitated piety as ever trod the halls of justice. When he ascended the steps and seated himself in the witness chair, he threw his long bony pedestals into a double twist, folded his arms majestically and assumed the air of one of those grand, gloomy and peculiar geniuses, who are given to the habit of wrapping themselves, Napoleon like, in the solitude of their own originality. His whole bearing seemed to say, "Here I am, Mr. Moore, and this is my inning." Revenge, which is always the weak

193

pleasure of a little and narrow mind, was written all over his furrowed face. There is no passion of the human heart that promises so much and pays so little as revenge. It is at first sweet, but becomes bitter ere long and recoils back on itself. Bacon better explained it in these words, "A man that studieth revenge keepeth his own wounds green, which otherwise would heal and do well."

If Prof. Rucker sought revenge, he is now tasting its first sweets. He should be satisfied. He took advantage of Mr. Moore's weakness to write and print unguarded thoughts, and he has been the means of sending him to the penitentiary for two long years. In doing this, he has broken up a happy home, and saddened the hearts of Mrs. Moore and others who never did him wrong. "Christian charity!" "Do unto others as ye would have others do unto you!" When he sits around his comfortable fire-side at night, if he has a conscience above an adder, he will think of the fire-side he has made desolate, and the sad hearts that sit around it. If down in the cold storage of his bleak anatomy there be a single warm spot, when he reclines on his comfortable couch at night, the vision of an aged prisoner stretched on the iron cot of his narrow, stony cell will haunt and haunt his wandering thoughts. But such a vision may possibly never disturb his dreams. The grace of God, which aboundeth so fully in his heart, and that love which passeth all understanding, may give him such perfect peace, as will enable him to sleep well. He has had his Christian revenge — that revenge which the Lord claimed as his own, and with which man should not repay.

In a strange contrast, let me describe another scene. When Mr. Moore was led from the court room to one adjoining, containing a cell, a number of friends followed to express their sympathy and bid him farewell. Fearing that his son, Leland, a manly young fellow, was nursing revengeful thoughts, he said, "Son, I fear you are meditating revenge. Go home, and take no further action in the case. Whatever you do, I would not have you hurt Prof. Rucker or bring sorrow to his family. If you would please me in one thing more than another, observe this request. I would rather go to prison than have you hurt Prof. Rucker." In a moment like this a man's true nature comes to the surface. I have deviated from my report of the prosecution to introduce the Christian and the Infidel, in the light of the revenge, as they appear in this trial.

The District Attorney upon opening the trial introduced Mr. Moore to the Judge's attention as a Free Lover, and editor of a Free Love paper. Mr. Moore arose to object, but was called down by the court. The District Attorney questioned Mr. Rucker as to receiving certain copies of the Blue Grass Blade through the mail, and as to his marking certain items in these particular copies and forwarding the paper to Washington. Rucker identified the paper which he had thus mailed to the postal department.

Mr. Moore in cross examination received not a single direct reply to a question that he had asked. Rucker was quick to see that the charge and evidence so far, proclaimed Mr. Moore the advocate and publisher of a Free Love paper. He knew the effect this would have on a jury, and questioning him as closely as he could, Mr. Moore did not succeed in getting Rucker to state the principles advocated and known all over Kentucky to be advocated, by the Blue Grass Blade. The following is the questioning in part:

Moore — "How long have you been a subscriber to the Blue Grass Blade?"

Rucker — "Well, for a number of years."

Moore — "How many years?"

Rucker — "Well, I don't know just exactly."

Moore — "Did you take it when it was first published?"

Rucker — "I guess I began taking it about that time."

Moore — "How long ago was that?"

Rucker — "Several years ago."

Moore — "Do you not distinctly know that it was just thirteen years ago?"

Rucker — "I am not certain of the date."

Moore — "Did it advocate Free Love when you first subscribed for it?"

Rucker — "I cannot say."

Moore — "Have you read it closely enough to know what it has advocated?"

Rucker — "I cannot say that I have?"

Moore — "Have you read it as closely as you do the ordinary newspapers?"

Rucker — "Well, yes, at times."

Moore — "And you don't know the principles that it advocates?"

Rucker — "Well, I have noticed that it advocates a variety of things."

Moore — "Do you not know, as well as you know you are sitting there, that my paper is an Infidel-Prohibitionist paper, that it is now such, has always been such, and is now regarded by everybody as such?"

To this Rucker gave some evasive reply, and Moore again pinned him to the question. The court here interfered and protected Rucker. "But, your Honor." said Mr. Moore, "the District Attorney charged me with being a Free Lover, and a publisher of a Free Love paper. It is false, every word of it, and I want to prove it by Prof. Rucker himself, who, if he tells the truth, will say that it is false."

Here Moore lost his head; the unfairness exasperated him and his address to the Court was impertinent, but just and natural enough under the circumstances. The Court reminded him that he was at liberty to conduct his own case, but he must observe the usual rules of propriety; that a fair trial would be given him, and there was no inclination on the part of the Court to persecute him. Moore asked His Honor if he would again be permitted to question Prof. Rucker. The court replied that he could summon him if he wished. Later on, when Mr. Moore asked that Prof. Rucker be called to the stand, it was found that Prof. Rucker had drawn his witness fees and taken his departure for home. Moore said, "Why, Your Honor, you told me that I would be permitted to question him again." "Well," said His Honor, "I guess he has gone home. You ought to have —" (the rest I did not hear). This is some of the guaranteed "fairness." After that Mr. Moore became rattled and an Indian statue in front of a cigar store could have put up almost as able a defense; that is from a legal standpoint.

Here was a man who had been taking the Blade most of the time for thirteen years and didn't know what it advocated. If Rucker ever knew much of anything he don't look like it. Maybe when he is called to the witness stand again he'll know something about it. In my opinion, the worst reflection that can be cast upon Mr. Moore is that he should ever have had anything to do with a man who knows so little.

During the noon recess, I talked to the District Attorney, and told him that his charge that the Blue Grass Blade is a Free Love paper was absolutely false; that he certainly was misinformed; that he could not afford to have it known to the thousands of Liberals in this city that he had misrepresented Mr. Moore; that it was very evident that he would succeed in convicting Mr. Moore anyhow, without misrepresenting him and convicting him on a false charge; that it looked to me that it was the Infidel aimed at.

He replied: "If it is not a Free Love paper, I would like to know what you call it?" I answered, "These two papers you have in your possession are the only issues ever sent out by Mr. Moore which contained articles on Free Love, except issues in which he had scathingly denounced it, and to my knowledge no man in the country had more forcibly denounced it than Mr. Moore. I asked him if he considered the Enquirer a Christian paper, because it inserts church notes in its columns every week, and occasionally prints Talmage's sermons, or, if he called the Times-Star an infidel paper, because it always inserts Ingersoll's lectures when he appears here?" When the court was called at 2 p.m., Mr. Bundy began his speech by stating that he had been told that the Blue Grass Blade was not a Free Love paper, that he did not want to misrepresent Mr. Moore, or prosecute any man for his peculiar beliefs, but if those two copies before him were not Free Love papers, he didn't know what to call them.

It is thus seen that he started out seemingly to correct the charge, but in the end made it more forcible than ever. Some more "fairness." Then he read the passages upon which the indictment was made, and called attention to some other articles in the paper upon which he was not indicted. These he had no business to introduce, for they were not pertinent to the case. If Mr. Moore had introduced foreign matter he would have been called down abruptly. He called the jury's attention to the first article in the paper, in which Mr. Moore discussed some atheistic question, and said the "paper was full of blasphemous articles like that, and if he was not mistaken, he (Moore) could be indicted for blasphemy as well as Free Love. It was a terrible thing for Mr. Moore to "insinuate" Free Love doctrines in his paper, but all right for Mr. Bundy to "insinuate" the crime of atheism and blasphemy against Mr. Moore, in his speech to the jury, when Mr. Moore was being tried only for Free Love statements. Some more "fairness." What would more prejudice a Christian jury against a man than to be charged with atheism? Was Mr. Moore on trial for atheism? Then Mr. Bundy launched out in a spread eagle speech about "the American home," that would have done credit to Ben Butterworth in his palmiest days, when addressing a country political meeting. It was the same old speech, almost word for word, that I have heard McKinley, Foraker, and a dozen other politicians give when addressing the hay-seed audiences I used to attend. He told how the statute had been provided for just such cases as this, to protect the American youth and the American home from such "vile, lascivious, lewd and indecent stuff," as charged in this indictment.

Mr. Bundy well knew, and I subsequently told him so, that the mails are loaded to the guards with the Bible, which contains such "vile, lascivious, lewd and indecent stuff" that the clergy of Michigan and other States are having this "vile, lascivious, lewd and indecent stuff" eliminated for an abbreviated Bible, so it will be fit to put in the hands of school children; that this abbreviated Bible is for the purpose of concealing "the vile, lascivious, lewd and indecent stuff" from the pure minds of childhood. He knows that this book contains among its grand pages a record of all the vile practices of primitive times; that this is the advocate and source of polygamy, that it contains the "nasty, dirty, lewd, lascivious and indecent" songs of Solomon; the suggestive amours of David; the incest of Lot; the crime of Onan, and what not that is viciously and immorally suggestive. He knows that this book is in his own home, and in nearly every "American home" for the preservation of whose morals he is so tenderly sensitive. He knows, too, that the commercial press sends through the mails into American homes all the dirty rape, divorce and other morbid, suggestive and criminal news it can rake up; and that many of them contain column after column of plain assignations, and that these papers go into his own home and into the hands of his own children.

Mr. Moore has not been very choice in his language; but if he had ever printed and sent through the mails half as dirty stuff as is contained in the Bible and the commercial press, I would not be losing my sleep to defend him to-night. I do not approve of Mr. Moore's slangy style of expression. I do not excuse him. Because the Bible is nasty in parts, is no reason that he should be uncouth in some instances in his paper. All the more shame to the infidel who fails to dignify and exalt speech. He is supposed to have progressed beyond Bible influence. The trouble with Moore is that he was a preacher once and has never gotten out of the rut.

Mr. Bundy's talk about the American home was pretty enough, and no doubt touched the right spot in the jury's hearts. But considering the passage through the mails of the indecent stuff in the Bible, and the columns of assignations, sent right into American homes, it sounded strangely inconsistent, when he declared that the law provided that statute purposely to cover such ideas as those for which Mr. Moore stood indicted. But Bundy had a duty to perform; and that was to send an old man on the down grade of life to the penitentiary — for what? For murder, theft, slander, burglary, or vice of any kind? No! What then? Why for sending through the mails a private opinion upon a social question which many people dispute about — a question that does not come up to the standard of Bible purity (?).

Bundy, like Rucker, went about his duty as systematically as determinedly. He, a young man of health and promise. To me it was a strange sight to see a youth, almost, bending his best energies to imprison a man whose years are few, for a most trifling offense, as compared to some which are committed against the postal law, and which go unnoticed day by day. I could not have done it. I doubt if Bundy sleeps well over it. I have this now to ask of every friend of Freethought:

"What has the gray-haired prisoner done?
Has murder stained his hands with gore?
Not so; his crime's a fouler one."

He is an infidel. That appears to be Moore's chief crime, all the way from Rucker to the penitentiary. That was Paine's crime, for which a nation he almost created has condemned him to hate and infamy. It was the crime of Copernicus and Galileo, and Vanini and Bruno and Servetus.

I do not know that it is so, but from my close observation of this trial I am impressed with the belief that it was not a fair one, but had the object in view of suppressing Moore by confining him. Anyhow, I believe it was Rucker's object. Bundy, in one sentence, called the jury's attention to Moore's atheism, and his liability to indictment for blasphemy, and in the next declared "that Mr. Moore was not being prosecuted for his peculiar beliefs." Whether this was intentional upon the part of Mr. Bundy or not, I do not know. But I do know the effect that such an "insinuation" will have upon a Christian jury, and I know it was not fair, and I know that if Moore had had a capable lawyer, Bundy would have been compelled to confine himself to the Free Love indictment. It is this, along with some other things, that impresses me as I have stated.

Mr. Moore's defense in reply to Mr. Bundy's speech was about as weak an effort as a man could possibly make. He seemed rattled and talked incoherently, and more about himself than the indictment. But there was some excuse for this. He knew he was going to be sent to prison. At the noon recess he told me that he felt it in the Judge's countenance; and that the accusation of publishing a Free Love paper, which he felt he would not be given a chance to disprove, depressed him greatly. What with the pugnaciousness of the District Attorney and a Christian jury to face, he felt that he was already condemned. He began to realize his position, and thought his best plan was to appeal to the jury and tell them about himself and his family, and impress them, if he could, that he was something more than a Kentucky moonshiner or counterfeiter. His talk excited more amusement than sympathy, as was plainly seen in the faces of the jury. The Judge leaned his head upon his hand, and to all appearances went to sleep. Likewise, a juryman inclined his head and appeared to be asleep. Moore was allowed to talk fifteen minutes, when the Judge stopped him and reminded him that he was not talking to the point and asked him how much time he expected. Mr. Moore told him "that he had not even begun yet, but if he wanted to stop him at any time just to say the word and he would quit." "All right," said the Judge, "I will take you at your word and tell you when you have exhausted your time."

Mr. Moore took up his paper which contained the language so offensive to Rucker's pious optics, and, beginning with the first article, attempted to show that his paper was not a Free Love paper, but that it was an Infidel-Prohibition paper. He took up each article separately, read the headings, and commented on the matter discussed, doing his best in his feeble and choked up way to prove to the jury, none of whom knew anything about his paper, that it was not a Free Love journal. Why should not a man have the right and be granted the time to disprove a false charge against him?

The Court permitted him to talk fifteen minutes, and abruptly told him that his time was up, and to sit down. He then charged the jury, and sent them off to the jury-room. It only required five minutes for them to declare a verdict of guilty.

I have this now to say about Mr. Moore's trial. I have been in the Police Court in this city, where a thief, with only a thirty days' workhouse sentence confronting him, was given more respectful consideration than was given Mr. Moore in this trial. I have seen old bums tried for loitering, and their rambling tales told, without the Judge resting his head as inclined to sleep, or to express his weariness.

I have attended trials where a man was being tried for sheep stealing, trials lasting more than a week — yes, for weeks at a time — with the examination of many witnesses to go through with, and lawyers spending a half a day at a time in a single speech, but Mr. Moore was allowed a little pitiful thirty minutes to go over a defense which involved a far-reaching and critical examination, which required the most delicate handling before a jury, which, from appearance, would be slow in comprehension of an analytical subject of any kind. When time was called on Mr. Moore, he had come to himself and was presenting a good argument.

Mr. Moore did not summon a single witness, while he might have had fifty if he had so chosen. Since he occupied no time in his defense by the examination of the witnesses, it looks as though he ought, at least, to have had a reasonable amount of time generally occupied in taking testimony.

Whether Mr. Moore presented his case in a rustic manner or not; whether he was a little uncouth in observing the dignified proprieties of a United States Court, still he is an American citizen, and without witnesses, and a Christian jury to face, his very weakness should have been his defense. He was acting as his own lawyer, and he had a right to tell it in his own way, and a right to the time to tell it — that is, if free speech and the right of defense are still one of the guarantees of American citizenship.

When the jury's verdict of "guilty" was handed in, the District Attorney asked for sentence at once. The Judge said he wanted some time to consider it, and would give it at ten o'clock the next morning, at which time Moore and Hughes were called before His Honor. In passing sentence the judge said: "Mr. Moore, I am inclined to be more lenient with you than you deserve. You knew the law, you had been warned that you were violating it, you continued to violate it, and you still boast of it." "Yes," said Mr. Moore, "I am proud of everything I have done." "Well, then, I will not give you half of what you ought to have. Your sentence is that you will be confined in the Ohio Penitentiary for two years and stand charged with the cost of indictment until it can be paid." This is the sentence as near as I can remember it. I am writing this report entirely from memory, as I took no notes.

I had expected Mr. Moore to receive a stiff fine, but I was not prepared for a sentence like that. And when that sentence fell from the Judge's lips, I said to myself, "Verily there is no more mercy in the hearts of some men than there is milk in a male tiger."

Previous to this sentence Mr. Moore was asked if he had anything to say why sentence should not be passed upon him. He said he had, and was told to take oath. "Your Honor," he said, "I have some scruples about taking oath as it is generally given." Here he was interrupted by the judge, saying, "I don't want any more trifling here." "Well," said Mr. Moore, "I don't believe in a God, and will not take the oath; I wish to affirm." "Affirm him!" said the Judge, impatiently.

Then Mr. Moore said that he had been indicted and prosecuted on a false charge, that he was neither a Free Lover, nor the editor of a Free Love paper; but since he had been declared guilty, he appealed to the Court's mercy, saying that a heavy fine would bankrupt his family, that his farm was mortgaged for $5,000, which was one-third of its valuation; that he neither raised race horses, nor corn for whisky, and a farmer in his part of the country who discarded these markets, had a hard time to get along. "Above all," said he, "I want to take all the responsibility of this case upon my shoulders. Whatever fine or imprisonment is to be meted out, let it fall upon me, and not upon Mr. Hughes. I want him to go back home to-night to his wife and baby."

Then, to the consternation of all the Liberals present, as well as to many others, the awful sentence of imprisonment for two years was given. Mr. Hughes was then fined $25.00 and costs, [amounting] to

201

$76.00. It was the quiet, skillful work of Judge Feland, and fine legal tactics, that saved Hughes. If Mr. Moore had employed Judge Feland, who had studied the case and came prepared for it, this defense would have been at least presented with dignity and ability, even if he did not escape imprisonment. But every Liberal present believes that it is doubtful whether legal talent would have greatly mitigated the sentence.

After the trial was over a lawyer present stepped up to me and said, "Men will fight and die for liberty, and then put men into office who will rob them of it."

I left the court-room and followed Mr. Bundy to his office, five or six doors away. While sitting in the waiting-room another lawyer, whom I had seen in the court-room all the morning, stepped to the telephone and communicated with someone about the Moore trial. He said, "It is the most outrageous sentence ever given in that court-room."

I waited till I got opportunity to see Mr. Bundy, and told him that the sentence imposed was cruel, and that I intended to appeal, and wanted to know what time I had, and what would be the bond. He replied that he "did not think that Judge Thompson would grant an appeal; that it lay entirely with the Judge to fix the bond; that Moore had gotten a fair trial, and that he came off easy, as the Chicago Record man was imprisoned two years for a much less offense." From this I judge a precedent had been looked up, and confirms my impression that he was doomed to imprisonment from the start. I asked what steps I should take in making an appeal. He said, "I advise you to get a lawyer, and you can only get an appeal on a Writ of Error granted by Judge Thompson, but I don't think it will do any good."

"All right," said I, "[I'll] get the lawyer, and there is plenty of error to appeal from. All I want is the time to make it, and secure bondsmen."

I sent Clark and Kaplun and other members of the Ohio Liberal Society out to communicate with other influential Liberals, while I went to see a legal adviser, Judge Feland unfortunately having gone home the night before. I returned in one hour and found that Moore had been handcuffed and hustled off to Columbus just thirty minutes after I left Bundy's office. Whether the haste to get him away was due to the prospective appeal, I do not know. I would not do Mr. Bundy the injustice to insinuate it. This case was a legacy to him from his predecessor in office. As District Attorney it was his duty to prosecute it. If he did so conscientiously, he but performed his duty.

As to the injustice of his methods, and the justice of the sentence, that is another thing, and this is what I want to call to the attention of Liberals throughout the country.

In justice to the Court, I will say that Mr. Moore was offered the services of a lawyer, which he refused, and if he had argued more to the point in the beginning, I am satisfied the Court would have given him more time. I want to say, too, that Mr. Moore has very few friends among the Liberals in this city. He has lambasted them as much as ever he did Rucker, and alienated most of them, and they do not regard him as a representative Freethought propagandist. Whatever action they may take in this case, then, cannot be regarded as due to personal attachment to Mr. Moore. The principle involved is more to them than the man. The Ohio Liberal Society has already entered an appeal, and intends to fight the case. As this Society is not particularly friendly to Mr. Moore, and as it is here on the ground, the Freethinkers throughout the country can trust to its actions and believe that its condemnation of this sentence merits the help and assistance of every organized Society and individual Liberalist. For myself, I say that Mr. Moore deserves censure. He had been warned by Mr. Betts, the Postoffice Inspector, but did not heed it, and thus exposed himself to prosecution.

He had been appealed to by his best friends, and time and again rebuked by his subscribers for using language neither dignified nor refined. But he is imprisoned under a false charge. The language upon which he was indicted was neither "lewd," "obscene," nor "lascivious," as charged by the District Attorney. In fact, the words themselves are as chaste as a paragraph from Addison. The substance of the speech is all that can be called into question, whether or not it is of an "indecent character." You will notice, if you refer back to the statute previously quoted, that an offense of this kind involves the use of words and language which are "obscene, lewd, lascivious, or of indecent character." If Mr. Moore's language, for which he was indicted, was all of these, his sentence was just under the law. But it was certainly neither of the first three, and as to being of an "indecent character," that is a debatable question. Is an opinion, clothed in chaste words, expressed of any of the natural appetites, regarded by the law as indecent? That is the question. If not, Mr. Moore is a wrongly-imprisoned man, and the charge against him is as false as the statement that he is a Free Lover and editor of a Free Love paper. I understand it was decided by the Superior Court of Illinois that the public discussion of love, free or otherwise, is not "indecent."

Mr. Bundy dwelt largely upon the "suggestiveness" of Mr. Moore's language, saying that "it suggested indiscriminate relation of the sexes, and therefore damnable, lewd and indecent." What is "suggestion"? "To the pure all things are pure." "Evil to him who evil thinks." Where does the law draw the line at "suggestion"? Marriage itself is only legalized sexuality, and why may not the "suggestion" of marriage itself incline to the thought of lasciviousness? Why may not the discussion of love after marriage be as "suggestive of indecency" as before marriage?

When closely analyzed, as between Bundy's speech and Moore's, it is hard to tell which one is to be pitied most for its weakness. Moore's was incoherent, and Bundy's puerile and merely assertive. It proved nothing. Mr. Moore, in his defense, was not allowed the time to define, weigh and analyze the words which are charged to be obscene. When ordered to stop by the court, he was making what I thought was a very good argument. He was endeavoring to prove to the jury, by showing them the contents of the paper that it was not a "Free Love" journal. It was a new thing to me, to see a man on trial, with his liberty involved, called down while he was making his best point to prove his innocence. Suppose he had been indicted for advocating a Christian principle such as Paul advocated — that "it is best for a man not to marry at all." Is there anything more offensive to our marriage laws than that? Can anything be more "suggestive" of Free Love than that?

The Ohio Liberal Society intends to carry this question to the Supreme Court and test it. The question, more than the man, it thinks vital. It involves free speech and a fair trial. It concerns every Agnostic, Atheist, Deist, Socialist, Spiritualist, Materialist, and Freethinker of every description in this country. If this Comstock law is to be pushed with such vigor as to send men to the penitentiary for mailing such language as Mr. Moore used, it must also be applied as vigorously in other directions. We demand fair play. Obscenity, lasciviousness and suggestiveness in the Bible are ranker in quality than any that ever appeared in the Blue Grass Blade, or in most any other print for that matter. We want to know if this Comstock law is made for the infidel and not for the preacher. We want to know just what and who it covers. We want to know and have it settled whether sacred vulgarity has privilege before the law that is not to be granted to the plain, ordinary kind. We want to know if the infidel has the right to a fair trial. Infidels furnished the hands and the brains and the money when the foundations of this country were laid. The whole Republican principles of government as adopted were the outgrowth of the teachings of Thomas Paine, an infidel. Jefferson, an infidel, wrote its Declaration of Independence, Girard, an infidel, supplied its treasury, and Washington, an infidel, fought its battles. Christianity is essentially monarchical. It never had any idea of government above the aristocratic. It has a king at its head. It expects to live in a kingdom in the world to come, where Rucker and all the rest will wear crowns.

The principles of this government were not conceived in the head of a Bishop. They were conceived in the head, the glorious head, of Thomas Paine. Freethought is the child of that conception. It wants now, to know whether it has any rights of that inheritance in this country; whether it is to be brow-beaten in our courts; whether it is to be made a foot-ball of for pious pastime.

We do not propose to make a martyr of Mr. Moore. If he inclines to pose as such, he will lose the respect of his friends. It is charged by the District Attorney, the newspapers and his enemies that Mr. Moore is assuming a martyr's role. While he exhibited a foolish egotism in choosing to act as his own lawyer, I will say that his actions before the Court, his manner and emotions, and his child-like appeal to the jury and to the Judge for clemency, all evinced a desire to escape punishment. He showed an eagerness to put the legality of free speech to the test, and this eagerness, I think, was construed by the Court to be an insolence and a desire to pose as a persecuted individual. Mr. Moore has always been a man who has been willing to put his principles to a legal test, no matter what personal sacrifices he might be called upon to make. Many of his friends, as well as his enemies, have thought that he courted imprisonment for notoriety. I am led to believe by his actions in this trial, and by my conversations with him, that in this case this was a mistake. But when it comes to making a legal test of free speech, he has always been on hand. Considering the hundreds of thousands of Freethinkers who cowardly remain under cover, for myself I respect the one man who is brave enough, reckless enough if you will, to charge down the front line of battle, even if he has no other object in view than notoriety. The front is the most respectable place for a man to go down. This fight is on and must be settled in the courts. It may as well be settled right now. I ask the Liberals of this country if it isn't about time that men should cease being sent to the penitentiary for their free opinions and open assertions upon dogmatic theology. If it isn't about time that a man can express his views about one of the human emotions without being deprived of his liberty.

The Ohio Liberal Society has employed the law firm of Phares & Keller, of Cincinnati, to test the case. It has already put up $100.00. It will probably cost two or three times that amount, and maybe more, to carry the case to a Superior Court. It needs this extra amount and doubts not that it will be forthcoming. The treasurer of the Ohio Liberal Society, J.C. Wilms, Northwest corner Eighth and Vine, will receive contributions.

I call upon the Liberal organizations and all Liberal papers of this country to rise up as one in protest that will be heard and felt. Christianity when passive and tolerant is docile enough, and develops many of the humane instincts. But let it feel the intoxication of power, and it develops at once the brutal instincts which inbred superstition always excites. Many people in this country think an Atheist or Agnostic has no right to citizenship whatever. Let cases like Mr. Moore's go unchallenged, and it is only a question of time until the Agnostic, if he dares express himself, will follow him.

Back in the days of Bloody Mary, the Catholic savages of England killed off the Protestant savages by thousands. In course of time it came the Protestant's turn, and Catholic property was confiscated, and every offensive Catholic priest executed. Down in Cornwall, a mining region, was a priest by the name of Trelawny, who was much beloved by the miners, and who was ordered to be taken and executed. His people flocked around him and the local authorities found that he could not be taken. The King found it necessary to send an army down there. About thirty thousand of the rough miners gathered together as one man, and with nothing but their picks and such rude instruments as they could quickly manufacture, defied the King's army. As they marched in procession, they sang this verse:

> "And shall Trelawny die?
> And shall Trelawny die?
> When thirty thousand Cornishmen
> Will know the reason why?"

Their determined opposition dissuaded the King from making any further effort to get Trelawny. The stubborn protest of Freethinkers will arouse a sentiment that will likewise have its effect.

Will the Liberals of this country allow Mr. Moore to lie in the Ohio penitentiary for two years, without rising up as one man and asking "the reason why?"

J. B. WILSON, M. D.

The Lexington Standard, edited by a Negro, in the interest of Negroes, printed the following:

206

A PETITION TO THE PRESIDENT
OF THE UNITED STATES ASKING FOR THE PARDON
OF C.C. MOORE FROM THE OHIO PENITENTIARY

The Blue Grass Blade came back at us rather savagely last week in reply to our little squib regarding Editor C. C. Moore's probable incarceration by the Federal Courts for the offense charged against him of misusing the mails. The fact is, what we said was merely in a Pickwickian sense — in the usual spirit of editorial picket-firing. We felt no animus toward Editor Moore, and have none now. On the contrary, we deeply sympathize with him in his present misfortune, feeling that he has been unjustly incarcerated.

We appreciate the moral courage and integrity of the man who, in ante-bellum days, could stand up and denounce slavery as wrong. Such men belong to the class of true friends of the Negro race. We appreciate all the good qualities that shine like stars through and from behind Editor Moore's eccentricities. We believe him to be strictly honest and courageous in all that he advocates, and do not feel like joining in with the preachers and professors of religion who are crying, "Crucify him."

To show that we are in earnest in this matter, we start a petition for the pardon of Editor Moore, beginning the list with our signature, and we ask every Negro in Kentucky to sign it. We have no doubt that we will get more than a thousand names. To insure bona fide signatures we shall canvass the State in person while traveling in the interest of The Standard, and by correspondence through the medium of friends, giving the movement our unqualified editorial endorsement until success is attained, and our white brother of the press breathes the pure air of freedom again. The following is the form of the petition we shall circulate:

To William McKinley, President of the United States:
YOUR EXCELLENCY — Charles Chilton Moore, of Lexington, Kentucky, editor of the Blue Grass Blade, formerly published in Cincinnati, having been indicted by a Federal Grand Jury, charged with sending obscene matter through the mails, upon which charge the said Charles Chilton Moore was tried in the said city of Cincinnati and sentenced to two years' imprisonment in the Ohio penitentiary; now, therefore,

We, the undersigned, Negro citizens of Kentucky, petition Your Excellency to pardon Charles Chilton Moore for these reasons: We are of the opinion that the offense was of a technical character and not sufficient to warrant the punishment inflicted; that the person, or persons, who brought said charge and prosecuted the same did so on account of prejudice to said Moore. His long service in the cause of temperance, the exposure of shams and frauds, and the unmasking of charlatans, by his trenchant pen, should entitle him to clemency. Mr. Moore is an old man, and incarceration in the penitentiary will not only impair his already precarious health, but it is liable to cause his premature death.

We desire, further, to call your attention to the fact that Mr. Moore has a family dependent upon him for support, and his absence from home is not only liable to cause domestic suffering but serious anguish, which in all probability will shorten the life of his aged wife.

We hope, after a careful reading of this petition and accompanying letters, you will not hesitate to grant the pardon sought.

R. C. O. BENJAMIN, Editor Standard, Lexington, Ky.

With this closes my book to the point that I wrote it in the penitentiary, I having completed it and sent it to my family in one month after I had been imprisoned. Since that time I have been liberated, and I am writing now at my home, "Quakeracre," on the farm, eight miles north of Lexington. I am writing now on Sunday, December 17, 1899, my book having been printed nearly up to this point.

I will end this story of my life by telling, in one chapter, an outline of my experience from the time I was sent to the penitentiary up to the date, and that will be —

Chapter XI

When I was sentenced to the penitentiary at Columbus, I had never seen any penitentiary except the very common one at Frankfort, Kentucky, from a distance, and once, twenty years before, for hardly more than five minutes, inside. A prisoner had just cut a guard when I got there, and I heard him telling how he was going to whip the prisoner. Naturally, my impressions of penitentiaries were not very pleasant. I got to Columbus about 4 o'clock in the evening of February 8, 1899. The train stopped and let me and the officer off near the penitentiary, before getting to the station. The thermometer stood then, or very soon after, from 15° to 20° below zero.

When I came in sight of the building I found it a very large and a very elegant house. It had then over 2,300 prisoners in it. When I came into the office the warm air felt pleasant. The officer who had charge of me took the handcuffs off of me, and I was told to take off my overcoat, and I, of course, did so. A man, whom I subsequently found to be Warden E. G. Coffin, said to me, in rather a rough voice and manner, "What were you sent here for?" I said, "I don't know." He said, "Another innocent man sent here, ha!" in a tone of irony. I said nothing. He was a man fully six feet high, and weighed 200 pounds. He seemed to have an ordinarily good face. He was about 70 years old, and well preserved for a man of his years.

He said to a guard, who was waiting to take charge of me, "He is too old to work." I said to him, "You see that my hair and beard are very long; please do not cut them off until the weather moderates, as it would endanger my health; my habit is to wear my hair and beard long in the cold weather, and cut them off only once a year, at sheep-shearing time." He said to the guard, "Tell them not to cut his hair and beard without further orders from me."

The guard took me into a hall in an old part of the prison, and allowed me to stand by a stove in the hall. I knew nothing at all about regulations, but, of course, conducted myself like a gentleman. Some prisoners who had special privileges, a dozen or two of them, came to me, and, in the presence of the guards, talked to me. They were anxious to know about me, and I talked to them perfectly freely, the guards hearing or not hearing, as suited them. A prisoner who had listened to me said, "You won't be here long." That same thing was said to me by several prisoners. I do not know, to this day, whether they meant I would not be in the penitentiary at all, or would not be in that particular division of the prison. I did not then know that there was any better part of the prison, and from the fact that all of them said it was an outrage that I had been sent there, I rather thought they meant to say that I would not be in the penitentiary long. Several of them told me in a quarter of an hour after they saw me and heard me talk, that my case was not at all like that of any body there, and they condemned the court that had sentenced me in bitter terms. I saw at once that there was a general understanding among the prisoners that I had been falsely imprisoned, and they showed me their sympathy and respect in every way. I talked just as freely as I wanted to do, the guards not seeming to want to stop me, but plainly being interested in all that I said. The prisoners were ordered to fall into line for supper, and I went with them into the dining room, where all but fifty or one hundred ate. I had not eaten anything since breakfast, but was not hungry. All of the supper that anybody there had was some stewed raisins, cold baker's bread and coffee, or imitation of coffee, with neither milk nor sugar in it. I could not eat it, and sat waiting for the order to rise. Nobody was allowed to speak a word. When we were all marched back I was directed by the guard to follow him to my cell. His name was Kolb, and he was always a good friend to me. The cell ranges were five stories high, and I was in the second story. My cell was about four feet broad, seven feet long and six feet high to the lowest part of the arched roof. The door to it was about two feet wide and five feet high.

There was an iron bed, three feet wide, with coarse covering on it, and a straw pillow. There was no furniture but a wooden stool. There was a small gas jet. On a small shelf, above the door, I saw a book, and took it down. It was a Bible. I opened it at random. It was at the story of "Ezekiel's vision of the dry bones in the valley of Jehoshaphat." It seemed to me something of a coincidence. I had several times in print alluded to that story as a sample of the dull reading of the Bible. I laid the book back upon the shelf, and did not touch it any more.

I was locked in my cell about 6 o'clock. I had not been there more than a half hour before a bright-faced young man came to my cell-door, and was introduced to me by the guard as Howard, reporter for the Press-Post of Columbus. His face and manner and talk and everything showed that he was much interested in my case. He knew I was a newspaper man, and asked me to give him a full report of my case, and of my antecedents and of myself. I did so, he taking notes rapidly, occasionally asking me to stop a little when he could not keep up with his notes. The article for his paper next day was two and a half columns of fine print, and pictures of me, representing me as a prisoner, as a preacher, as an editor, and as a pedestrian tourist. It was exceedingly complimentary of me. There were one or two small mistakes that did me a little injustice, and one or two that did me more than justice — said good things about me, regarded morally and intellectually, that were more than I deserved, so that as a whole the report was at least fair to me, and possibly a little more than I deserved. He brought me a copy of it next day, and we were friends as long as I was in prison.

I soon saw that the papers of the city were divided in their estimate of Warden Coffin. Those that were for him were for me, and those that were against him were against me, but the preponderance of newspaper influence of the city was for both of us.

I soon noticed that all officers and prisoners spoke in complimentary terms of the Warden. I supposed that was policy, and it did not affect my estimate of him. I was not entirely pleased with his manner to me, but noticed that all he did was fully as kind, or more so, than I had expected.

Before 8 o'clock, the time at which a bell rang for us to go to bed, and the gas was turned off, a young boy who was a prisoner there from Lexington, Ky., and who had been sent there from some far Western State, and who had a hall permit, came to my door, and told me that he had brought me a sandwich. He broke it into two pieces, so as to get it through the grates of my cell-door. It was of light bread and potted ham. I thanked him heartily, of course. It refreshed me, and I enjoyed it the more because I thought a guard must be conniving at his giving it to me, showing that the guard was friendly to me.

When I was finally left to myself, I sat on the side of my bed to think over the situation and to realize that I was really in the penitentiary[.] There was not a single unhappy thought about it except the unhappiness that I knew my condition was giving my wife and children. I cried some when I thought about that, but except that, I felt proud and happy that I had stood by the convictions of my conscience until it had taken me to where I was. I felt convinced that good people everywhere would honor me, and that as soon as I could get a letter to my wife and family, I would greatly relieve their minds. I went to sleep feeling quite happy, but believing that I would wake some time during the night and be horrified that I was in a penitentiary cell. I did wake, I suppose about midnight; the whole situation flashed through my mind in a second. I just said to myself, "I am here for having done right, and the world will be better and happier that it is so," and I dropped into a sweet sleep in a few minutes, and slept until the bell aroused me in the morning.

The guard said to me, "We will make better arrangements for you in a day or two."

The next morning for my breakfast I was taken to a place they call "Jericho," where an average of about 75 prisoners ate, and the eating was a good deal better than in the regular place for the other prisoners to eat, and we were not marched into and out of it, and could sit and eat as long as we cared to. Only prisoners who were to be treated better than others were taken there. But they were black, white, Indians and Chinese. A good many of those who ate there were there for only short times, but I ate there, until one day the Warden gave me permission to go outside the prison and take my meals at a restaurant that belonged to the prison if I would pay fifteen cents for each meal, and I ate there the last month of my imprisonment, though I could have eaten there sooner than that if I had cared to do so.

The second day of my imprisonment I was taken to the room for the identification of prisoners by the Bertillon method. My photograph was taken with my glasses off, front and side view, with my prison number 31498 fastened across my breast. Then I was weighed and measured in many dimensions, and my own clothes were taken from me, except my underclothing and shoes, and I was put into the gray uniform of the highest grade the rules allowed to be given to any prisoner on his first coming there. It had a military cap and a suit much like the Confederate uniform, the only stripe on it being a blue military stripe down the sides of the legs of the pants. The very highest grade uniform was just like that, except that the stripe was black. No prisoner could have the black stripe until he had been there six months with the highest grade of conduct.

There were two other prisoners examined when I was. They were stripped nude, but I was not made to take off my underclothing. Their heads and beards were shaved. Neither my hair nor beard was cut while I was there, and they were both very long.

For the first two days that I was there I was frequently taken to the main office of the prison, and the Warden and other high officers talked with me for hours, most of the time listening to me. They seemed unusually interested.

The third day I was taken out of my cell, and given one of 31 cells that were much more comfortable than any others in the whole prison, and I thought mine was the best situated of them all. It was about six feet broad, nine feet long, and ten feet high, and it had a large latticed door, and the whole front was latticed, and I had a nice bed, and nice gas and heat. A prisoner, for 50 cents a month, took care of my cell. He put in it a carpet, and another prisoner, just as a kindness, brought me a nice table, and I had books and papers and writing apparatus in abundance.

The average good prisoner could write one page only twice a month. I was given permission to write as many letters as I wanted every day, and as long as I wanted to, and I received an average of five letters a day while I stayed there. In a few days after getting there I was put to writing on the prison paper, and to doing the principal part of its editing, and to reading the proof of a book the Warden was publishing, and to general literary work, using my spare time for a month to write all of this book, except this last chapter which I am writing at my home in Kentucky.

My new cell was in a new and very handsome part of the prison, and I was given a hall permit that allowed me to walk in a hall of the prison, the hall being 500 feet long, 20 feet broad, and 50 feet high. I could spend my time walking in that hall, or talking with some privileged prisoners, from 5 o'clock each evening until 8:30 o'clock, when we had to go to bed.

I found among the prisoners a man of 70 years of age, who was a fine thinker, and a man of pretty broad reading, and he and I spent a good deal of our spare time in walking in the hall and in conversation. There were others of the prisoners and some of the guards who were interesting, and some of the guards and officers showed me distinguished kindness; some of them an affection that surprised me. I never was treated by prisoners or officers like any other man in the whole prison.

Everybody seemed to regard my case exactly like I did. Other prisoners could only have their friends at stated times, and they were members of their families. There were people coming to see me almost any day, and I have had as high as thirty visitors — gentlemen and ladies

— to come and see me at once, and they would bring me nice things to eat. There was no guard with them, and the Warden told me, after the warm weather came, to take my friends out on the grass in the large court of several acres of pretty trees and fountains and flowers and a library, and my friends and I would talk as long as we wanted, and sometimes the Warden would come and talk with us. He called me once to introduce me to Governor Bushnell, whom I found to be a splendid and affable gentleman. Among my callers were Catholic priests and Protestant clergymen.

When the pretty season came on, the Warden gave me a permit to spend a good part of every day in the prison yard, which was quite beautiful. This was a privilege which was granted to about 30 prisoners, and among them there were men who were as intelligent and cultivated, so far as I could see, as the best in our free society. In order to get to stay out in the fresh air in the pleasant weather, I asked the Warden to let me work with the gardener, and the Warden fixed it so that I could stay out in the yard or in the greenhouse, and work, or not work, as it suited me.

The head gardener and I soon got to be good friends. He was a prisoner, and used to be gardener for Booth, who killed Lincoln, and he spoke affectionately of Booth.

One day the Warden came to me out in the yard, and asked me to let him see my yard permit. He took it and wrote something on it, and told me that would allow me to go outside of the prison whenever I wanted to, so that I stayed on the prison grounds. There was a beautiful yard in front of the prison outside, about six hundred feet long and one hundred feet wide. I had simply to walk to the prison gates and they would fly open, and I went out whenever I wanted to; never less than once each day. Nobody was allowed in that ground but some trusty prisoners, when they came there sometimes to work on it, and excepting myself and my friends from the outside. I would frequently lie down on the grass under the shade and go to sleep, and my friends, nice ladies and gentlemen, and little children, would come and sit with me.

The friendship between Warden Coffin and myself seemed to grow stronger all the time I was there, and he would frequently bring me, or send me, letters that he would receive from various parts of the United States, thanking him for his kindness to me.

All the time I was there I edited my paper the Blue Grass Blade, and it came to the prison, the Warden telling me to send it to him, and its coming each week was watched for with interest by its coterie of

214

readers there.

I could have avoided going to church if I had tried to, but the exercises were nearly always interesting, and frequently very funny; the fun being made by music and speeches of visitors and prisoners and the Chaplain and the Warden. The music and the floral displays were beautiful. Soon after I was sent there the Warden alluded to me one day in a speech in the chapel in the most complimentary terms, saying that I was a man who knew a thousand times as much as he did.

After I had been there about three months, one day my young friend, Howard, of the Press-Post, came running into the printing office to be the first to bring me some good news, and, as soon as he could get his breath, he told me that President McKinley had commuted my sentence to six months, with all the benefits of "good time," for good behavior, so that my whole imprisonment would be only five months. He had learned it by telegraph from Washington, and the Warden said he had been so informed, and in a few days he handed me my commutation papers, and I was to be liberated on the 7th of July.

From that time on the dear ones at my home counted the days when I would be at home, and my good friend, Warden E. G. Coffin, who had defeated the purpose of my Christian enemies to make me suffer, or probably kill me, in the penitentiary, because I did not believe their religion, promised to come home with me. He did not do it, however, owing to unusual stress of business just about the time I started home, but I still have his promise to visit me.

I received congratulations from many sources, including my prison companions. The 4th of July was a holiday for all the prisoners. Over 2,300 of them were allowed to come out and have a grand picnic with their friends on the grass, inside the walls, the women prisoners being allowed to spend the day in the beautiful yard outside the prison, to which I was the only prisoner that had access. It was such a sight as cannot be witnessed anywhere else in the whole world.

There was an old guard named Frankhauser, whose kindness to me was remarkable. He never locked my cell at night that he did not say to me, "Good night, Brother Moore."

According to the rules of the prison, only the very best prisoners could have their permits for a month at a time, and then they were renewed, if they had done right. When mine expired, toward the close of my imprisonment, I handed the expired permits to old Brother Frankhauser to get them renewed by the Warden. The kind old guard said to me, "Oh, you don't have to have any permit; you just go ahead like you had one, and I will stand between you and any danger." I said

"No, I don't want to do that; I want to abide by the rules of the prison."
He laughed and said, "You are right," and took my expired permits and
had them fixed at his leisure, I enjoying all privileges without them in the
meantime.

A day or so before my day to be released I asked old Brother Frankhauser at what time he would unlock my cell in the morning of the day
my time expired, and he said, "At any time you say after the clock strikes
twelve in the night." I arranged to have him unlock me at the usual time,
five o'clock in the morning, and he was there with a happy smile on his
face to congratulate me.

Many of the prisoners along in the thirty-one cells of the "Banker's
Row" that I was in, were there for life, and some of their cells were
luxuriously furnished, and had curtains that they drew down over their
doors and gratings. They furnished these themselves, but though I had
plenty of friends at home and in Columbus, and almost anywhere who
would have been glad to furnish me all of those, I never had anything
in my cell but the simple things I have told you of. The Warden had told
me that if I preferred it he would have me a sleeping room fixed in the
printing office, so that I need not go into a cell at all, but the cell had
so many advantages that I did not care to make the change.

I was the only prisoner who could be in my cell when I wanted to, at
the hours when visitors were passing through the wards, as they did by
hundreds, almost every day. Sometimes a crowd of gentlemen and
ladies would gather at my cell door, and talk to me a long time, and beg
for "just any old copy of the Blue Grass Blade" that I could find, and
I generally had a package to distribute.

On the morning of my liberation I bade good-bye to many officers and
prisoners, and went out in the same suit of citizen's clothes that I had
worn to the prison. Ordinarily the suit worn there by prisoners is given
out to any prisoner that may be going out, but mine was nicely put away
for me and was returned to me all cleaned and pressed in nice style, a
banker prisoner from Cincinnati, who had charge of that department,
taking great interest in having me provided for.

The Warden was going to have a nice citizen's suit made for me by
the fine tailor prisoners, but I told him I would rather have a nicely made
prison uniform, so he had the tailors to take my measure, and they made
and gave me the nicest prison suit they could make, taking extra pains
with it, and putting the black stripe down the pants, instead of the blue,
making it the highest grade, though I had only constructively been there
six months.

By previous arrangement I was to meet my friend, F. S. Montgomery, who lived at Shepard, four miles from Columbus, on the steps of the State Capitol. He came there for me with his carriage, and drove me and some gentlemen friends around the city, and then took me to dinner at the home of Mr. J. M. Byler and wife, who had been good friends to me, and who would come to see me on the lawn in front of the prison, and bring me nice things to eat. We had a delicious dinner and a delightful time. His wife and little children are all beautiful and sweet.

When we had talked an hour or so after dinner, it was train time, and [they] took me to the elegant station, the Government having given me a ticket to Lexington.

At Cincinnati there were friends who live in that city who met me, and the reporters for the big papers had long interviews with me, and wrote long and complimentary accounts of me.

My reception at Lexington was the most remarkable thing in that line ever given any prisoner in the world. I had been told by my wife that there would be a demonstration in Lexington, on my return, but I had supposed that in consequence of a two hours delay of the train upon which I was, in consequence of a freight wreck, probably there would hardly be anybody at the train, which did not get in until nine o'clock P.M.

When the train rolled into the station I heard a band playing "My Old Kentucky Home," and looked out upon the perfect throng of people, and soon saw that they were all there to meet and welcome me. It was hard for me to realize that it was possible.

I am writing these lines at my home, "Quakeracre," on December 26, 1899. I will close this book with the account of my reception at home by reprinting from the Blue Grass Blade of July 16, E. M. 299, what I there reprinted from other newspapers.

Before printing these I have the following to say regarding my whole life up to the hour at which I am writing. I am now 62 years and 6 days old. I am enjoying remarkable health and strength. I do not regret a single thing in my whole life. I am glad that it has all been just as it has been, and I would not change a single thing in it, if I had miraculous power with which to do it. I would not exchange my life for that of any President of the United States. I may yet do that which I will deeply regret. I shall labor not to do so. My highest ambition has been far more than realized. I have believed all my life, that to act just as I have done would enable me to say that I was proud of my record, in my old days. I now say that with a deeper appreciation of its significance than I had ever dreamed of. I would not exchange the rewards of my conscience that are now mine for all the money of Rockefeller. I am assured that after I am dead I will be honored even more than while I was living. I believe that my life has been such as to make my race better and happier. I believe that my being sent to the penitentiary was fortunate for me and all others.

While I have had many Christian friends who were and are as good people as ever lived, the most dangerous citizens that we have — the greatest enemies to public liberty, intelligence and morals, and the greatest tyrants and hypocrites on earth are men and women who are not only in the churches, but who are so prominent and active in their work that the church is a public enemy.

The whole Bible is a bundle of errors, except a few moral precepts that are found in all religions, which are very fine and which we should try to practice.

Before Ingersoll died it was hard for me to forgive him that he had never come to my assistance, but after his great death, which ended the greatest life of any man known to history, I have mingled all my reproaches of him with his ashes and scattered them to the winds.

The greatest sentence ever uttered was when Tom Paine said, "The world is my country, humanity my brethren, and to do good is my religion."

I close my book, like the great Infidel, Lincoln, "with charity to all and malice to none."

Chapter XII

[From the Lexington Leader]
MADE HERO OF THE HEATHEN

EDITOR MOORE RETURNS FROM
THE PENITENTIARY AND IS ACCORDED AN OVATION.
— A GALA NIGHT FOR FREETHINKERS.

E ditor C. C. Moore is home again after a six months term in the Ohio State Penitentiary.

He came in last night wearing a low-crowned straw hat and a smile, and in one hand he carried a box containing his prison suit.

The train was two hours late, owing to a small wreck of three lumber cars at Blanchett Station on the Cincinnati Southern, but the crowd that had begun to assemble long before the regular time of arrival stuck it out to the last and seemed determined not to be deprived of being present at the home-coming of the "Heathen."

Saxton's band played "My Old Kentucky Home" when the editor alighted, and the crowd which had accumulated until it reached nearly 500 people, yelled and shouted as friends grasped the editor's hand and told him how glad they were to see him back again.

THE FIRST HANDSHAKE.

Editor Moore came in on the Blue Grass Special, and was seen first by the crowd at the station through the plate glass windows of the parlor car in the rear.

He came out of the train onto the rear platform as the crowd surged quickly around that end of the car, and pushed and shoved for places to see and greet him.

The first man to shake his hand was Mr. Letcher Lusby, an old-time friend. The greeting was most cordial.

The next hand Editor Moore received to shake was that of Hon. Moses Kaufman, a leading member of the Reception Committee. Then

219

came a series of his warmest friends, among whom was Mr. W. W. Goddard, of Harrodsburg, a particular admirer. When Editor Moore saw him he fell on his shoulders and embraced him like a brother.

RECEPTION TOUCHED HIM.

It was with difficulty that the venerable editor of the Blade could refrain from shedding tears as he exclaimed that he had no idea he was to be honored by such an enthusiastic reception.

It was fully five minutes before he could be gotten through the crowd to the carriages in the rear of the station, where he was again detained by hand-shaking on all sides.

Editor Moore tipped his hat and bowed graciously to the throng in response to their shouting.

When the procession of carriages formed, making five altogether, the band boarded one of the new electric cars, which had been especially chartered for the purpose, and in a few moments more the receiving party was on its way to the Phoenix Hotel.

STREETS WERE CROWDED.

The streets along the line of the march were crowded, and the people shouted to Editor Moore as he passed. On South Broadway at each street intersection were lines of persons, both white and black, sometimes three and four deep. The band played as the procession proceeded, and behind the carriages gathered a big following. At Main and Broadway, as the car turned it was confronted with a long line of people who had assembled along the edge of the sidewalk, and as the procession passed up Main Street the shouts echoed for half a block at a time. Editor Moore was obliged to tip his hat and bow again and again, passing Mill, Upper and Limestone Streets. At the Phoenix Hotel the car with Saxton's band stopped, and the carriage containing Editor Moore, who had ridden with Mr. Kaufman, Mr. Julius Marks and Mrs. Josephine K. Henry, drew up at the ladies' entrance.

MET BY HIS WIFE.

At the entrance of the hotel Editor Moore was met by his wife. The crowd here was bigger than at any other point. The scene accompanying the meeting was very affecting. Editor Moore fell upon his wife's neck and wept for joy. His daughter, Miss Lucile Moore, was there also, and with her Miss Nannie St. Clair, of Georgetown. Editor Moore met his son Leland, when he reached the parlors upstairs and embraced him for the first time since he was released from the prison. He introduced his wife to the crowd and told them he was glad to present to them the woman who had said she was not ashamed of being a convict's wife.

SPEAKS TO A LARGE CROWD.

After Mr. Moore had been escorted to the parlor and been welcomed by many handshakes, cries went up from the crowds in front of the hotel for a speech.

The white-haired and white-bearded editor soon appeared on the porch and at once all were attention.

"I thank you," said the venerable gentleman, "from the very depths of my heart for this reception. It more than atones for confinement in the penitentiary. In fact, I would have been willing to spend my life in the penitentiary to know that I had so many and such faithful friends in my home place.

"All of you have been true to me and from now on I shall devote all my energies toward the uplifting of everyone, the aiding and benefiting of everyone — even the preachers.

"I have been one of the most honored prisoners ever confined. My lot in the penitentiary might have been a very different one, but I found in the Warden a man who thought of religion much as I do.

"I am no martyr, but I willingly and cheerfully suffered for what I believed to be the truth and would have died for it had it been required of me.

"Dreyfus[1] and I, prisoners as we have been, and as he is now, are more honored than any prisoners in history, and we were both persecuted for religion's sake, he by Catholics —"

At this a female voice from the crowd cried out:

"That's a lie."

Editor Moore concluding the sentence said:

"And I by Protestants."

"I have no animosity toward anyone, and rejoice to be once more among you."

---

[1]Dreyfus, Alfred (1859-1935), a French military officer wrongly accused of being traitorous and sentenced to life imprisonment. He was finally pardoned and released despite protests from reactionary anti-Semites throughout Europe.

221

THE FORMAL RECEPTION.

After delivering the short speech from the balcony the Heathen Editor stepped back into the parlor, his friends there closing around the center table. Editor Moore was shown a chair by the side of his wife and family, where he sat down to wait for the ceremonies to proceed. The editor was as picturesque as ever, with a wealth of long curly hair and whiskers just inclined to gray, which he said Warden Coffin had kindly spared. "I intended to trim them," he said, laughing, "as I have made it a practice to cut them once a year, and that at sheep-shearing time, but I thought I'd wear them home this way to show you that they haven't been tampered with by the prison officials." When Mr. P. Parrott rapped for order, Hon. Moses Kaufman was introduced and he made the following address of welcome:

MR. KAUFMAN'S WELCOME.

This reception on your return home, Mr. Moore, is tendered you by your friends, not because of any views they may hold in common with you — for there are those among us who do not agree with you in all things — but because of the esteem we hold you in, and because of the love we bear you.

It is not Charles Moore, the rationalist, but Charles Moore, the model husband, the loving father, the kind neighbor, and respected fellow-townsman whom we welcome.

We want to show to the world, persecuted and hounded by your enemies as you have been, that we, who know you best, love you none the less and honor you more for the wrongs you have been made to suffer.

You are neither the first, nor will you be the last, who has thus been made to feel the fangs of those who are tolerant of no opinions except their own.

The pages of history are filled with the illustrious names of those who thought, and uttered truths, beyond the limits placed by their generations. Socrates dared to go beyond, and was condemned to death, Spinoza was excommunicated, Galileo was imprisoned, and Michael Servetus and Bruno died at the stake. Yet to-day monuments are erected to their memory, and a grateful world acknowledges the service rendered civilization by them.

Even Jesus, for teaching a loftier morality, broader views and newer thoughts, was condemned to death by an intolerant priesthood; and yet to-day, after 1900 years, more than one-third of all the world worships at his shrine.

222

France has its Dreyfus; Kentucky has her Moore. Innocent of crime, and accused by those whom he had reason to believe to be his friends, Capt. Dreyfus was cruelly sentenced to a punishment worse than death. But at this very moment all France is ringing with the cry of "A bas l'arme — Vive la Justice!" And taking up that cry, reverberating through the corridors of the world, and as it comes to us, borne on the crests of the ocean waves, we too shout: "Down with bigotry! Down with hypocrisy! Long live liberty! Long live free speech!"

There may be Ruckers to accuse, and courts found to condemn, but nothing shall ever stop the avalanche of truth as it rushes upon the century at our doors.

"Forward, forward, let us range,
Let this great world spin forever down
The ringing grooves of change."

Mr. Moore, on behalf of your friends of the city of Lexington, I bid you welcome back to your home — your home which your enemies had nigh made desolate — and back to our hearts, from which, however, you have never for a single moment been absent.

A STRONG LETTER.

Mr. Kaufman was applauded when asked that he be allowed to read a letter which had been received from Dr. J. B. Wilson, of Cincinnati, who was not able to be present, and, in addition, present some resolutions passed by Lexington friends thanking Dr. Wilson and others for kindness shown. Dr. Wilson's letter was read as follows:

Cincinnati, O., July 7, 1899.

TO HON. MOSES KAUFMAN:

I regret that I cannot attend the banquet which yourself and other citizens of Lexington will tender Mr. Moore on his arrival home Saturday evening. I had a little to say about the injustice which compelled him to leave home, and if I could have the pleasure of attending the banquet, I would have something to say about the triumph of his return.

I congratulate the Liberals of Lexington upon this occasion, which is a notice to the clergy that the day has passed when religious persecution can go unchallenged; that Freethought is a power that is beginning to be recognized and felt; that it is rapidly drifting toward organization, and that all future attempts to suppress free speech and free press immediately becomes a National issue — an issue that reaches even to the Presidential ear, and becomes a responsibility that even he cannot avoid. The fear of offending the Liberals of this country, which doubtless chiefly influenced the President to grant commutation of sentence, is indication of our growing importance and strength.

Your welcome to Mr. Moore is a merited rebuke to all who were instrumental in depriving him of his liberty, a just rebuke to the ignorance of Judge Thompson and Attorney Bundy. I say "ignorance and incapacity," because these men are fitted neither by study, practice nor experience for such eminent judicial positions.

They are politicians, and only occupy their positions as the result of squaring political obligations. Neither of them seemed to comprehend the relation of free government, this far-reaching principle which involves the very birthright of free government. Neither of them seemed to know that a United States Court is a tribunal, not for the special purpose of convicting offenders, but for dispensing justice. They made a foolish blunder, and that, too, at the beginning of their judicial career.

The indictment and imprisonment of Mr. Moore has not been in vain; for through it notice has been served to religious fanatics, and to all prejudiced courts, that every such challenge to the right of free speech and free press, from this on, will become a national issue, and will be defiantly met by a stubborn opposition.

Mr. Moore was indicted and sentenced simply because he is an infidel. His right to discuss sex and other social issues would never have been questioned if he had given Jesus all the honor and glory.

I congratulate the state of Kentucky for the broad and liberal-mindedness of so many of her eminent public men, who, in the sentence of Mr. Moore, felt that justice was outraged and made his cause their own.

But above all, we may congratulate ourselves upon the larger and fuller liberality of the times; upon that growing liberality which is beginning to realize that the right of free speech in one person involves the same right in all; that freedom cannot exist in the same government with slavery; that man cannot be politically free, and woman politically enslaved; that justice cannot prevail with the superfluities of the land in the hands of a few, and labor begging for something to do; that political freedom alone is not the full measure of government, but only government in name, when not equally allied with religious and economic freedom; that freedom of conscience under a free government does not mean that the Christian clergy alone are entitled to the exercise of it; but that the holiness of the Christian's belief shall stand upon the same footing and no higher than the holiness of the skeptic's belief. We congratulate ourselves that, more and more, men and women are inclined to do their own thinking, and bravely to speak their honest opinions, and that they are inspired to so act just as Burns says, "for the glorious privilege [of] being independent."

I will see that Mr. Moore leaves Ohio in a sober condition, and hope he will reach Lexington in good shape for a great speech.

Sincerely yours,
J. B. WILSON, M. D.

THE RESOLUTIONS.
The resolutions were as follows:

Whereas, Dr. J. B. Wilson of Cincinnati, O., and Warden Coffin of Columbus, O., in their several capacities have extended favors to our fellow-townsman, Mr. C. C. Moore, at a time when he most needed favors — the one by his loyal and moral support, coming fearlessly to Mr. Moore's defense, by denouncing in unmeasured terms the injustice done Mr. Moore, and aiding and sustaining him in every way; and the other by his sympathy, universal courtesy, timely kindness and considerate treatment during Mr. Moore's imprisonment; therefore

Resolved, That we, the personal friends of Mr. Moore in his home here in Lexington, gratefully acknowledge the favors shown Mr. Moore, with the same gratitude as if shown to us in person, and herewith tender the gentlemen above named a vote of our deepest and profoundest thanks.

MRS[.] HENRY'S ADDRESS.
Mrs. Josephine K. Henry followed Mr. Kaufman with a strong address, saying:

This is an occasion unparalleled in the history of Kentucky. It does not conflict, however, with the logic of events nor the law of progress. Though it may seem to many an unimportant event, yet it bears with tremendous force upon the progress of intellectual liberty, and the protection of free speech and free press in the American republic. This occasion emphasizes humanity's demand for justice, and extracts the sting of dishonor from outlawed innocence. It emphasizes the fact, too, that freedom of speech is every American citizen's right, and cannot be

225

infringed upon, even though its exercise destroy the idols of the past and endanger the most cherished ideas. In this government of the people, by the people, and for the people, every man and woman has the inalienable right to give to the world his or her best thought, and when written or unwritten law attempts to destroy that right, it undermines the very foundations of American democracy.

Five months ago, under the pretext of violating a national law, the man whom we honor to-night was taken from the bosom of his family, from his daily pursuits and the society of his friends, and imprisoned among felons in the United States penitentiary at Columbus, Ohio. He had committed no crime, save the expression of a thought. In the abounding flow of his pent-up soul, and in a moment of indignant defiance of laws and customs, which through ignorance and intolerance have so oppressed and degraded humanity, he expressed a thought, and the iron hand of religious tyranny invoked the law by stealth to clothe this man in a convict's garb and place him behind prison bars. Like a wounded eagle which surrenders to its captors, this prisoner accepted his sentence with sublime courage and resignation. The love for humanity, for truth, for honor, for justice, flashed from his eye as American freedom was shackled in his person, and he was borne away to a convict cell.

The court which sentenced this man, in whose honor this assemblage of intellectually free men and free women is gathered, builded wiser than it knew. The decree of the court, though stimulated by religious rancor and endorsed by organized hypocrisy, was so contrary to the American ideal of individual liberty, that even conservatives denounced it as not only cruel and unjust, but exceedingly unwise. Public opinion was seconded by a decree from the White House that Charles C. Moore be restored to liberty.

It is a fact seldom recorded in the history of the human race that a warm welcome and manifestations of joy await a liberated convict.

If Charles C. Moore's accusers can present themselves mentally and morally unsullied as he is, even in his convict's garb, let them come out of their "coward's castle," and meet him in noble, honorable, intellectual battle. Their silence will be their own accuser, and let them forever afterward hold their peace, and employ their time in "making their own calling and election sure."

Free thought, free speech and free press have been defended and preserved by the ablest of earth. Through ignorance and mental darkness, through bloody wars, through torture, terror and tyranny, free thought has upheld the Promethean Torch of Reason with steady hand,

and undeciding step, until now it is leading the world with victorious colors. Those who have advanced and labored for better things for humanity have ever been the victims of religious prejudice and tyranny; yet, through all the ages, Freethinkers have kept their hands unstained with human blood, and have never persecuted a human being for opinion's sake; but let history tell of the sufferings and persecutions of Freethinkers, from the burning of Bruno to the imprisonment of the editor of the Blue Grass Blade. But for the battle fought for free speech and free press by that splendid trinity of Freethinkers — Benjamin Franklin, Thomas Jefferson and Thomas Paine — the human mind to-day would be in chains, and the printing press the exclusive property of those in ecclesiastical and civil power.

The superstitions, fables and fears of the past are steadily retreating before the "march of mind," and the banner of Rationalism is now thrown to the breeze by the scholars, poets, orators, editors and brain-workers of our time, and it is even being grasped by clerical hands in cathedrals, churches and chapels, and being waved in synods, conferences, and ecclesiastical battle-grounds. Rationalism has advanced this far in the United States. The newspaper is far more powerful than the pulpit. The monopoly of the pulpit has been destroyed by the press, which is the greatest lever of civilization.

This released prisoner was the last man in the American republic who was tried for the alleged crime of blasphemy. The decision of Judge Parker, rendered here in the city of Lexington in this case, is one of the ablest in American jurisprudence, and it was so favorably commented on by the press of our community, and commended for its true American ring, that it is conceded no man in the United States will ever again be tried for blasphemy. Such a barbarism is sleeping in the grave with witch-burning, and now the President of the United States has condemned the outrage of imprisoning an American citizen for printing his honest thoughts by releasing this editor from prison, and let us hope that this alleged crime will slumber in the grave of the cruel past, and in the future Lexington will be crowned with honor for the triumph of true American principles all through the martyrdom of Charles C. Moore. President McKinley has planted himself on the foundation stone of our Government in releasing this prisoner.

The students, not of theology, but of sociology, are the greatest benefactors of our race, and here in this American republic, with its millions of dollars' worth of untaxed churches, and law the echo of religious dogma, we need a Secretary of Sociology in the President's Cabinet much more than a Secretary of War, who calls the flower of

227

young manhood to the battlefield and arms them with deadly weapons to take the lives of their brothers, or wrest from unoffending people their religion, their property, their homes, their hopes and their lives.

We need education, investigation and free discussion on all the problems and mysteries of this strange existence we call life, and it is a crime to persecute scientists, sociologists and thinkers who are seeking a way to elevate and liberate the race from degrading conditions. Our whole educational system needs to be reconstructed, and the young instructed in all the facts in nature that affect their lives, and the lives of generations yet to be born, that they may not be launched upon the tempestuous, treacherous sea of life without rudder or compass. Facing actual conditions as they are to-day under our present system, what do we find?

After 1900 years of organized theology humanity is full of fears to-day. The world is filled with sad hearts, with sighs and tears. Our civilization is mentally[,] morally and physically diseased. There is a rapidly increasing demand for insane asylums, prisons and scaffolds. All pitiless the usurer demands his pound of flesh. The brothel thrives in the shadow of the church, society tramples mental and moral worth under foot and bows to mammon. All the Christian nations have standing armies and sailing navies armed to the teeth with the most powerful death-dealing weapons human ingenuity can devise, ready to throttle the life out of each other, or dismember the kingdoms and empires of so-called heathen nations, and reduce these unoffending people to serfdom to satisfy insatiable avarice. Ignorance, vice and poverty, the Shylocks of our race, are populating the world. Poverty is the toiling, cringing, helpless slave to wealth, and a wail arises from Christendom:

"Oh! for the rarity
Of Christian charity,
Under the sun."

The priest, the law, and the hangman seem as powerless against the forces of evil as a feeble human hand against the law of gravitation. With all these sad facts before us, is it a crime to seek a better way to bring hope and happiness to this sad old world? This is what Rationalists are trying to do, though they too often receive condemnation and sometimes a prison for their service. To elevate his fellows and to remove some of the tragedy of life, Charles C. Moore has lived and labored, sacrificed and suffered.

If to avow your principles and discharge your duty to your fellows in the face of prison, or impending death, is to be a hero, this released prisoner is a hero. If to love your fellow creatures better than yourself is goodness, he has shown this self-sacrifice. Like the immortal Bruno, this released prisoner appeared before his time, and was born for agitation, and as well try to stay the eternal forces of nature as to bring this intrepid soul to bay. From Bruno's stake to Voltaire's lustrous star, from Thomas Paine's liberty cry mid the storms of war, to the imprisonment of Charles C. Moore, the star of Rationalism has been ascending and shedding its light upon the next man's mind. The able liberal press of the United States and Europe is bringing into the ranks of Rationalism the superior intelligence of all nations and professions, and the brainiest ecclesiastics of our time are falling into line. The reign of reason is at last being ushered in. There is hope for our race as long as one proud head is above the waves of superstition. Science, the great iconoclast, is breaking the idols of the past, and with her torch she is chasing fear from the human heart and illuminating the caverns of superstition and transforming them into temples of thought.

Rationalism has discovered that knowledge, and not faith, is the salvation of humanity, and Rationalism is saying to Orthodoxy, "We are weary of hearing what you believe; tell us what you know."

Intolerance alone prevents intellectual hospitality between orthodoxy and free thought. This should not be. If we knew each other better, we would love each other more. We are all but compassless mariners over life's unsounded sea, and under our present system the fears, responsibilities, cares and sorrows laid upon human hearts are enough to swing the planet from its orbit. If we could all exemplify in our lives the lines of the immortal Pope,

"Teach me to feel another's woe,
To hide the fault I see,
That mercy I to others show,
That mercy show to me,"

there would be no more intolerance, persecution or imprisonment for opinion's sake. To-night I believe that after suffering injustice, persecution and imprisonment, Charles C. Moore would extend all the kindness in his great nature to those who have so deeply wronged him. He is built just that way. Yet, do we claim that this editor has no faults? No. And now to you, our friend, who has been made to suffer so much, we say, Hail! and thrice welcome to [your] old Kentucky home from your prison exile. Your persecutors sought to cover your name and fame with infamy, but instead you return to your devoted and heroic wife and children, to your friends upon your native heath with your silvered locks covered with honor. Your release from prison, by the order of the President of the United States, vindicates the right of free mails, free speech and free press. You were the victim of religious prejudice, because you lacked broad-minded, liberty-loving, constitution-reviving men for prosecutor, judge and jury; yet these men had sworn on taking their offices to uphold the Constitution which declares, "No human authority can in any case whatever control or interfere with the rights of conscience," and that free speech and free press are inalienable rights of American citizens. Standing on the broad platform of Rationalism, let us not be uncharitable to your accusers or persecutors. Let us recognize the fact that they are the product of heredity and environment, of a diseased religious and social system. It would be unphilosophical to cherish hard or revengeful feelings against any concerned in placing you in a convict's cell. Let us be charitable, even if they were cruel and unjust. You were too short-sighted to discover the gravity of such a proceeding. Your conviction has advanced the cause of Rationalism and proven that the power of American principles for the protection of human rights is invariable and will endure as long as the love of liberty dwells in the human heart.

The hosts of Rationalists and lovers of justice rejoice in the triumph of American principles, and greet you with gratitude and hope. Return to your ancestral home and to your peaceful pursuits an honored man. Follow the plow and guide the mighty pen by reason driven, remembering that our civilization begins and ends with the plow and the pen, and when sophistries and myths have vanished, when the methods of statesmen and politicians have passed into oblivion, and the sword of the soldier rusted in its scabbard, your words and deeds will speak and live in the lives of the generations of the coming century, and it will be told of you that you did what you could to wrest the iron hand of superstition from the enslaved human mind and trembling human heart, and write in the eternal firmament in glittering stars the magical word "Liberty."

HON. WOOD DUNLAP'S ADDRESS.

I am surprised at being called upon to deliver an address this evening, because I do not think I agree with our distinguished guest upon any proposition he has advanced through the columns of the Blue Grass Blade. I do not hesitate to say, however, that I regard him as one of the best men, morally, and one of the greatest men intellectually, the State has ever produced. I am simply here to assist in the welcome of C. C. Moore, a citizen, from imprisonment that I have always thought unjust and uncalled for.

The beautiful address delivered by Mrs. Henry suggests a thought with which I am in harmony, in regard to the freedom of the press.

Toleration is the keystone upon which is founded our American institutions; toleration in its broadest and most glorious sense. In colonial times it was intolerance that embittered the lives of our ancestors, and even now its baneful shadow is upon the land.

The proscriptive vices of the middle ages have flowed down with the blood of the race, and have tainted the life that now is with a suspicion and distrust of freedom. Liberty in the eyes of men has meant the privilege of agreeing with the majority. Men have desired for free thought, but fear has stood at the door.

It remains for the United States, the greatest advocate of freedom, and the grandest country on God's foot-stool, to build a highway broad and free, into every field of liberal inquiry, so that the poorest of men who walk therein will be more secure in his life and liberty and pursuit of happiness than the soldiers who sleep behind the rampart.

Persecution has no part nor lot on this side of the sea; the pillory nor the thumbscrew. Essential freedom is the right to differ. Nor must this right be conceded with coldness nor disdain, but freely, cordially, and with utmost good will. No loss of rank nor social ostracism must darken the pathway of the humblest seeker after truth. The right of freethought, free speech and free inquiry is as clear as the noon-day sun, and as bounteous as the waters of the sea. Without a full and cheerful recognition of this right, America is only a name, her glories a dream, her institutions a mockery.

EDITOR MOORE TALKS.

Editor Moore was modest in his response. He said he did not intend to make a speech, but would give a short talk. He thanked his friends for their kindness, and said that he felt that his imprisonment had not been without its rewards in more ways than one. He would not take $100,000 for his experience. He wanted nothing but kind words to be spoken of his persecutors, and made that special request of his friends. He had been treated with every kindness and consideration by Warden Coffin, and had enjoyed unusual privileges while in the Ohio State Penitentiary. He would take the lecture platform soon — not because

231

he cared for public advertising, but because he would have something to say. "I have been the best treated prisoner from Socrates to Dreyfus," repeated he. After the reception and addresses the banquet was served in the main dining room of the hotel, plates being laid for 75 people. Hon. Wood Dunlap and J. Hub Prather were among the speakers at the close, after which Editor Moore and his family drove out to their farm, "Quakeracre."

Warden Coffin was unable to accompany Editor Moore to Lexington, as anticipated, but will come later.

The Committee on Reception last night was composed of Messrs. M. Kaufman, Julius Marks, P. Parrott, E. B. Wrenn, W. W. Goddard and Mrs. Josephine K. Henry.

[From the Lexington Herald.]
TEARS AND MUSIC
MINGLE AS EDITOR MOORE RETURNS HOME.
— A WELCOME FIT FOR A KING.

Charles Chilton Moore has returned to Lexington.

His return was marked by a demonstration which would have done honor to a conquering army returning from some field of battle with its flag unfurled and proudly flying to the breeze.

Mr. Moore returned at 9:16 o'clock Saturday night from Columbus, Ohio, where he has served five months as a convict for daring to express his opinion through the columns of his paper.

The reception he was accorded at the depot showed how many of the citizens of Lexington honored this erratic and singular character. The train was due to arrive shortly after 6 o'clock, but because of an accident it was delayed almost three hours.

The news that Mr. Moore was to come spread rapidly, and when the appointed time for the train to arrive came about two hundred persons had assembled at the depot. When it was reported that the train was late the crowd began to thicken, and when it finally arrived more than one thousand people were at the depot waiting to extend a cordial welcome to Mr. Moore. Saxton's band was there and made the wait less tedious by playing several selections; finally "My Old Kentucky Home," and the crowd cheered. When Mr. Moore appeared on the platform a shout went from the gathering which completely drowned the music. As he stepped to the platform, friends rushed toward him, all eager to grasp him by the hand.

AFFECTING SCENES.

The first person to reach his side was W. W. Goddard, a lifelong friend. As he grasped the hand of the aged journalist, tears sprang to his eyes, and one of the most pathetic scenes followed. The two old men, both far past the noontide of life, clasped each other in a loving embrace, and their tears were mingled. Mr. Moore caught sight of his wife in the crowd, and as he made way to her side tears sprang afresh to his eyes, and with voice filled with emotion, he clasped her in his arms, and those present bowed their heads in reverent silence.

With his arm around the neck of his wife, Mr. Moore pushed his way through the crowd to the waiting carriage on the opposite side of the depot, stopping at every step to grasp the hand of some friend who bade him a hearty welcome. When the carriage was finally reached, he entered it with a number of friends, and other carriages filled with friends and newspaper men started for the city.

A special car had been chartered for the band, and as it was whirled down Broadway it played inspiring strains, and shouts of welcome came from every throat. The streets were crowded, and all along the route people stood on all the sidewalks and in doorways, and applauded him, and when the carriages finally drew up in front of the Phoenix Hotel the crowd was so dense that it was impossible to force a passage-way through it. Finally an entrance was gained, and Mr. Moore and his friends went to the parlor on the second floor, while the band began to play on the sidewalk in front of the building. The crowd grew denser each moment, and when Mr. Moore stepped to the balcony cheering broke out again, drowning the sound of the music.

MADE A SHORT SPEECH.

He was called on for a speech, and, with hat in hand, he leaned far over the balustrade and made a few touching remarks, thanking everybody for the cordial welcome extended to him. He said that he forgave everybody for the alleged wrongs that had been done him, even the preachers, and wished to be forgiven by all for anything he may have done wrong.

He said that he was the most honored prisoner that ever lived, from Socrates to Dreyfus, because of the liberties he had been granted while in prison, and the favors he had been shown. He told of the treatment he received while confined, and spoke in eulogizing terms of the Warden. He told of the meeting with his wife, and that she had said to him that she was glad, under the circumstances, to be the wife of a convict.

While he was speaking a street car filled with pleasure seekers stopped in front of the hotel, and the young ladies and gentlemen aboard cheered him to the echo. Mr. Moore then bade the large crowd on the sidewalk good-night and retired to the parlor, which was full of friends. A general handshaking followed. Mr. P. Parrott, one of Mr. Moore's warmest friends, and who had been instrumental in getting up the celebration, led him to the center of the floor and bade him be seated. He then, in a few brief remarks, introduced Hon. Moses Kaufman, who delivered the address of welcome.

MRS. HENRY SPEAKS.
When Mr. Kaufman concluded, Mrs. Josephine K. Henry, of Versailles, was introduced, and for more than a half hour she spoke. She was interrupted several times with applause, and when she concluded Mr. Moore arose and briefly addressed the assemblage. He recited his trial and conviction and his confinement in the penitentiary, and the treatment he received. He said that he had been allowed privileges which had never been extended to a man who had been confined in the Ohio Penitentiary. He said he was proud of his prison garb, and would have worn it at the reception had it not been for his wife.

EVEN LOVES RUCKER.
He said that he intended to go on the lecture platform and would wear the stripes. He said that he had become so accustomed to the prison suit that he felt lost without it, and citizen's clothing made him feel like he was dressed up. He said that he bore malice toward none, not even to Mr. Rucker. He said that he forgave all, and that in the future he would live for his friends. He referred to the fact that he had been allowed to retain his hair and beard, and said that he was the most honored prisoner alive, from the fact that every prisoner in the penitentiary was made to obey the rules, and yet he was shown favors from the moment he entered the walls until he left.

THE WARDEN THANKED.
After the reading of the letter a resolution, which had been adopted by a number of friends, was read, thanking Warden Coffin and Dr. Wilson for many kindnesses shown. The reading of the resolution concluded the ceremonies and the party then adjourned to the dining room, where a sumptuous banquet had been spread. About seventy-five guests sat at the table and several speeches of welcome were made.

234

[Special to the Cincinnati Enquirer]
WELCOME

FIT FOR A KING GIVEN INFIDEL MOORE AT LEXINGTON.

Lexington, Ky., July 8, 1899. — Stripped of a felon's garb Thursday, Charles Chilton Moore, freethinker, free-love advocate, editor, ex-preacher and literary eccentric returned home at 9:30 o'clock to-night from the Ohio Penitentiary and received a welcome fit for a king. Five hundred people — men, women and children — waited for two long hours at the depot to greet the gray-haired Kentuckian. As the train rattled into the city the strains of "My Old Kentucky Home" were blended with hurrahs, and when the infidel alighted he was almost torn to pieces by his friends.

Entering a carriage, drawn by two white horses, and headed by a brass band, he was driven to the Phoenix Hotel. A dozen carriages filled with Freethinkers and newspaper men followed. Every street corner was a "jam," and the ex-convict's return was like a triumphant entry into a conquered city.

At the hotel Editor Moore made a speech to two thousand people in which he said that he and Dreyfus were the two most famous people in the world, both being prosecuted by religionists.

A reception and banquet followed, which lasted until midnight. Mr. Moore was convicted in the United States Court at Cincinnati in February for sending obscene matter through the mails. His sentence was commuted to six months by the President.

[From the Cincinnati Times-Star]
THEY FLOCKED ABOUT THE BLUE GRASS EDITOR.

C. C. MOORE, JUST RELEASED FROM PRISON, IS WELCOMED BY HIS FRIENDS.

Scores of admirers flocked about Editor C. C. Moore at the Palace Hotel Saturday, congratulating him on his release from the Ohio Penitentiary. Mr. Moore was sent up from Cincinnati by Judge A. C. Thompson, of the United States Court, for sending obscene publications through the mails. Despite the charges made against him, Mr. Moore had many friends and admirers who stuck to him, and finally succeeded in getting a commutation of his sentence.

Editor Moore wrote a book while in prison, which he calls "Behind the Bars; 31498." While in the penitentiary he still edited his paper, the Blue Grass Blade, in which he published sharp criticisms on the Federal officials who prosecuted him. He left for Lexington Saturday, where he was met by a band. A banquet was tendered him at the Phoenix Hotel.

[From the Blue Grass Blade.]
OVATION AND ORATION

MEET ME AT MY "OLD KENTUCKY HOME".

I write this before having had time to read what the newspapers have had to say about the very remarkable demonstration in the city of Lexington that welcomed me back from the Ohio Penitentiary to my own home.

It had seemed to me probably unnecessary to describe what so many others had so —

At that black mark I was taken so sick while I was writing this in the Lexington Library that I had to quit and go to a hospital. Of the two hospitals in the city, one is managed by the Protestants and the other by the Catholics, and I was watched all night and fed on ice by a sweet Sister Pachomia, and now about fifteen hours after coming here I am able to write again. The Herald of this morning will kindly give an account of my illness. It seems hardly possible, but it looks to me that it is a recurrence of an illness that I had from poisoned milk in the penitentiary, in which a number of persons were sick from poisonous fungus growth in the milk.

At Columbus, for days before my release, I was continually congratulated by friends, officers, and prisoners inside and by persons who came to see me from the outside, and on my release a carriage under the management of Brother F. S. Montgomery was waiting for me, and he took me and a party of my friends on a drive to see the attractions of the beautiful city of Columbus, and then drove us to the home of Brother J. M. Byler and his lovely wife and children, and they all escorted me to the "Big Four" train at 12:45. We had an elegant dinner at Brother Byler's.

At Cincinnati I was met at the depot by friends, and at the business house of Brother Kauplin and at the Palace Hotel we had a nice and joyous reunion.

At 4 o'clock P.M. Saturday, July 8, I started over the Queen & Crescent for Lexington, having purposely delayed my departure in order to arrive at Lexington at the time to suit the program of my reception. Our train was due at Lexington at 6:45 P.M., but we were delayed three hours by a freight wreck.

I had anticipated that there would perhaps be about fifty people to meet me, and supposed they would have gone away when the train was found to be so much behind time. But the scene that greeted me was like a dream that so dazed me that, to this time, I have not been able to realize it.

As the train came up to the station with its spacious and handsome surroundings, I heard a splendid brass band playing "My Old Kentucky Home," and on looking out of the large palace-car window I saw a crowd of people of all ages, races, sexes and conditions, that was the beginning of an ovation such as was never accorded any citizen of Lexington, not even Henry Clay when he would come home from the United States Senate.

The crowd had been waiting for three hours, and were standing just as thick as people could stand — so thick and so pressed up against the sides of the train that it could not move out until the crowd began to follow the carriages that took the reception committee and the orators of the occasion and myself to the Phoenix Hotel, nearly a mile and a half away.

The route was down South Broadway to Main, the handsomest two streets in the city, and then up Main to the Phoenix, the handsomest hotel in the city. The procession of handsome carriages, with their tops turned back, and elegantly caparisoned horses and liveried drivers, was preceded by a large, open electric car, upon which was the band, and that ran slowly to allow the carriages to keep up, and to avoid danger in the crowd of people.

The streets were lined with people of all kinds, from highest to poorest and most humble, for that distance of nearly a mile and a half, and one continuous cheer greeted us all the way.

Mrs. Josephine K. Henry and I occupied the back seat of the carriage, and Senator Moses Kaufman and Col. Julius Marks the front seat.

Mrs. Henry looked just as pretty as she did when I was a preacher, and she one of my sweethearts during the civil war, and Hon. Moses Kaufman is called a "lovely man" by more women than any other man in Lexington. As for myself I was looking just as usual, and of course my modesty forbids me to say exactly how that was. I had the very pretty straw hat that they had given me as a part of my parting wardrobe on leaving the penitentiary, and I used that hat in recognition of

237

salutations all along the route.

There was only one drawback to the pleasure of the occasion, and that was the absence of Warden Coffin and Dr. Wilson, and there is a general feeling that a large part of this demonstration will have to be done over again when those two gentlemen get here, as they are booked to do before long.

Those two men have simply captured the hearts of the people of this city, and they will have to come here, even if it becomes necessary for Kentucky to issue a requisition on Governor Bushnell to bring them here. Nothing but most urgent stress of business kept them from coming, and I can assure our people here that they will soon be with us, and a banquet at the Phoenix will be given them. Apart from the interest they have shown in me, they are two men that Kentucky honors herself in honoring.

Main street was thronged with cheering people, including the best ladies and gentlemen of the city, and in the vicinity of the Phoenix the people were packed as thick as they could stand in every foot of standing room, from one side of the street to the other.

My wife and family stood in the front door that led to the parlors of the hotel, to meet me. That is the woman who had immortalized herself by saying, "Under the circumstances, I am proud to be a convict's wife," — words that will live in history along with my own words, when they put the handcuffs on me, "You are shackling American liberty, not me," and I believe the reception that I have had at Lexington is a notification to the church that no other man in America will ever be imprisoned by the United States government for his religious opinions.

I have repeatedly warned the clergy of this country of what their interference with the civil rights of this country is liable to bring upon them. None of them, I suppose, dared to venture out to witness my welcome home, but they can imagine from the newspaper accounts that the consequences to them will be as fearful as when in the French Revolution the people rose against the clergy and cut off the heads of 12,000 of them, if they persist in meddling with the secular affairs of this country.

It is significant that in the pulpits of this city, the next day (Sunday), no priest or preacher dared to utter a protest against a demonstration that, of course, was an open and public rebuke of them.

Soon after I got into the parlors on the second floor of the hotel, into which only as many were admitted as would comfortably fill the parlors, there was a shout from the crowd out in the street, demanding that I should speak to them. I stepped out upon the beautiful balcony and

238

made them a little talk, which, though in my loudest voice, could not be heard to the limits of the crowd, and though my reputation is that I am the only living Kentuckian who is neither a Colonel nor an orator, they cheered, with one exception, as enthusiastically as if I were saying it as well as Billy Breckinridge could do it. The one exception that I did not hear, but only know of from newspaper reports, was a female voice, which seemed to be that of some Catholic, when I said, "Just as Dreyfus was persecuted by Catholic Jesuits in Europe, so was I imprisoned by Protestant Jesuits in America."

The fact that the voice said "That is a lie," as soon as I had finished the sentence about Dreyfus, and before I had mentioned my own case, indicated that it was from a Catholic. But, apart from this, there has been no difference between Catholics and Protestants in their treatment of me from the day I started to prison until now, while in the whole of my career, from my beginning of the Blue Grass Blade to this date, the Catholics have done me far less injustice than Protestants have done.

The addresses of welcome in the parlors of the hotel were gems of beauty, and all appear in this issue of the Blade except that of Hon. J. Hub Prather. In my reply they did not

"View me with a critic's eye,
But passed my imperfections by."

I telephoned Mr. Prather and got his promise to write me his address for publication, but have now received the following note:

MR. MOORE. — The Courier-Journal telegraphed that papers would arrive by a special. Cincinnati Tribune man and Louisville Commercial representative, respectively, are here, and I have engagements with each of them this morning. I have to meet the C.-J. train. These things happen unexpectedly, and, almost necessarily, preclude the possibility of my writing anything for publication, and force me to ask to be absolved, or, at least, great indulgence.

I do not recollect any special thing that I said.

I consider you a great hero, and that you are of the immortal few who are not born to die, and I said that when other names were erased from history, yours would live through the endless ages of eternity.

Your name needs no shrill clarion to hand it down to time's remotest bounds.

Your friend,
"Hub."

I said, among other things in my talk, that I had sometimes dreamed that after I was dead, it was possible that somebody might say of me as was then being said, but that I should live to see and hear such honor to me, was something that I had never anticipated in my most enthusiastic aspiration, and that were I to die now, I would not only die satisfied, but realizing that I had already received more of honor than I deserved or ever expected.

I impressed upon my hearers that now more than ever, that we had triumphed over my few enemies, all of whom were of the clergy, I did not feel unkindly to any human being on the earth, and I thought that now was the grand opportunity for us to show to the world that the philosophy of rationalism has in it more to make men and women good and happy than there is in the best of the religions.

My allusions to Col. Ingersoll and to Charles Watts, respectively the leaders of infidelity in America and in Europe, were not unpremeditated. I can, and will, forgive Ingersoll, but I can never forget that in the hour of my need of his friendship, he deserted me as no brave and grand and generous and bold man would have done.

As for Watts, intellectual giant that he is, his attack on me while I was in prison, through Editor Foote's paper the "Freethinker," London, England, was simply brutal.

My experience has shown me that while infidels, as a mass, have stood by me like friends tried and true, there are among infidels, as among Christians, some people who are not what I would have them to be, and I am going to cooperate with all, religious or irreligious, who are impelled by that sentence of Paine, "The world is my country — to do good my religion," and that sentiment of Confucius and Jesus, "Do unto others as you would have them do unto you."

My reception at Lexington was the most signal declaration that the world has ever witnessed since Christianity began under Constantine 1,500 years ago, that at last the time has come to the "land of the free and the home of the brave" when an infidel has as much right to think and to say what he thinks, as the Christian has, and while my policy is for peace, and I believe in conquering by argument rather than by arms, I warn the clergy that we are going to maintain this right by force if that be necessary, and when this last is appealed to, the clergy can have some conception of the outcome of the conflict by imagining what would have been the result had they attempted to stop by force this demonstration on the night of July 8, 1899.

240

[Cincinnati (O.) Commercial-Tribune.]
IS JUST OUT OF PRISON.

EDITOR MOORE, OF THE BLUE GRASS BLADE, IN TOWN. — JUST OUT OF THE COLUMBUS PENITENTIARY — HE TALKS OF THE PAST AND THE FUTURE.

Editor Charles C. Moore, of the famous Blue Grass Blade, of Lexington, Ky., arrived in Cincinnati yesterday afternoon from Columbus, where he had just been released from the penitentiary, and was seen last night at the Palace Hotel by a Commercial-Tribune reporter. Mr. Moore looks little the worse for his imprisonment, and has his usual patriarchal appearance; a great shock of gray hair and a long, full beard, tall and lean of figure. He spoke with his old-time vigor and his spirit was as aggressive as ever.

"My prosecution," he said, "was plainly a religious persecution, and I predict that it will be the last to occur to any one in this country. Even men who inspired it, such as Prof. Rucker, now express regret at their course.

"While in the penitentiary Warden Coffin treated me with the greatest consideration, and he and the other officers gave no hint of feeling disrespect for me. No one seemed to think that any odium attached to me, as they knew I was simply a victim of religious prejudice. It is a fact that on the prison register no charge was placed against my name, and I had the greatest liberty of action. While in confinement I wrote the manuscript of a book to be entitled 'Behind the Bars; 31498,' that I will now publish.

"After a short time I shall take the lecture platform and deliver my speeches in the stripes I wore. Senator Lindsay had little trouble in bringing President McKinley to see the real reason for my conviction, and then he pardoned me. I husband no malice toward any one, but as long as life shall last I shall never cease to work with voice and pen against what I hold to be wrong. I wear this Toledo Jones button because I admire the mental and moral courage of the man.

"On my arrival here I was met at the depot by many of my loyal friends, and to-morrow I shall hold a little informal reception here in the hotel. When I reach my home in Lexington to-morrow I will be met by a brass band and escorted to the Phoenix Hotel, where I am to be tendered a banquet, and the address of welcome will be delivered by Mrs. Josephine K. Henry, of Versailles, Ky."

241

[From the Cleveland Gatling Gun.]
THE HOME-COMING OF A HEATHEN.

BY JUDGE J. SOULE SMITH

It was my pleasure to witness the home-coming of my heathen friend, C. C. Moore, editor of the Blue Grass Blade, and bishop of a somewhat diversified flock. He was just out of the Ohio Penitentiary, where he had been serving Uncle Sam and enjoying himself at said Uncle's expense; and though he had been treated like a lord by the Warden, yet he was exceedingly glad to get back once more to God's country, where he could smell once more the breath of red clover and feel under his foot the soft sward of Kentucky blue grass.

I have rarely written anything concerning Mr. Moore, though I have known him for thirty years in more or less intimacy. His religious views and mine are entirely antagonistic. I am a free-thinker, and, as such, a believer in Jesus Christ, not because other people claim to believe, but because of my own convictions maturely and calmly adopted. Infidels, as a rule, are not freethinkers — they adopt a negative belief and are as sensitive about it, and as easily angered by opposition as the most bigoted preacher of an unscriptural gospel. And I think Mr. Moore and many of his admirers are bigots, just as surely as Parson Rucker, who caused the heathen editor to be sent to the penitentiary.

But Mr. Moore's imprisonment and return home are matters of broader scope and deeper import than Mr. Moore's belief or Mr. Moore's personality; and the narrowness of Prof. Rucker, his accuser, demands more than local rebuke. The trial and conviction of Charlie Moore have become a pregnant issue in our national affairs, and the reception accorded him at Lexington, by the most conservative community in the United States, was the verdict of that people on that issue. Before his trial he would pass quietly along the streets, rarely speaking or spoken to; on his return from prison, late at night, on a long delayed train, a thousand people waited at the depot for hours to greet him, and the open carriage in which he sat passed for a mile through lines of others shouting a welcome to him. At the hotel traffic was blocked on the broad street until he appeared on the balcony and made a speech, and hundreds filed past him in the hotel parlors to take his hand. No wonder tears dimmed his eyes and choked his utterances! He had not dreamed of such a magnificent reception.

In that crowd there were hardly fifty people who agreed with him in his religious opinions, and, in all the crowd, there was not one who believed that Prof. Rucker had sent Charlie Moore to prison from a sincere desire to protect the morals of himself or somebody else. And therein was the meat of the whole demonstration. Had people thought that Prof. Rucker was honestly mistaken, that he really believed that the punishment of Mr. Moore would conserve the interest of morality, they would have deplored the occurrence, felt sorry for Charlie Moore, and gone on about their business. But nobody believed that then, and nobody is ever likely to believe it hereafter.

I took some interest in the trial of this heathen man at Cincinnati. I knew something of the people who were behind the prosecution; I have read nearly every copy of his paper since he began publishing it — in fact, procured and read one copy of an issue that never went through the mails; and, as I have said before, I have known him for thirty years; however greatly I may, and do, condemn much that he has said and more that he has printed, I never knew him to speak or print anything that was obscene or calculated to excite lust in the breast of any auditor or reader. I read the article for which he was indicted. I think they said it was too lewd and obscene to be copied into the indictment — though may be I am mistaken about that. So far from being a defense of free love, it was an argument for the marital relation, a plea for the hearth-stone, and a demand for sexual purity. It was not lewd, it was not obscene, it was not erotic — no man nor maiden could be harmed by reading it. It could not be called indecent, except by someone with a soul morbidly alive to the possibilities of filth. The reader of this may pick at random the "family" magazines of this or next month and on the advertising pages find pictures of young women clothed in net undergarments, trying on corsets, washing with Smear's soap, or shaking Snook's foot-powder into their shoes — all intended to be attractive by appealing to the sensual passion. He may see on every book-stall periodicals only attractive by reason of nude or semi-nude pictures of actresses, or groups of women in bathing costumes lying about on the sand. Almost any breezy day he may see young and old women on bicycles, in the public streets, exposing their persons above the knee to the gaze of every passer-by. Every one of these sights is expected and intended to arouse sexual passion, and any one of them compares to Charlie Moore's "indecency" just as the undraped Cyprian of the slums does to the marble nudity of the Greek Slave. Yet this indecency goes unrebuked!

So that the welcome given to Editor Moore by a pious, conservative people is more significant than all the speeches made by his especial friends. It was a protest against that short-sighted and narrow-minded bigotry which made him a victim; against that hypocrisy which allows the brothel and the assignation house to advertise in the daily papers alongside the abortionist and the wealthy voluptuary, and threatens with fetters and a convict's garb the writer who was bold enough to denounce them. It was a magnificent and spontaneous demand for freethought, and free expression of that thought.

More significance than the surface shows appears to me in this remarkable demonstration. Nobody "worked up" the popular enthusiasm. A few friends hired a brass band and a half-dozen carriages, and 5,000 people did the rest. Believing as I do in Almighty God, I can but see that the arrest, conviction and imprisonment of Charlie Moore — yes, even the contemptible rancor of Prof. Rucker — was a wise design of Providence for working out great and good results. As to Mr. Moore himself, that one day was worth living all his life for, and the only dark thread in its warp and woof was that none of his friends could with uplifted heart thank God that such a day dawned. I listened to their speeches with the shadow of that sorrow upon me.

LEXINGTON, KY.

[From the Cincinnati Enquirer.]
THE ENQUIRER INTERVIEWS MR. MOORE.

"I would not take $10,000 for the five months I have spent in the penitentiary," was the extraordinary statement made by Charles C. Moore, editor of the Blue Grass Blade, published at Lexington, Ky. Mr. Moore was a Federal prisoner, sentenced to serve a term of two years for improper use of the United States mails, the same consisting in circulating his paper by this means, which was held to contain matter that the Government should not be utilized in its dissemination. He was pardoned, and on account of good behavior was credited with a month's time, reducing his imprisonment to five months.

"My paper is better off financially to-day than it ever was. If I had been confined ten years, it occurs to me that it would have had the largest circulation of any paper in America. Moreover, I have made friends. I have more than I ever had. The journals of Kentucky which were against me, because they did not understand me, are now for me. They have come to know that even an infidel may not be all bad. I edited two papers while in prison, my own at Lexington, and the other the official publication at the institution where I was a convict. I have been well employed and have profited by my segregation from the world. I have reflected and am stronger, if possible, in my views, than before my trial and conviction.

"Even the Ohio press is treating me with more tolerance. We heathens are softening the hearts of you Christians, and we are acquiring traits of charity and liberality, which secure to every man the right to think and speak for himself."

Mr. Moore left for his home near Lexington at 4 o'clock yesterday evening. When seen at the Palace Hotel he was surrounded by a group of fellow-believers, who hung on every word he uttered and evinced unbounded love and confidence in him.

"When I arrive at home a great concourse of people will receive and greet me, and a banquet will be tendered me at the Phoenix Hotel. An address of welcome will be delivered by Mrs. Josephine K. Henry, the most talented woman I ever met. She was a music teacher when but a girl, and one of my congregation when I preached. She was converted to our faith. Once I advocated her as a candidate for President. The noblest and the best rulers of any and all ages were Queen Elizabeth and Queen Victoria. We will be better off when we shall install the lady of the White House and the President of the Nation at the same time in one and the same person.

"As to my plans for the future, they are all mapped out. I am going to lecture and edit my paper, too. As lecturer, I shall appear in my prison garb. Ere long I am coming to Cincinnati, and shall be heard on the rostrum."

Mr. Moore holds Warden Coffin, of the Ohio Penitentiary, in the highest regard. "He believes," said the infidel, "that the object of the penal institution is to make good men of bad ones. Eight or nine out of every ten are susceptible to the influence of reform. Warden Coffin is doing a grand work in treating convicts as human beings who are capable of being brought to a realization of their errors, and endeavor to get away from the wicked, and to follow along the path of right. Unfortunately, some of his associates proceed on the theory once a criminal always a criminal, and have no idea of humanity in the management of convicts."

[From the Light of Truth.]
A VICTIM OF A BAD COMBINATION.

Charles C. Moore, the freethought prisoner and publisher of the Blue Grass Blade, whose sentence of two years in the Ohio Penitentiary was commuted by the President, was released from that institution last

Friday, and proceeded to his home near Lexington, Ky. A large company of his friends in this city met him on his release and bade him goodbye. An ovation was extended to him at Cincinnati and Lexington.

Moore was the victim of a bad combination, viz. — Comstockism and Kentucky orthodoxy. Few survive such an ordeal as he has encountered, and had it not been for the humane condition of the society in the big prison he would undoubtedly have perished. From this we conclude that as a place of residence for a freethinker the Ohio Penitentiary is to be preferred to the state of Kentucky.

When Mr. Moore was publishing his paper in Cincinnati, the Light of Truth Publishing Company did his printing for a time, and we came to know the fearlessness of the man's nature, and, while admiring it, prophesied that the Colonels, Majors and parsons of Kentucky would have him behind the bars again if he ever returned there. They had previously imprisoned him, so he knew their peculiarities, but he went back, and finally an accommodating judge sequestrated him where the manly offices of Warden Coffin could lighten his burdens. The logic of the situation is, as we see it, that President McKinley, in the goodness of his heart, has dealt out a hardship to Mr. Moore in expelling him from the penitentiary because he has gone right back to his "Old Kentucky Home," where the Lord's own, together with such aid as the devil can render, will make life miserable for the venerable humanitarian.

COPY OF LETTER SENT TO ATTORNEY-GENERAL GRIGGS.

VERSAILLES, KY., April 14, '99.

U.S. ATTORNEY-GENERAL GRIGGS Washington, D.C.:

Dear Sir: — I write you this letter in behalf of a U. S. prisoner, under sentence of two years at the Columbus, Ohio, penitentiary, charged with sending objectionable matter through the U. S. mails.

The prisoner in question is Editor Charles C. Moore, of Lexington, Ky.

I am a Kentucky woman who has made a study of the principles of government. I am loyal to true American principles, and have profound respect for the dignity of the law when justly administered.

The trial and conviction of Charles C. Moore is one of the most remarkable cases in American jurisprudence, and in view of the evidence, the motives and character of the prisoner, this conviction strikes a deadly blow at free press, free speech, and the individual rights of American citizens.

Thousands of disinterested persons throughout the United States recognize the fact that the U. S. prisoner, C. C. Moore, is a mental giant, a humanitarian, and, above all things, a moral Titan, whose character is without blemish, whose life is devoted to making the world nobler and better.

His crime is that he spoke in perfectly chaste language on a sociological question, the one of all others which demands the investigation and best efforts of all thinkers and sociologists, in view of the fact that the ignorance upon this vital question has filled our social system with misery and domestic warfare, and is peopling the world with mental dwarfs, physical wrecks, and moral monstrosities.

There is danger indeed to the stability of the American Government when an American citizen can be branded as a convict for seeking to elevate our social status.

If we could add to the President's Cabinet a Secretary of Sociology, whose duty it should be to devise ways and means to educate the people of the United States on the vital question of Sociology, thus elevating the morals of our nation, which would lead to higher thinking and nobler living, our Government could then, indeed, protect life, liberty, and the pursuit of happiness much more effectually than by sentencing and imprisoning the students of Sociology.

In the name of liberty and justice I plead with you to examine into this case, and I feel assured that you will discover that this man has been most unjustly dealt with.

Pleading with the highest judicial power in our land for a practical application of American principles, I ask that you recommend an immediate and unconditional release for the United States prisoner, Charles C. Moore.

Very respectfully,   JOSEPHINE K. HENRY

WARDEN COFFIN

TELLS MY WIFE WHAT HE THINKS OF ME AND MY IMPRISONMENT.

COLUMBUS, O., June 26, 1899.

MRS. LUCY P. MOORE:

Madam — I am in receipt of your kind favor, and am pleased to hear from you on account of the friendly feeling that has existed between your husband and myself since he has been in this institution. I also thank you for the kind manner in which you speak of me on account, as you allege, of the generous treatment of your husband since he has

247

been under my charge.

Whatever I have done for him, in the way of making his imprisonment as pleasant as possible, consistent with maintaining good discipline, has been for the reason that I recognized in him the elements of a highly-cultured gentleman, worthy [of] the confidence and respect of all good citizens, and for the further reason that I did not consider that the offense of which he was charged was one that demanded harsh and severe treatment, and I think that the Government finally came to the same conclusion, or it would not have consented to commute and reduce his sentence from two years to six months.

A man like Mr. Moore fully appreciates any kindness that is extended to him, or to any friend of his. He is a big, noble-hearted man, with nothing but kindness in his heart for the whole human family.

I greatly fear that I will not be able to comply with your and Mr. Moore's wishes by going home with him, as the time he leaves will find me very much engaged in matters pertaining to the management of the prison, but I promise that I will visit your part of Kentucky this summer, and will be pleased to call and see you.

The ovation that Mr. Moore's friends will extend to him on his arrival at home will be a pleasant greeting to him, and one that I would be pleased to witness.

He understands that his friends desire him to arrive at home on the 8th instead of the 7th of July, and he will comply with these wishes.

With my best wishes for your future happiness, I am

Respectfully yours,   E. G. COFFIN

DECISION OF JUDGE WATTS PARKER.

IN THE CASE OF THE COMMONWEALTH OF KENTUCKY VS.
C. C. MOORE, CHARGED WITH BLASPHEMY.

COMMONWEALTH OF KENTUCKY,...................... Plaintiff
         VS.
CHARLES C. MOORE,................................Defendant
                INDICTMENT NO. 1.

The defendant, C.C. Moore, is charged with having committed the offense of blasphemy.

It is alleged in the indictment that the defendant intended to treat with offensive levity and ridicule the scriptural account of the divine conception and birth, and, to bring contempt upon Almighty God and his divine purpose in causing the birth of Christ, did maliciously and blasphemously publish in a newspaper known as the Blue Grass Blade the following words:

> "When I say that Jesus Christ was a man exactly like I am and had a human father and mother exactly like I had, some of the pious call it blasphemy. When they say that Jesus Christ was born as the result of a sort of Breckinridge-Pollard hyphenation between God and a Jew woman, I call it blasphemy; so you can see there is a stand-off."

It is further charged that by his language the defendant meant that pious and religious persons stated and believed that the birth of Jesus Christ was the result of an unholy and illicit connection between Almighty God and Mary, the mother of Christ.

To this indictment the defendant has filed a demurrer and thereby made the claim that no offense against the laws of Kentucky has been charged against him.

This demurrer having been argued with singular earnestness and ability by counsel both for the prosecution and the defense, and the question presented being a new one in the State, the Court has given the case unusual consideration. We have no statute against blasphemy, and our Court of Appeals, so far as we know, has never passed upon this or any similar question. We must, therefore, in our investigations have recourse to the common law and to the judicial decisions of other States and counties.

Blackstone, in treating of offenses against God and religion, speaks of this offense as blasphemy against the Almighty by denying his being or providence or by contumelious reproaches of our Savior Christ. The punishment, he says, is by fine or imprisonment or other infamous corporal punishment. The ground upon which blasphemy is treated as an offense is that "Christianity is a part of the law of England." The leading case, in this country, in which the crime of blasphemy was discussed was that of the People vs. Ruggles, decided by the Supreme Court of New York in 1810, Chief Justice Kent delivering the opinion. In this case it was decided that the common law against blasphemy was still in force, and a judgment to pay a fine of $500 and be imprisoned three months was affirmed. The Court in this opinion, cited with approval of a number of English cases, in which the right to punish blasphemy had been vigorously upheld, and quoted the words of Lord Bacon, "profane scoffing doth, by little and little, deface the reverence of religion," and "two principal causes I have and know of Atheism — curious controversies and profane scoffing." Whilst this opinion did not declare that Christianity was part of the laws of the State of New York, but expressly disclaimed that there was an established religion in that State, yet the closeness with which it adhered to the definition of blasphemy as laid down by Blackstone, and the great reliance placed upon the English decisions make us hesitate to walk in the path trod by Chief Justice Kent himself.

For, in England there was an established church. The church was part of the State. Apostasy and heresy were punished — the first commission of either offense disqualifying the offender for holding office and the second being punished by three years imprisonment without bail. Even witchcraft was claimed by Blackstone to be an offense against God and religion, and to deny the existence of such a crime, he said, was "at once to flatly contradict the revealed word of God," though he appeared to think it well that the punishment of this crime had fallen into disuse, as there had been no well authenticated modern instance of its commission.

In this country where the divorce between the church and State is complete and final, we should examine with care and accept with caution, any law framed and intended for a country where church and State are one. The difficulties in reconciling religious freedom with the right to punish for an offense against any given religion are manifest.

From the opinion in the People vs. Ruggles we may deduce as conclusions of the Court, the people generally in this country are Christians; that Christianity is engrafted upon the morality of the country; that all religions are tolerated, but that this toleration, as to false religions, means immunity from test oaths, disabilities and the burdens of church establishments; that to revile the Christian religion is an offense, but that to revile other religions is not an offense punishable by law.

In the Bill of Rights, in the Kentucky Constitution, it is declared that all persons have "the right to worship Almighty God according to the dictates of their consciences"; that "no preference shall be given by law to any religious sect, society or denomination, nor to any particular system of ecclesiastical policy," and that the civil rights, privileges or capacities of no person shall be taken away, or in any way diminished or enlarged on account of his belief or disbelief of any religious tenet, dogma or teaching.

It is difficult to conceive how language could be made plainer. If the framers of the Constitution intended to place all religions on an exact equality before the law, they appear to have employed language well calculated to express their purpose. They recognized the fact that men were religious; that they had different religious views, and some had no religious faith, and granting the fullest religious freedom, they declared that the rights of none should be "diminished or enlarged on account of his belief or disbelief of any religious tenet, dogma, or teaching."

Under this Constitution no form of religion can claim to be under the special guardianship of the law. The common law of England, whence our law of blasphemy is derived, did have a certain religion under its guardianship, and this religion was part of the law. The greatest concession made to religious liberty was the right of learned persons to decently debate upon controverted points.

The essence of the law against blasphemy was that the offense, like apostasy and heresy, was against religion, and it was to uphold the Established Church, and not, in any sense, to maintain good order, that there was a law against blasphemy.

The most superficial examination of the chapter in Blackstone treating of offenses against God and religion, must convince any mind that the sole aim and object of these laws was to preserve the Christian faith, as it was then understood and accepted by the Established Church. It may seem to us that the punishment of these offenses were severe in the time of Blackstone, but they had been greatly mitigated, as the stake and fagot had been of far too frequent use in propagating what was deemed to be the true religion. Even Blackstone complains that the definition of heresy had been too uncertain, and that the subject had been liable to be burnt for what he had not understood to be heresy, until it was decided to be so by the ecclesiastical judge who interpreted the canonical Scriptures. To deny any one of the persons of the Trinity, or to allege that there were more gods than one, was a heresy, and was punished in the same manner as apostasy.

Blasphemy is a crime grown from the same parent stem as apostasy and heresy. It is one of a class of offenses assigned for the same general purpose, the fostering and protecting of a religion accepted by the State as the true religion, whose precepts and tenets it was thought all good subjects should observe.

In the case of laws of a country enjoying absolute religious freedom, there is no place for the common law crime of blasphemy. Unsuited to the spirit of the age, its enforcement would be in contravention of the Constitution of the State, and the crime must be considered a stranger to the laws of Kentucky.

Wherefore, it is adjudged that the demurrer be and is hereby sustained, the indictment is dismissed, the defendant's bail bond is quashed, and the defendant is dismissed hence without delay.

[From Freethought Magazine (Chicago), of April, 1895.]

CHARLES C. MOORE.

Charles C. Moore, whose portrait appears as the frontispiece of this number of this magazine, is the editor and publisher of the Blue Grass Blade of Lexington, Ky.

It has been but a short time since we made the acquaintance of Mr. Moore and his journal, but we must confess we have become much interested in the editor and the paper. We feel confident that every intelligent person who is acquainted with Mr. Moore and the Blade will agree with us when we say that we are sure that there is no other man like Charles C. Moore on the face of the globe, and no other paper that is anything like the Blue Grass Blade published in the English language. As for ourselves, we can best express our opinion of the Blade by saying that it is the only paper that we have on our exchange list that we read each week from beginning to end — every article.

As before stated, not having known Editor Moore but a short time, we are not prepared to write a sketch of his life, but that well-known and distinguished woman of the South, Mrs. Josephine K. Henry, of Versailles, Ky., has furnished us with the following sketch which we are sure will much interest any reader of this magazine:

EDITOR FREETHOUGHT MAGAZINE: — I hereby gladly present to your intelligent readers the following brief life sketch of Charles Chilton Moore, the infidel prohibition editor of the Blue Grass Blade of Lexington, Ky.

Civilization is calling for intellectual liberty, therefore, as a Kentucky woman, I esteem it an honor and a privilege to pay a tribute to this man, who is one of the grandest champions of intellectual freedom, justice and morality, that has arisen in the American republic.

The maternal grandfather of Charles C. Moore was Barton W. Stone, who was the founder of the "Christian," or Reform church, whose initiative work was carried to completion by Alexander Campbell. He is the son of Charles Chilton Moore, Sr., and Maryanne Harrison Stone, natives of Virginia. The striking individuality and stainless lives of the grandparents and parents of Mr. Moore have, under the laws of heredity, given the world this great souled man, with purity in his heart and life, and truth upon his lips. Born the child of fortune, and nurtured in the lap of luxury, with all that wealth and social prestige could give to make life happy and successful, after graduating at Bethany College, Va., he entered the ministry of the Christian church, and brought the ability and enthusiasm that have characterized his entire life into his work.

He began preaching just before the civil war, and preached almost to its end. Possessing ample means, he never accepted a penny for his ministerial services. His desire to do good to his fellows was so intense that he abandoned a prosperous charge, and went on foot through the mountain regions of Kentucky, carrying, as he then thought, the true gospel to the poor and ignorant, and while ministering to them spiritually, his great heart went out to them in their poverty, and he gave liberally of his abundance to supply their material needs.

The subject of this sketch being a great student, and even in young manhood, a profound thinker, doubts arose in his mind, and he began to question the truth and efficacy of doctrinal religion, and the authenticity of the Bible. In his attempt to convert to the Christian religion, a very scholarly young Confederate soldier — William J. Hatch — the two young men agreed to study both sides of the Christian religion, reading and arguing assiduously together for a number of weeks. The remarkable result of this investigation was that the young [soldier] was converted to the Christian religion and the young minister renounced Christianity, and became an infidel. Once convinced of the error of dogma, in agony of soul he renounced the faith of his ancestors, and repudiating the idea of the merciless, blood-thirsty, revengeful Jehovah of the Bible as the only hope of humanity, in its hopelessness and ignorance, he counted no sacrifice too great to try and lead humanity to a grander life than dogmatism and priestcraft will ever allow the race to enjoy. With stern conviction and magnificent courage, he turned his back upon the taper-lighted altar of faith and walked into the illimitable realm where the god of reason reigns, and for more than a quarter of a century he has proven himself a moral and intellectual hero, standing in solitary grandeur amidst the storms of obloquy, ridicule, calumny and ostracism, undismayed by church, State and society, as they pour their anathemas upon him, imprison him, threaten his life, and rob him of the fruit of his honest toil, and his right of liberty of conscience guaranteed to every citizen of the American Republic.

The intensity of the life of Charles C. Moore cannot be portrayed by language. His great heart so overflows with sympathy to deluded and suffering humanity, that, counting not the cost, he springs with the spirit of the Nazarene carpenter to the defense of the victims of tyranny and avarice which surge through our civilization, making a travesty and caricature of dogmatic religion, and a monstrous deformity of civil and social codes. When the press, pulpit and people are silent in the presence of public and private wrongs, he comes alike to the victims of poverty and strong drink, the ill-paid slaves of avarice, abused and neglected motherhood, the fallen women, the wronged Negro, calling on bishop, priest and deacon, judge and jurist to prove the wisdom of retaining religious and civil codes that fill the world with moral monstrosities, mental dwarfs and spiritual paralytics.

It is absolutely true that the infidel Charles C. Moore is a "man in whom there is no guile." His paper, the Blue Grass Blade, is the most unique sheet that ever came from a printing press, and he richly deserves the royal title of the phenomenal truth teller. All questions bearing upon the moral uplift of the race are freely discussed, and his trenchant pen sways from the height of an Emerson or Ingersoll, and the pathos and polish of a Washington Irving, to the keenest wit, satire and sarcasm of the masters of those arts. He writes from twelve to sixteen columns a week, the entire paper, save correspondence and advertisements, and many of his articles on vexed problems that are now up for solution, which he dashes off while the typos wait, are worthy of a place in our best magazines.

The Blue Grass Blade is read in Europe, India, and in the iles of the sea, and in every State of the Union, and as an evidence that this unique editor who ably advocates infidelity, prohibition and woman suffrage, has something to say, when the weekly issue arrives at the many homes it enters, every member of the household desires it first. The Liberals read it aloud to their friends, and the illiberals borrow it and read it on the sly and get some new ideas.

This eccentric editor is generally censured for his personal journalism, for laying bare the sins that curse society, but the truth is that the man in "whom there is no guile" rebels so against the shams and tyranny of the church, State and society that his soul chaffs and his heart bleeds over wrongs and sufferings that might, under a regime of reason, common sense and common humanity, be averted, and he, therefore, speaks without fear, because he must, but is ever ready to right any wrong and openly acknowledge his fault.

Charles C. Moore is the author of a book entitled "The Rational View," which is a modern rationalistic view of theology. Being a learned theologian and Bible student, and having taken a calm survey of orthodoxy, heterodoxy and rank infidelity, the author of "The Rational View" uses most forcible reasoning for the conclusions he reaches. Mr.

254

Moore said in a recent issue of the Blue Grass Blade:

"If the Bible were universally known to be true, it is doubtful if a system of rewards and punishments that are only to be realized after death, could influence any man to do good. But when any man who has any capacity to think at all, realizes that he can have no substantial and sound reasons for believing the Bible is true, though you may intimidate him so that he will not say what he really believes, the alleged system of rewards and punishments after death will not influence his conduct. Orthodox preaching and churches do no good. They never make men any better. Nobody ever saw a man made any better by becoming a churchman. There are good men in the churches, but their belief did not make them so."

Having reached the age of 57 without a blemish on his life, which has been read of all men in domestic, social and civil relations, Editor Moore is constantly pleading for some learned ecclesiastic to meet him in oral or written debate on the authenticity of the Bible and the value of dogmatic Christianity; in other words, a fair contest between Orthodoxy and Rationalism, delineating the uses and abuses, success or failure of Bible Christianity. So far the clergy have barricaded themselves behind the reeling towers of faith, saying in undertones, that infidels, guided by reason, are unworthy to meet ecclesiastical giants who walk by faith alone, but whose lives are often misfits that would not show up well under the searchlight of reason, forgetting that what civil and religious liberty we enjoy to-day has been won for us, and every round in the ladder of human progress has been placed there by the misunderstood and persecuted infidel.

Mr. Moore has a book ready for the press, entitled "Behind the Bars," written while in jail by the so-called Christians, who arrested, tried and imprisoned him in the jail at Paris, Kentucky, for telling the truth in regard to that uncertain quantity that often masquerades as religion in the cloak of Christianity.

A few months ago Charles C. Moore was indicted by the grand jury of Lexington, Kentucky, and imprisoned in the jail of that city at the instigation of a minister of the gospel, on the charge of blasphemy, because he said, in the Blade, that "Jesus was not God, but a man who had a human father and mother."

His arrest attracted wide attention, and when the case came to trial, Judge J. Watts Parker, who was on the bench, proved himself a correct interpreter of American principles and an able jurist, by deciding that there can be no such crime as blasphemy in Kentucky, as the new

Constitution guarantees to all persons, liberty of conscience.

The prosecutors of Mr. Moore carried his case to the Supreme Court of Kentucky, where it is now pending. Thus, through the fire of persecution, is the Infidel, Charles C. Moore, making religious intolerance quail before the magnificent heritage of freedom of conscience, guaranteed to all in this government. When the world is ready to hear the truth, persecution will find a resurrectionless grave, but that time is not yet.

The man or woman who dares to think or reason, and refuses to conform to superstitions and cruelties that, after nineteen hundred years, find the world in sin and sorrow, suffering and subjection to tyrannical man-made creeds and codes, must have the splendid courage manifested by this man to stand undismayed against the tides of opposition that flow from the springs of ignorance and intolerance.

The South has always been the stronghold of conservatism, and even to-day it is considered almost a crime to have a new idea. But times are changed, and evolution is doing its perfect work, even here in the South; and when the names of statesmen and heroes who purchased fame by fitting their ideas to public sentiment, or taking the lives of their fellows on the field of battle, will have passed into oblivion, the names of the intellectual liberators of the race, of which Charles C. Moore is one, will go ringing down the corridors of time, laden with the gratitude of all lovers of liberty and justice.

> "For while the Rabbis, with their thumb-worn creeds,
> Their loud professions and their little deeds,
> Mingle in selfish strife, lo! freedom weeps;
> Wrong rules the land, and waiting justice sleeps."

The subject of this sketch lives at his old ancestral home, on a beautiful farm, near Lexington, Kentucky. His devoted wife, who was Miss Lucy George Peak, of Scott county, Kentucky, has sustained him with her love and counsel through the tempests that, for twenty-eight years, have raged around their path, and at times her life has been a long-drawn agony, because of the persecutions to which Mr. Moore has been subjected. Three sons and a daughter arise and call them blessed, and delight the hearts of their parents by possessing to a remarkable degree, the virtues of truth, kindness and integrity of life.

If Christians who persecute the Infidel for non-belief in creeds that breed dissention and hatred, would take his life as a model, then there would be no need of religious revivals, no sin-laden soul at the mourner's bench, no drunkards to curse society, no moral lepers at the matrimonial altar, no prisoners at the bar, no need of priests to groom poor cowering humanity for heaven; for all would be busy being happy and making others so by rendering justice and humanity to fellow-creatures on the shores of time, serene in the conviction that eternity will take care of itself. The all hopeful word of the Bible Christianity to-day is "revision." Is it not an infidel trend to revise the infallible word of God as men grow wiser? The strictly orthodox to-day would have been rank infidels a decade ago. The harshly grating word "damned" in Mark's gospel has been revised to read "condemned;" the place where the worm dieth not is in the Gehenna Valley, Hinnom, and the "Prince of Darkness" is now minimized to Diabolus, which rendition is equally as instructive, but a little more comforting.

The thinkers of the world have been the revisionists, and they have brought us all the light we have; but how they have been made to suffer! The Kentucky infidel, Charles C. Moore, has had his share of persecution, but he has started rills of thought that are now rising into streams.

> "This man with moral zeal is burning,
>   For right some word to speak, some blow to strike,
>   And with the plow of reason he is turning
>   The stubborn glebe of church and State alike."

JOSEPHINE K. HENRY.

March 15, 1895.

Charles C. Moore, as is well known, is the publisher and editor of the Blue Grass Blade, of Lexington, Ky. The portrait of Mr. Moore appears as the frontispiece of this number of this magazine — also in this number is a life-sketch of the eccentric editor, by Mrs. Josephine K. Henry, of Versailles, Ky., one of the ablest and most distinguished women of the South. A correspondent of the Chicago Times, in describing the leading women who attended the late Suffrage Convention, at Atlanta, Georgia, says of Mrs. Henry:

"Mrs. Josephine K. Henry of Versailles, Ky., possibly stands at the head of this trio of women orators, by virtue of her remarkable eloquence, her personal magnetism, and the power she has of swaying and electrifying her audiences.

"Of slender, almost frail physique, Mrs. Henry's personnel does not impress a stranger with the full idea of her abilities. But the moment she

arises to speak on the stage and the tones of her magnetic vibrant voice are heard, the audience falls under her spell, and as she proceeds in her address they are invariably carried along with her. She has been called the "Woman Henry Clay of Kentucky," and those who have heard her will not dispute her title. In private life Mrs. Henry is a devoted wife and mother, and is simply adored by her family and hundreds of admirers." —
(Freethought Magazine)

HANDCUFFS — "GOOD-BYE."

When we came to print the very last pages of this book, January 18, E.M. 300, (A.D. 1900)[,] my printers said that in the mechanical get-up of the book two or three more pages were desirable, and asked me to furnish copy for them and I write the following. The words for which I was fined and put in jail in Paris, Ky., by the "Christian" church were as follows:

"If I had a contract to bore for hell-fire, I would pick the place where the earth's crust is thinnest, and rig my derrick right in front of that Christian church in Paris."

A saloon keeper sent me word that he would build a saloon to be called "The Derrick," right in front of that church and that I might drink there free, the balance of my life.

The words for which I was put in the penitentiary, I have never seen in the paper from the time I wrote them, over two years ago, to this date. The paper was taken from my file and I have none. I had a copy of that paper in my hand at my trial (?) and expected to read it, for the first time after I wrote it, to the Court and jury; but in what was practically only fifteen minutes that was allowed me to defend myself, I never got an opportunity to see it, and about the time I expected to read it, I had the handcuffs on and was on my way to the penitentiary.

Just as I am writing the closing pages, I get a letter which I print to show the esteem in which I was held by my fellow-prisoners:

PENITENTIARY, COLUMBUS, OHIO.
January 14, 1900.

MR. C. C. MOORE, Lexington, Ky.

Dear Sir: — I hope you will pardon me for this liberty I take in addressing you, as we never had any acquaintance with each other, yet

I saw you nearly every day while you were in prison, and got very well acquainted with you through others.

As all the boys speak only in the highest terms of you — at least those that were acquainted with you — I have heard, through some of them, that the editor of the "News" had refused to send you a paper, [and], as I am an assistant at the Postoffice Department, I took it on myself to send you one, as I think you are entitled to one for what you did for it while you were here.

Perhaps Walker does not think so, but I do, and I will continue to send you one every week, as long as I am in a position where I can.

Remember, Mr. Moore, that you have a world of friends in this place — men whom you never met.

Now, Mr. Moore, I will not take up any more of your valuable time with my letter, but hope you will appreciate this favor, which, though it is not much, you may rest assured is from the heart.

Hoping to hear from you whenever it is convenient I remain

Yours truly,

W. F. RAIDLER, 28161, O. P.

_____

"You shackle American liberty, not me."

"Under the circumstances I am proud to be a convict's wife."

I bid you an affectionate "Goodbye," and this brings us to

THE END.

"AIMS AND PURPOSES"
(as recorded in documents of incorporation)
AMERICAN ATHEISTS ARE ORGANIZED:

(1) to stimulate and promote freedom of thought and inquiry concerning religious beliefs, creeds, dogmas, tenets, rituals, and practices;

(2) to collect and disseminate information, data, and literature on all religions and promote a more thorough understanding of them, their origins, and their histories;

(3) to advocate, labor for, and promote in all lawful ways the complete and absolute separation of state and church;

(4) to advocate, labor for, and promote in all lawful ways the establishment and maintenance of a thoroughly secular system of education available to all;

(5) to encourage the development and public acceptance of a humane ethical system, stressing the mutual sympathy, understanding, and interdependence of all people and the corresponding responsibility of each individual in relation to society;

(6) to develop and propagate a social philosophy in which man is the central figure, who alone must be the source of strength, progress, and ideals for the well-being and happiness of humanity;

(7) to promote the study of the arts and sciences and of all problems affecting the maintenance, perpetuation, and enrichment of human (and other) life; and

(8) to engage in such social, educational, legal, and cultural activity as will be useful and beneficial to members of American Atheists and to society as a whole.

"DEFINITIONS"

Atheism is the *Weltanschauung* (comprehensive conception of the world and of total human life value systems) of persons who are *free* from theism — *i.e.*, free *from* religion. It is predicated on ancient Greek Materialism.

American Atheism may be defined as the mental attitude that unreservedly accepts the supremacy of reason and aims at establishing a life-style and ethical outlook verifiable by experience and the scientific method, independent of all arbitrary assumptions of authority or creeds.

Materialism declares that the cosmos is devoid of immanent conscious purpose; that it is governed by its own inherent, immutable, and impersonal laws; that there is no supernatural interference in human life; that man — finding his resources within himself — can and must create his own destiny. Materialism restores to man his dignity and his intellectual integrity. It teaches that we must prize our life on earth and strive always to improve it. It holds that man is capable of creating a social system based on reason and justice. Materialism's "faith" is in man and man's ability to transform the world culture by his own efforts. This is a commitment which is in every essence life-asserting. It considers the struggle for progress as a moral obligation and impossible without noble ideas that inspire man to struggle and bold creative works. Materialism holds that humankind's potential for good and for an outreach to more fulfilling cultural development is, for all practical purposes, unlimited.

American Atheists is a nonpolitical, nonprofit, educational organization. Another of its functions is to act as a "watchdog" to challenge any attempted breach of what Thomas Jefferson called "the wall of separation between state and church," upon which principle our nation was founded.

Membership is open only to those who are in accord with the "Aims and Purposes" indicated above and who are Atheist Materialists. Membership in the national organization is a prerequisite for membership in state, county, city, or local chapters. Membership fee categories are reflected on the reverse side of this sheet (American Atheists Membership Application form).

American Atheists, Inc.
P. O. Box 140195
Austin, TX 78714-0195

Membership Application For American Atheists

Last name _____ First name _____

Companion's name (if family or couple membership)

Last name _____ First name _____

Address _____

City/State/Zip _____

This is to certify that I am/we are in agreement with the "Aims and Purposes" and the "Definitions" of American Atheists. I/We consider myself/ourselves to be Materialist or Non-theist (i.e., A-theist) and I/we have, therefore, a particular interest in the separation of state and church and American Atheists' efforts on behalf of that principle.

I/We usually identify myself/ourselves for public purposes as (check one):

☐ Atheist   ☐ Objectivist   ☐ Agnostic
☐ Freethinker   ☐ Ethical Culturist   ☐ Realist
☐ Humanist   ☐ Unitarian   ☐ I/We evade any re-
☐ Rationalist   ☐ Secularist   ply to a query
☐ Other: _____

I am/We are, however, an Atheist(s) and I/we hereby make application for membership in American Atheists. Both dues and contributions are to a tax-exempt organization and I/we may claim these amounts as tax deductions on my/our income tax return(s). *(This application must be dated and signed by the applicant[s] to be accepted.)*

Signature _____ Date _____

Signature _____ Date _____

Membership in American Atheists includes a subscription to the monthly journal *American Atheist* and the monthly *Insider's Newsletter* as well as all the other rights and privileges of membership. Please indicate your choice of membership dues:

☐ Life, $750
☐ Couple Life, $1,000 (Please give both names above.)
☐ Sustaining, $150/year
☐ Couple/Family, $75/year (Please give all names above.)

☐ Individual, $50/year
☐ Age 65 or over, $25/year (Photocopy of ID required.)
☐ Student, $20/year (Photo-copy of ID required.)

Upon your acceptance into membership, you will receive a handsome gold embossed membership card, a membership certificate personally signed by Jon G. Murray, president of American Atheists, our special monthly *Insider's Newsletter* to keep you informed of the activities of American Atheists, and a subscription to *American Atheist*. Life members receive a specially embossed pen and pencil set; sustaining members receive a commemorative pen. Your name will be sent to the Chapter in your local area if there currently is one, and you will be contacted so you may become a part of the many local activities. Memberships and subscriptions are nonrefundable.

☐ I am/We are enclosing a check or money order for $ _____ payable to American Atheists

☐ Please charge my/our charge card for $ _____. ☐ Visa or ☐ MasterCard

Card # _____

Bank Name _____

Expiration date _____

Signature _____

Return form to:
American Atheists, Inc., P. O. Box 140195, Austin, TX 78714-0195

Don't Miss The
American Atheist

Founded by the first lady of Atheism, Dr. Madalyn O'Hair, the *American Atheist* is the magazine of the modern Atheist. From the latest deeds of Atheist activists to the last antics of the religious right, its articles run the gamut of issues important to Atheists. Skirmishes in the state/church separation battle, the life-style and history of Atheism, religious criticism, current events are all included in the focus of this journal. The nation's hottest topics — school prayer, abortion, creationism — are all covered in its pages from the Atheist's viewpoint.

This magazine's writers bring readers a unique spectrum of viewpoints from literally all over the world. Examples? One columnist offers glimpses into the religions of India. Another highlights the pain of women in the Arab world. Jon Murray, president of American Atheists, spotlights the progress of Atheism (and religion) in the United States.

So why miss any more of this fascinating magazine? Though it is free to members of American Atheists, it is also available to nonmembers on a yearly subscription basis. Go ahead: Check off a box below and head into the wonderful world of Atheism.

☐ Regular subscription, $25   ☐ Sustaining subscription, $50
☐ Foreign subscription, $35   (tax-deductible)
☐ Sample copy, $2

Last name ——————————— First name ———————————

Address ————————————————————————————

City/State/Zip ————————————————————————

☐ I am enclosing a check or money order for $ ——————— payable to American Atheists.

☐ Please charge my credit card for $ ———————. ☐ Visa or ☐ MasterCard

Card # ———————————————————————————

Bank Name ——————————————————————————

Expiration date ————————————————————————

Signature —————————————————————————————

Return form to:
American Atheists, Inc., P. O. Box 140195, Austin, TX 78714-0195

OTHER BOOKS FROM AMERICAN ATHEIST PRESS

The Bible Handbook by G. W. Foote & W. P. Ball_____$9.00
Everything is here: absurdities, indecencies, contradictions, unfulfilled prophecies, broken promises of god, obscenities, sado-masochisms, impossibilities. Paperback. 372 pp. (5008)

All the Questions You Ever Wanted to Ask American Atheists — with All the Answers by Madalyn O'Hair & Jon G. Murray_____$9.00
The experience of 20 years of Atheist work is distilled into this 248-page paperback. (5356)

Pagan Origins of the Christ Myth by John G. Jackson_____$4.00
This is one of the American Atheist Press' best-selling books. No wonder, since it takes on the question most historians of the Roman empire era have not had the guts to ask — did Christ exist? The answer is NO! Find out why. Paperback. 32 pp. (5204)

Ingersoll the Magnificent by Joseph Lewis_____$10.00
Twenty-four classic orations by Robert Ingersoll, nemesis of the nineteenth-century American clergy, demolishing organized religion. Paperback. 342 pp. (5216)

Women and Atheism: The Ultimate Liberation by Madalyn O'Hair_____$3.50
This is the unexpurgated chapter of *Freedom Under Siege*, which was seriously censored in that publication. The full story of Christianity's oppression, suppression, and repression of women. Paperback. 21 pp. (5420)

The Case Against Religion by Dr. Albert Ellis_____$4.00
Religion is a mental illness — and this famous psychiatrist proves it! Paperback. 57 pp. (5096)

Why I Am an Atheist by Madalyn O'Hair_____$4.00
Basic American Atheism combined with a history of Materialism, upon which Atheism is predicated. Paperback. 39 pp. (5416)

Why I Left the Roman Catholic Church by Charles Davis_____$4.00
A damning condemnation by the man who had risen to head the Roman Catholic church in England, then quit in disgust. Learn why. Paperback. 22 pp. (5080)

Atheist Primer by Madalyn O'Hair_____$4.00
Gods are figments of human imagination. This fact is clearly and humorously explained in simple language a small child can easily understand. Illustrated children's book. Paperback. 30 pp. (5372)

Unzipped: The Popes Bare All by Arthur Frederick Ide_____$8.00
A dispassionate, documented, and devastatingly detailed examination of all the gluttons, rapists, necrophiliacs, hedonists, slave-owners, pedophiliacs, tyrants, murderers, and drug abusers presented by the Roman Catholic church as its Vicars of Christ. Paperback. 189 pp. (5510)

(Texas residents please add 7¾% sales tax.)

Order from:
American Atheist Press, P. O. Box 140195, Austin, TX 78714-0195